EXPRESSION

Freedom of

EDITED BY HAIG A. BOSMAJIAN

NEAL-SCHUMAN PUBLISHERS, INC.
NEW YORK   LONDON

THE FIRST AMENDMENT IN THE CLASSROOM SERIES
Edited by Haig A. Bosmajian

The Freedom to Read Books, Films and Plays. The First Amendment in the Classroom Series, No. 1. Foreword by Ken Donelson. ISBN 1-55570-001-2.

Freedom of Religion. The First Amendment in the Classroom Series, No. 2. ISBN 1-55570-002-0.

Freedom of Expression. The First Amendment in the Classroom Series, No. 3. ISBN 1-55570-003-9.

Academic Freedom. The First Amendment in the Classroom Series, No. 4. ISBN 1-55570-004-7.

The Freedom to Publish. The First Amendment in the Classroom Series, No. 5. ISBN 1-55570-005-5.

Published by Neal-Schuman Publishers, Inc.
23 Leonard Street
New York, NY 10013

Printed and bound in the United States of America.

Library of Congress Cataloging-in-Publication Data

The Freedom of expression.

  (The First Amendment in the classroom series ; no. 3
Includes index.
  1. Freedom of speech—United States—Cases.
2. Educational law and legislation—United States—Cases.
I. Bosmajian, Haig A. II. Series: 1st Amendment in the classroom series ; no. 3.
KF4772.A7F74 1988   342.73′0853   87-28131
ISBN 1-55570-003-9   347.302853

Contents

Preface

THE *First Amendment in the Classroom Series* responds to the need for teachers, students, parents, and school board members to become more aware of how First Amendment rights apply to the classrooms of a free society. Those cherished rights, if they have any meaning, are directly relevant and essential to our schools. What is especially needed is a wider familiarity with and understanding of the arguments and reasoning used to reach judgments regarding First Amendment issues, so often controversial and divisive, affecting what goes on in the classroom. To be unfamiliar with those arguments is to be unprepared to defend the First Amendment rights of students and teachers. Those arguments will be found in this series devoted to (1) the banning of books, plays, and films; (2) religion and prayer in the classroom; (3) symbolic speech; (4) teaching methods and teachers' classroom behavior; and (5) school publications and underground newspapers. My earlier volume, *Censorship, Libraries, and the Law*, covers cases of school library censorship.

When United States District Judge Hugh Bownes declared unconstitutional a Portsmouth, New Hampshire, Board of Education rule forbidding "distribution of non-school sponsored written materials within the Portsmouth schools and on school grounds for a distance of 200 feet from school entrances," he declared in the order of the court that "this opinion and Order is to be posted on the school bulletin board in a prominent place, and copies of this opinion and Order are to be made available to the students in the school library."[1]

This was a reminder to students, teachers, and school board members—but especially to the students—that First Amendment rights applied to them. As the United States Supreme Court had put it exactly thirty years earlier in *Barnette*, the First Amendment rights need to be practiced in our schools "if we are not to strangle the free mind at its source and teach youth to discount important principles of our government as mere platitudes."[2]

While the actual decisions in the cases involving the First Amendment rights of students and teachers in the classroom are crucial, the arguments and reasoning in the opinions are equally important. *Why* did the court decide that students could not be prohibited from distributing their literature? *Why* did the court decide that students could not be compelled to salute the flag? *Why* could the teacher not be dismissed for using books containing "offensive" language? *Why* could not the school board dismiss the teacher for using "unorthodox" teaching methods? *Why* could not parents have sex education banned from the school? *Why* did the court decide that prayer in the classroom was unconstitutional? Understanding the "whys" leads to an understanding of the workings of a democratic society.

In 1937, when throughout the world democratic institutions were being threatened and some were being destroyed, John Dewey observed that wherever political democracy has fallen, "it was too exclusively political in nature. It had not become part of the bone and blood of the people in daily conduct of life. Democratic forms were limited to Parliament, elections, and combats between parties. What is happening proves conclusively, I think, that unless democratic habits of thought and action are part of the fibre of a people, political democracy is insecure. It cannot stand in isolation. It must be buttressed by the presence of democratic methods in all social relationships."[3]

When the students, teachers, school boards, and parents involved in these cases insisted on exercising their First Amendment freedoms, they learned that the principles of our democracy are not "mere platitudes." For the students especially, the cases helped demonstrate that the Bill of Rights and "democratic habits of thought and action are part of the fibre of a people." These cases show political democracy "buttressed by the presence of democratic methods" in one realm of our society—the classroom.

It has been clearly established at several levels of our judicial system that protecting the First Amendment freedoms of teachers and students is crucial in a free society. In *Barnette,* the United States Supreme Court declared: "The Fourteenth Amendment, as now applied to the States, protects the citizen against the State itself and all of its creatures—Boards of Education not excepted. These have, of course, important, delicate, and highly discretionary functions, but none that they may not perform within the limits of the Bill of Rights. That they are educating the young for citizenship is reason for scrupulous protection of Constitutional freedoms of the individual, if we are not to to strangle the free mind at its source and teach youth to discount important principles of our government as mere platitudes."

In giving First Amendment protection to junior and senior high school students who had worn black armbands to school to protest U.S. involvement in the Vietnam War, the United States Supreme Court spoke most clearly in *Tinker* on the issue of the First Amendment rights of teachers and students. Justice Abe Fortas, delivering the opinion of the Court, said in 1969: "First Amendment rights, applied in light of the special characteristics of the school environment, are available to teachers and students. It can hardly be argued that either students or teachers shed their constitutional rights to freedom of speech or expression at the schoolhouse gate. This has been the unmistakable holding of this Court for almost 50 years."[4]

When in 1978 United States District Court Judge Joseph Tauro ordered school authorities to return to the high school library a book which had been removed because it contained a "dirty, filthy" poem, he reiterated in his own words what had been declared in *Tinker:* ". . . the First Amendment is not merely a mantle which students and faculty doff when they take their places in the classroom."[5]

On these pages are the stories of students and teachers who risked much to fight for their First Amendment rights in the classroom, who did not "shed their constitutional rights to freedom of speech or expression at the schoolhouse gate" and did not see the First Amendment as "merely a mantle which students and teachers doff when they take their places in the classroom." What is encouraging is that in almost all the cases appearing in this series, students and teachers have been given First Amendment protection by the courts.

The reasons given in the opinions on these pages are applicable to many of those First Amendment controversies which may never reach the courts. Edward Jenkinson, who has done much research and writing on censorship in the schools and who chaired the National Council of Teachers of English Committee Against Censorship has reported: "During the early seventies, approximately one hundred censorship incidents were reported to the ALA [American Library Association]'s Office for Intellectual Freedom each year. By 1976, the number had risen to slightly less than two hundred and climbed to nearly three hundred in 1977." Shortly after the 1980 Presidential election, Judith Krug of the American Library Association estimated a threefold increase in reported censorship incidents, "which would mean roughly nine hundred reported incidents a year." But as Jenkinson points out, the reported incidents "are only a small part of the censorship attempts each year. . . . After talking with teachers, librarians and administrators in meetings in 33 states, I believe that for every reported incident of censorship at least fifty go unreported."[6]

The First Amendment in the Classroom makes available the many substantial arguments that can be used by students, teachers, and parents involved in First Amendment controversies surrounding teachers and students in the classroom. The reasons given by the judges on these pages are there for students, teachers, and parents to use in their efforts to persuade school boards and others that the First Amendment applies to the school environment and that the "Fourteenth Amendment, as now applied to the States, protects the citizen against the State itself and all of its creatures—Boards of Education not excepted."

In his discussion of the nature and function of the judicial court opinion, legal scholar Piero Calamandrei has observed that "the most important and most typical indication of the rationality of the judicial function is the reasoned opinion." Of the need for the judge to present the reasoned opinion, Calamandrei says that

> "ever since justice descended from heaven to earth and the idea gained ground that the judge is a human being and not a supernatural and infallible oracle to be adored, whose authority is beyond question, man has felt the need of a rational explanation to give validity to the word of the judge." [The major function of the reasoned opinion, explains Calamandrei,] "is an explanatory or, one might say, a pedagogical one. No longer content merely to command, to proclaim a *sic volo, sic iubeo* [So I wish, so I command] from his high bench, the judge descends to the level of the parties, and although still commanding, seeks to impress them with the reasonableness of the command. The reasoned opinion is above all the justification of the decision and as such it attempts to be as persuasive as it can."[7]

Like the judge, neither supernatural nor infallible, we are asked for rational explanations to justify our decisions. The judicial opinions on these pages provide useful and persuasive reasons.

I hope that readers of the books in this series—students, teachers, school board members, parents, and others—will develop their appreciation for and commitment to the First Amendment rights of students and teachers in the classroom and will recognize the variety of arguments available to counter those who would not have the First Amendment apply to teachers and students. The First Amendment freedoms were put into the Bill of Rights to be used; the court opinions in this book demonstrate that teachers and students usually get First Amendment protection from the courts. We must recognize, however, that freedoms not exercised by the citizenry lose their vitality. Teachers and students, said Chief Justice Earl Warren, "must always remain free to inquire, to study and to evaluate, to gain new maturity and understanding; otherwise our civilization will stagnate and die."[8]

NOTES

1. *Vail* v. *Bd. of Ed. of Portsmouth School Dist.*, 354 F. Supp. 592 (1973).
2. *West Virginia State Bd. of Ed.* v. *Barnette*, 319 U.S. 624 (1943).
3. John Dewey, "Democracy and Educational Administration," *School and Society*, 45(April 3, 1937), p. 462.
4. *Tinker* v. *Des Moines School Dist.*, 393 U.S. 503 (1969).
5. *Right to Read Defense Committee* v. *School Committee, Etc.*, 454 F. Supp. 703 (1978).
6. Edward Jenkinson, "Protecting Holden Caulfield and His Friends from the Censors," *English Journal*, 74(January 1985), p. 74.
7. Piero Calamandrei, *Procedure and Democracy*, trans. John C. Adams and Helen Adams (New York: New York University Press, 1956), p. 53.
8. *Sweezy* v. *New Hampshire*, 354 U.S. 234 (1957).

Constitutional Amendments

ARTICLE I

Congress shall make no law respecting an establishment of religion, or prohibiting the free exercise thereof; or abridging the freedom of speech, or of the press; or the right of the people peaceably to assemble, and to petition the government for a redress of grievances.

ARTICLE XIV

All persons born or naturalized in the United States, and subject to the jurisdiction thereof, are citizens of the United States and of the State wherein they reside. No State shall make or enforce any law which shall abridge the privileges or immunities of citizens of the United States; nor shall any State deprive any person of life, liberty or property, without due process of law; nor deny to any person within its jurisdiction the equal protection of the law.

Judicial Circuits

Circuits	*Composition*
District of Columbia	District of Columbia
First	Maine, Massachusetts, New Hampshire, Puerto Rico, Rhode Island
Second	Connecticut, New York, Vermont
Third	Delaware, New Jersey, Pennsylvania, Virgin Islands
Fourth	Maryland, North Carolina, South Carolina, Virginia, West Virginia
Fifth	Louisiana, Mississippi, Texas
Sixth	Kentucky, Michigan, Ohio, Tennessee
Seventh	Illinois, Indiana, Wisconsin
Eighth	Arkansas, Iowa, Minnesota, Missouri, Nebraska, North Dakota, South Dakota
Ninth	Alaska, Arizona, California, Idaho, Montana, Nevada, Oregon, Washington, Guam, Hawaii, Northern Marianna Islands
Tenth	Colorado, Kansas, New Mexico, Oklahoma, Utah, Wyoming
Eleventh	Alabama, Georgia, Florida

Foreword

by Alan H. Levine

GEORGE Washington. Thomas Jefferson. Benjamin Franklin. John Adams. Abraham Lincoln. All men who dedicated their lives to the struggle for freedom. They are also the names of public high schools across the country. Not one of these men was known as a disciplinarian, and yet our public high schools remain places more committed to enforcing discipline than practicing freedom.

There is, of course, substantial lip service given to teaching students about freedom and democratic values. Social studies and civics courses abound with references to the Bill of Rights and the blessings of liberty. But outside of the textbooks, a different lesson is taught by those who run the schools. Witness the response of school administrators to the stirrings of freedom that began to manifest themselves in the public schools during the 1960s and 1970s. Principals suspended boys who had long hair. Coaches kicked them off school teams. Girls who wore slacks in cold weather were suspended or sent home to change into dresses. Dress codes were enacted to outlaw unconventional dress. Underground newspapers were seized, controversial articles in school newspapers were censored. Deans wrote down names of students who walked picket lines.

Small wonder that students were seen wearing buttons saying "Free the New York 275,000." That was the approximate number of students in New York City's high schools in the sixties.

The most significant step towards liberating public school students from their condition of unfreedom began in Des Moines, Iowa, on December 15, 1965. On that day, Christopher Eckhardt, a 16-year old high school student, and Mary Beth Tinker, a 13-year old junior high school student, came to school wearing black arm bands in protest against the Vietnam War. Told by school officials to remove the arm bands or leave school, the students left—and sued the school officials. Their case made its way to the United States Supreme Court, where a majority of the justices held that students must be permitted to express their views on subjects of concern to them, so long as they did so without substantially disrupting school activities.

Despite the Court's ruling, school officials were reluctant to surrender any part of their authority. So when a group of New York City high school students, intent on spreading the Supreme Court's message to their fellow students, distributed copies of the *Tinker* decision outside the entrance to the school, they were threatened with suspension by their principal. And in New Jersey, a principal

---

Alan H. Levine, a New York City civil rights lawyer, has represented students and parents in cases involving a wide range of student rights issues. Some of those cases are reproduced in this and other volumes in this series. He is the co-author of "The Rights of Students" and is President of Advocates for Children, a New York-based educational advocacy and student rights organization.

took to the school's public-address system to warn his students—who had been impressed by the black-gloved, raised-fist protest registered by two black Olympic athletes—that the Supreme Court decision applied to black arm bands, not to black gloves.

In some school systems, *Tinker* began to have an impact, and student rights policies were adopted. Elsewhere, resistance continued and lawsuits were brought. They are the subject of this book.

You will notice that only one of the cases collected here is from the 1980s. There have been few such cases, not because the schools have changed—the students have. There has been less student protest. Fewer controversial articles have been submitted for publication. There has not been much for school officials to suppress.

This is partly because, despite favorable court decisions, most students remain acutely aware that principals retain alternative means of dealing with "troublemakers"—through, for example, job and college recommendations, membership on athletic teams, appointment to school offices, grades, and selective enforcement of school rules.

I once represented a high school student who had distributed leaflets in front of his school. His father received a letter from the principal the next day reassuring him that his son had a legal right to publicly express his opinions. But "naturally," the letter concluded, "our judgment of Robert, and the nature of his school references, will have to be influenced by such expressions of his opinions." The message is not lost on most students: the risks involved in challenging school administrations are simply too great.

Why should that be? Why have school administrators been so threatened by students' peaceful protests, even when they have not been directed against school policies? Perhaps more importantly, can public schools change? Will they ever be capable of instilling the habits of freedom? Will they, for example, be able to teach students to think critically about public issues, to challenge the current orthodoxy, to resist the pressures of conformity, to speak out on matters of conscience?

The great philosopher of individual liberty, John Stuart Mill, would have answered no. Government, Mill believed, did not establish public schools to teach about freedom and dissent. For Mill, a system of public education was "a mere contrivance for molding people to be exactly like one another," with its ultimate goal to "establish...a despotism over the mind."

Some might think that too harsh. School officials would surely disclaim any such intentions. But if the object is not to "mold people to be exactly like one another," then why enact dress codes and long hair regulations? And if the purpose is not to establish "a despotism over the mind," then why suspend students for wearing armbands and civil rights buttons or prohibit them from distributing underground newspapers or publishing articles about drugs or birth control or other issues that are rarely discussed in school?

The answer, I believe, is that Mill, however vivid his language, was essentially correct. Public schools, as creatures of the state, are inherently repressive places. Their mission is to transmit the values of the state—that is, majoritarian values. It is inevitable that the expression of dissenting values will be seen as a threat to that mission. That is why school boards order the removal of so many books and teaching materials that express controversial ideas.

Charles Silberman, in his three-year study of the nation's public schools, *Crisis in the Classroom*, observes that school administrators are preoccupied with control. The petty rules that govern most schools are but one example of what Silberman means. Consider also that in most schools insubordination—that is, disobedience alone—is grounds for suspension, no matter how absurd, or small-minded, or silly the rule or command.

School officials take the issue of disobedience seriously. Their authority is at stake. Deviations from the norm are viewed with suspicion, if not hostility. Let me illustrate by returning to the principal who wrote to Robert's father about his son's leafletting. There was another confrontation between Robert and the principal, and a letter to his father ensued:

> As you recall, when you were in my office with him last week he refused to use the word "yes" and insisted that he would only say "yeah". Since that is still his stand, and since I can see no prospect of controlling him in larger things if I cannot even succeed in changing one word, I have placed him in the Dean's Office for the day in the hope that you can get him straight.

> I hope you understand that I cannot possibly control the behavior of 4,000 pupils if they were permitted such stubborn refusals. It is hard for me to believe that during the week when he had been suspended from school, you have been unable to get him to change one word. I hope you recognize that what is actually involved is not the one word, but the question of whose will shall prevail. That is a matter that I cannot ignore, if I hope to remain in charge of this school.

In places where authority is threatened in ways such as this, strict control over what students say—and read and think—will be routinely exercised. Freedom will be, at best, tolerated, never encouraged.

Students will enjoy freedom only to the extent that they struggle for it. It is a lesson that has been learned by other powerless groups in our society. They have learned the further lesson that the rights they have won will endure only so long as the struggle endures.

One hopes that the cases in this series will be a source of guidance and inspiration for that struggle.

Introduction

RHETORIC, said Aristotle, is the art of discovering all the available means of persuasion in any given situation. In his *Rhetoric* he advises speakers and writers how to go about using logical proofs and emotional appeals and establishing *ethos* in their communication. Aristotle was referring, for the most part, to verbal discourse, written and oral persuasion. More recently, anthropologist and communication scholar Dr. Ray Birdwhistell has observed that the human being is a "multisensorial being. Occasionally he verbalizes." In fact, in order to communicate, to influence, to persuade, we use all means available to us, both verbal and nonverbal.

On various occasions the United States Supreme Court and the lower courts have recognized the importance of symbolic speech and have given it First Amendment protection. As the 20 cases reprinted in *Freedom of Expression* reveal, teachers and students have expressed their concerns, grievances, and protests through symbolic speech. Some have refused to salute the flag in the classroom; others have worn black armbands to protest United States participation in the Vietnam War; still others have worn "freedom buttons" to protest racial segregation. In almost all the cases, the lower courts and the United States Supreme Court have given constitutional protection to those students and teachers who chose to communicate through such symbolism.

In every case dealing with teachers and students refusing to participate in the flag salute, the courts have decided for the nonparticipants, whether their objections to the flag salute were religiously based or not. In every case dealing with wearing black armbands as a means of expressing protest, the courts have decided for the students and teachers.

In the 1943 landmark case *West Virginia State Board of Education* v. *Barnette* the majority of the Court decided to give constitutional protection to the students of the Jehovah's Witness faith who had refused to participate in the flag salute ritual. In so deciding, the Court provided us this explanation of symbolic speech:

> There is no doubt that, in connection with the pledges, the flag salute is a form of utterance. Symbolism is a primitive but effective way of communicating ideas. The use of an emblem or flag to symbolize some system, idea, institution, or personality, is a short cut from mind to mind. Causes and nations, political parties, lodges and ecclesiastical groups seek to knit the loyalty of their following to a flag or banner, a color or design. The State announces rank, function, and authority through crowns and maces, uniforms and black robes; the church speaks through the Cross, the Crucifix, the altar and shrine, and clerical raiment. . . . A person gets from a symbol the meaning he puts into it, and what is one man's comfort and inspiration is another's jest and scorn.

Writing for the Court, Justice Jackson said that "it is the State that employs a flag as a symbol of adherence to government as presently organized. It requires the individual to communicate by word and sign his acceptance of the political ideas it thus bespeaks. Objection to this form of communication when coerced is an old one, well known to the framers of the Bill of Rights."

During the 1960s Civil Rights Movement, the Court on several occasions gave

First Amendment protection to sit-ins, recognizing the communicative functions of such symbolic behavior. In 1963, Justice Harlan joined the Court in deciding for students who had participated in lunch-counter sit-ins in downtown Baton Rouge. In his concurring opinion in *Garner* v. *Louisiana* he wrote:

> Such a demonstration [sit-in], in the circumstances of these cases, is as much a part of the 'free trade of ideas' . . . as is verbal expression, more commonly thought of as speech. It, like speech, appeals to good sense and to 'the power of reason applied through public discussion' . . . just as much as, if not more than, a public oration delivered from a soapbox at a streetcorner. This Cout has never limited the right to speak, a protected liberty under the Fourteenth Amendment to mere verbal expression.

Three years later, in another sit-in case at a segregated library in Louisiana (*Brown* v. *Louisiana,* 1966), the Supreme Court majority declared:

> We are here dealing with an aspect of a basic constitutional right—the right under the First and Fourteenth Amendments guaranteeing freedom of speech and assembly, and freedom to petition the government for a redress of grievances. . . . As this Court has repeatedly stated, these rights are not confined to verbal expression. They embrace appropriate types of action which certainly includes the right in a peaceable and orderly manner to protest by silent and reproachful presence, in a place where the protestant has every right to be, the unconstitutional segregation of public facilities.

Another important aspect of *Barnette* is that the United States Supreme Court not only recognized the importance of symbolic speech in finding for the students, but it relied on the crucial argument that the nonverbal, symbolic conduct of the students of the Jehovah's Witness faith who had refused to salute the flag involved no disturbances in the schools. In giving constitutional protection to the students, the Court stated: "The freedom asserted by these appellees [the students] does not bring them into collision with rights asserted by any other individual. . . . Nor is there any question in this case that their behavior is peaceable and orderly."

In its *Barnette* opinion the Court also brought to bear the clear and present danger test:

> It is now a commonplace that censorship or suppression of expression of opinion is tolerated by our Constitution only when the expression presents a clear and present danger of action of a kind the State is empowered to prevent and punish. It would seem that involuntary affirmation could be commanded only on even more immediate and urgent grounds than silence. But here the power of compulsion is invoked without any allegation that remaining passive during a flag salute creates a clear and present danger that would justify an effort even to muffle expression. To sustain the compulsory flag salute we are required to say that a Bill of Rights which guards the individual's right to speak his own mind, left it open to public authorities to compel him to utter what is not in his mind.

If the clear and present danger test is to be applied in determining whether a speech or a piece of writing will get constitutional protection, the same test would be no less applicable in determining whether a silent, passive form of symbolic expression deserves protection.

A quarter century later, in *Tinker* v. *Des Moines School District* (1969), the Supreme Court again decided for students communicating through symbolic behavior, and in so deciding emphasized the fact that the school officials had no hard evidence that a disturbance in the school would likely result from the students' symbolic communication. The Court noted that *Tinker* "does not concern aggressive, disruptive action or even group demonstrations. Our problem involves direct, primary First Amendment rights akin to 'pure speech.'" Writing for the majority, Justice Fortas emphasized the nonviolent nature of the students' symbolic expression:

> The school officials banned and sought to punish petitioners for a silent, passive expression of opinion, unaccompanied by any disorder or disturbance on the part of petitioners. There is no evidence whatever of petitioners' interference, actual or nascent, with the schools' work or of collision with the rights of other students to be secure and to be left alone. Accordingly, this case does not concern speech or action that intrudes upon the work of the schools or the rights of other students.

Justice Fortas explained the Court's rejection of the school authorities' "undifferentiated" fear of a disturbance, which has subsequently been cited again and again in cases involving students' rights. He wrote: . . . in our system, undifferentiated fear or apprehension of disturbance is not enough to overcome the right of freedom of expression. At the conclusion of his opinion, Justice Fortas again observed that the students "neither interrupted school activities nor sought to intrude in the school affairs or the lives of others. They caused discussion outside of the classrooms, but no interference with work and no disorder. In the circumstances, our Constitution does not permit officials of the State to deny their form of expression.

The lower courts also have relied heavily on the "lack of disturbance" argument in deciding to give constitutional protection to the symbolic speech of teachers and students. A United States District Court in Connecticut, in giving First Amendment protection to a teacher who had refused to participate in the flag salute, said in *Hanover* v. *Northrup* (1970): "In the instant case, there was no suggestion that Mrs. Hanover's behavior resulted in any disruption of school activities, or that her behavior interfered with or denied the rights of other teachers or students."

Giving constitutional protection to a teacher who had worn a black armband to protest U.S. involvement in the Vietnam War, the United States Court of Appeals, Second Circuit, said in *James* v. *Board of Education* (1972): "It is to be noted that in this case, the Board of Education has made no showing whatsoever at any stage of the proceedings that Charles James, by wearing a black armband threatened to disrupt classroom activities or created any disruption in the school."

In *Russo* v. *Central School Dist. No. 1* (1972), the same court gave constitutional protection to a Henrietta, New York, art teacher who had refused to participate in the flag salute with her students. The court argued that "Mrs. Russo made no attempt to proselytize her students. Instead, she provided her high school students with a second, but quiet, side of the not altogether new flag-salute debate: one teacher led the class in recitation of the pledge, the other remained standing in respectful silence. There is nothing to indicate that this demonstration had any effect—certainly no evidence of a destructive sort—on Mrs. Russo's students."

Had it not been for the school board's dismissal of Mrs. Russo, said the Court of Appeals, the very fact that she "was permitted to refrain from saluting the flag would clearly have been evidence to her students that the injustice and intolerance against which she was quietly protesting was not merely not well-founded but a demonstrable falsehood at least within the confines of one school's homeroom class."

Students who have refused to participate in the flag salute ritual also have been given First Amendment protection by various lower courts because the students' symbolic communications have not led to any classroom disruption. In 1970, a United States District Court in Florida decided in *Banks* v. *Board of Public Instruction of Dade County* for a student who was suspended for refusing to stand during the pledge and salute. School authorities denied that Banks' "refusal to stand was an exercise of his constitutional right of free speech and expression" and argued that "there is a compelling governmental purpose to be served in requiring students to stand during the pledge." In deciding against the school officials, the District Court stated: "The conduct of Andrew Banks in refusing to stand during the pledge ceremony constituted an expression of his religious beliefs and political opinions. His refusal to stand was no less a form of expression than the wearing of the black armband was to Mary Beth Tinker. He was exercising a right 'akin to pure speech.'" The court pointed out that Banks' refusal to stand had not "caused any disruption in the educational process."

Three years after *Banks*, the United States Court of Appeals, Second Circuit, decided for a New York senior high school student who had refused to participate in the Pledge of Allegiance because he believed that there was not "liberty and justice for all in the United States." In deciding for Theodore Goetz, an honor student and president of his class, the court argued in *Goetz* v. *Ansell* (1973) that there was no evidence "of disruption of classwork or disorder or invasion of the rights of others," and concluded, "We do not believe that a silent, non-disruptive expression of belief by sitting down may . . . be prohibited."

Included in this volume are five cases in which the students did not receive First Amendment protection from the courts. The judges argued that the evidence indicated that the speech involved had led to disruptions and a breakdown in discipline. In *Blackwell* v. *Issaquena* (1966) the United States Court of Appeals, Fifth Circuit, stated:

> The facts demonstrate that during the time students wore freedom buttons to school, much disturbance was created by these students. Their actions in the school building are indeed reprehensible and the school officials certainly have the authority to mete out punishment as they deem appropriate for their discourteous behavior toward school authorities, their disregard for the orderly progression of classroom instruction, and their complete disregard for the rights of their fellow students.

In *Gerbert* v. *Hoffman* (1972) the United States District Court argued that a sit-in conducted by the students was not protected by the First Amendment. The court was especially concerned about the disruptive effects of the sit-in: "We find that the conduct of the sit-in participants did substantially interfere with appropriate school discipline. 'Appropriate discipline in the operation of the school' certainly requires students to attend their scheduled classes and to refrain from preventing other students from attending classes in their scheduled location. . . . We find that the actions of the students disrupted the educational program of the school and therefore that the action of the school officials in terminating the sit-in by suspending the students did not violate the First Amendment rights of the students."

It is important to note, however, that the court also said that "the fact that the school administrators could not attend to their normal duties cannot be a basis for suspending the students' First Amendment rights. . . . The fact that these administrators cannot . . . attend to their scheduled duties is not a basis for determining that the sit-in itself has materially disrupted the school program." The *Blackwell* court also was careful to distinguish between symbolic behavior which created disorder in the school and so interfered with the rights of others, and symbolic behavior which did not lead to disruption. Turning to *Barnette*, the *Blackwell* court declared: "In *West Virginia State Bd. of Educ.* v. *Barnette* . . . the Court was careful to note that the refusal of the students to participate in the ceremony did not interfere with or deny rights of others to do so and the behavior involved was 'peaceable and orderly.'"

As the United States Supreme Court made clear in *Tinker*, the commotion and the disturbance feared by the administrators must be based on something more than apprehension: " . . . in our system, undifferentiated fear of disturbance is not enough to overcome the right to freedom of expression. Any departure from absolute regimentation may cause trouble. Any variation from the majority's opinion may inspire fear. Any word spoken in class, in the lunchroom, or on the campus, that deviates from the views of another person may start an argument or cause a disturbance. But our Constitution says we must take this risk. . . . "

One risk the United States Supreme Court was not willing to take, however, was allowing high school students attending an assembly that "was part of a school-sponsored educational program in self-government" to be exposed to a nominating speech that included some figurative, metaphorical, symbolic expressions making use of the sexual double entendre. In April 1983, Matthew Fraser, a Washington State honor student who had won statewide honors as a debater, delivered his short nominating speech for a friend who was running for student body vice president. Fraser declared before the high school assembly: "I know a man who is firm—he's firm in his pants, he's firm in his shirt, his character is firm—but most of all, his belief in you, the students of Bethel, is firm. Jeff Kuhlman is a man who takes his point and pounds on it. If necessary, he'll take an issue and nail it to the wall. . . . "

Fraser's one-minute speech with its puns and double entendres led to his suspension from school and the removal of his name from the list of possible speakers at the school's commencement exercises. According to school officials, he had violated a Bethel High School rule which read: "Conduct which materially and substantially interferes with the educational process is prohibited, including the use of obscene, profane language or gestures."

Fraser served two days of his suspension and eventually was allowed to deliver the commencement address. However, the case did not end there. In fact, Fraser was allowed to deliver the address only after a United States District Court in Washington enjoined the school district from preventing him from speaking at the commencement ceremonies. The school officials appealed to the United States Court of Appeals, Ninth Circuit, which decided for Fraser. The court argued that the school district had failed "to demonstrate that the speech had a materially disruptive effect on the educational process." The court further rejected the school district's argument that it could "discipline Fraser for using language considered to be objectionable because the speech was made at a school-sponsored function and was an extension of the school program."

The school district then appealed to the United States Supreme Court which in July 1986 reversed the lower court's judgment. Writing for the majority in *Bethel School Dist. No. 403* v. *Fraser*, Chief Justice Burger stated that "the schools, as instruments of the state, may determine that the essential lessons of civil, mature conduct cannot be conveyed in a school that tolerates lewd, indecent, or offensive speech and conduct such as that indulged in by this confused boy. The pervasive sexual innuendo in Fraser's speech was plainly offensive to both teachers and students—indeed to any mature person."

The Chief Justice distinguished Fraser's speech from the protected expression in *Tinker*:

> We hold that petitioner School District acted entirely within its permissible authority in imposing sanctions upon Fraser in response to his offensively lewd and indecent speech. Unlike the sanctions imposed on the students wearing armbands in *Tinker*, the penalties imposed in this case were unrelated to any political viewpoint. The First Amendment does not prevent the school officials from determining that to permit a vulgar and lewd speech such as respondent's would undermine the school's basic educational mission. A high school assembly or classroom is no place for a sexually explicit monologue directed towards an unsuspecting audience of teenage students. Accordingly, it was perfectly appropriate for the school to disassociate itself to make the point to the pupils that vulgar speech and lewd conduct is wholly inconsistent with the 'fundamental values' of public school education.

While the Chief Justice dealt with "inculcating" in students habits of civility, protecting the sensibilities of listeners, and prohibiting the use of "vulgar and offensive" language in public discourse, Justice Brennan in his concurring opinion focused on the "disruptive" language. Fraser's speech, said Brennan, "may well have been protected had he given it in school but under different circumstances, where the school's legitimate interests in teaching and maintaining civil public discourse were less weighty. In the present case, school officials sought only to ensure that a high school assembly proceed in an orderly manner. . . . Thus, the Court's holding concerns only the authority that school officials have to restrict a high school student's use of disruptive language in a speech given to a high school assembly."

At the same time that he contended that Fraser's speech "was no more 'obscene,' 'lewd,' or 'sexually explicit' than the bulk of programs currently appearing on prime time television or in the local cinema," Brennan concluded that "school officials did not violate the First Amendment in determining that respondent should be disciplined for the disruptive language he used while addressing a high school assembly."

Justices Marshall and Stevens dissented, unconvinced that education at Bethel High School was disrupted by Fraser's one-minute speech and that Fraser could have known that his metaphorical expression was punishable. In his short, one-paragraph dissenting opinion, Marshall claimed that in his view "the school district failed to demonstrate that respondent's remarks were indeed disruptive. . . . Here the board, despite a clear opportunity to do so, failed to bring in evidence sufficient to convince either of the two lower courts that education at Bethel School was disrupted by respondent's speech." Justice Stevens, in addition to arguing that the school's disruptive behavior rule was too ambiguous, stated that "the most difficult question is whether the speech was so obviously offensive that an intelligent high school student must be presumed to have realized that he would be punished for giving it." As Stevens saw it, neither the comments Fraser received from the teachers prior to delivering the speech nor the student handbook itself gave him sufficient notice of the likelihood that he would be disciplined.

In his argument that students could be prohibited from communicating in the kind of language used by Fraser, Chief Justice Burger stated that "the process of educating our youth for citizenship in public schools is not confined to books, the curriculum, and the civics class; schools must teach by example the shared values of a civilized social order." But denying Fraser First Amendment protection also became a lesson by example—surely not missed by students—in that "process of educating our youth for citizenship." One is reminded of Justice Jackson's oft repeated lines from *Barnette*: "That they [Boards of Education] are educating the young for citizenship is reason for scrupulous protection of Constitutional freedoms of the individual, if we are not to strangle the free mind at its source and teach youth to discount important principles of our government as mere platitudes."

Students may indeed come to see Constitutional principles as "mere platitudes" with more Fraser-like decisions. Judges at various levels of our judicial system have warned against censorship of expression in our schools and the effects such censorship could have on students' perceptions of our democracy. In deciding for some Texas high school students who had been suspended for distributing their "underground" newspaper near their school, Judge Irving Goldberg of the United States Court of Appeals said in *Shanley* v. *Northeast Ind. School Dist.* (1972): "One of the great concerns of our time is that our young people, disillusioned by our political processes, are disengaging from political participation. It is most important that our young become convinced that our Constitution is a living reality, not parchment preserved under glass." "It is incredible to us," continued Judge Goldberg, "that in 1972 the First Amendment was deemed inapplicable under these circumstances to high school students living at the threshold of voting and dying for their country."

Goldberg admonished the school officials: "Perhaps it would be well if those entrusted to administer the teaching of American history and government to our students begin their efforts by practicing the document on which that history and government are based. Our eighteen-year-olds can now vote, serve on juries, and be drafted; yet the board fears the 'awakening' of their intellects without reasoned concern for its effect upon discipline. The First Amendment cannot tolerate such intolerance."

When in 1972 the United States Court of Appeals, Second Circuit, concluded that the Board of Education had arbitrarily and unjustifiably discharged high school English teacher Charles James for wearing a black armband to school as a symbolic protest against American involvement in the Vietnam War (*James* v. *Board of Education*), Judge Irving Kaufman declared, after noting that James' students were approximately sixteen or seventeen years of age:

> Recently, this country enfranchised 18-year-olds. It would be foolhardy to shield our children from political debate and issues until the eve of their first venture into the voting booth. Schools must play a central role in preparing their students to think and analyze and to recognize the demagogue. Under the circumstances present here, there was a greater danger that the school, by power of example, would appear to the students to be sanctioning the very 'pall of orthodoxy,' condemned in *Keyishian*, which chokes freedom of dissent.

In 15 of the 20 cases appearing in this volume the courts decided to give constitutional protection to the students and teachers, placing significant emphasis on the argument that the symbolic speech had resulted in no disruption of normal school activities. *Fraser*, however, places less emphasis on that argument and instead stresses the more vague criterion of whether the speech "would undermine the school's basic educational mission." It is one thing to determine that "disruption" occurred and hence the speech was not protected; it is something else to demonstrate that the speech "undermined the school's basic educational mission" and thus was not protected. Under the latter, much more teacher and student speech can be prohibited, especially when that "mission" includes "inculcating the habits and manners of civility," to use Chief Justice Burger's words in *Fraser*.

Oftentimes one person's "uncivil" speech may be another's most effective means of expression and communication. It remains to be seen to what extent *Fraser* undermines *Barnette*, and the large body of law established since *Barnette*, protecting the First Amendment rights of students and teachers. Several years of precedents, especially court opinions since *Tinker*, cannot be easily and judicially erased. As Supreme Court Justice Powell told the American Bar Association in a speech delivered at the ABA's 1986 annual convention, the Supreme Court hews to precedents rather than presidents and Justices are reluctant to overturn longstanding rulings.

In the symbolic speech cases, the following have been firmly established as guiding principles:

• Symbolism and symbolic speech are forms of communication.

• The Supreme Court has "never limited the right to speak . . . to mere verbal expression."

• Students and teachers do not "shed their constitutional rights to freedom of speech or expression at the schoolhouse gate."

• School boards have "important, delicate, and highly discretionary functions, but none that they may not perform within the limits of the Bill of Rights."

• The school officials' "undifferentiated fear or apprehension is not enough to overcome the right to freedom of expression."

• "In order for the State in the person of school officials to justify prohibition of a particular expression of opinion, it must be able to show that its action was caused by something more than a mere desire to avoid the discomfort and unpleasantness that always accompany an unpopular viewpoint."

• Conduct by the student which "materially disrupts classwork or involves substantial disorder or invasion of the rights of others is, of course, not immunized by the constitutional guarantee of freedom of speech."

• The First Amendment rights of students and teachers are not to be determined by majority vote: "The very purpose of the Bill of Rights was to withdraw certain subjects from the vicissitudes of political controversy, to place them beyond the reach of majorities and officials and to establish them as legal principles to be applied by the courts. One's right to life, liberty, and property, to free speech, a free press, freedom of worship and assembly, and other fundamental rights may not be submitted to vote; they depend on the outcome of no election."

THE United States Supreme Court decides for students of the Jehovah's Witness faith who had been expelled from school because they had refused to participate in the flag salute. Student participation in the flag salute had been made mandatory by the West Virginia board of education resolution stating in part that all teachers and students "shall be required to participate in the salute honoring the nation represented by the flag; provided, however, that refusal to salute the flag be regarded as an act of insubordination, and shall be dealt with accordingly." In deciding against West Virginia, the Court declared: "The Fourteenth Amendment, as now applied to the States, protects the citizen against the State itself and all of its creatures—Boards of Education not excepted. These have, of course, important, delicate, and highly discretionary functions, but none that they may not perform within the limits of the Bill of Rights. . . . The very purpose of a Bill of Rights was to withdraw certain subjects from the vicissitudes of political controversy, to place them beyond the reach of majorities and officials and to establish them as legal principles to be applied by the courts. One's right to life, liberty, and property, to free speech, a free press, freedom of worship and assembly, and other fundamental rights may not be submitted to vote; they depend on the outcome of no elections. . . . We think the action of the local authorities in compelling the flag salute and pledge transcends constitutional limitations on their power and invades the sphere of intellect and spirit which it is the purpose of the First Amendment to our Constitution to reserve from all official control."

West Virginia State Bd. of Ed. v. *Barnette*, 319 U.S. 624 (1943)

Mr. Justice Jackson delivered the opinion of the Court.

Following the decision by this Court on June 3, 1940, in *Minersville School District* v. *Gobitis,* 310 U.S. 586, the West Virginia legislature amended its statutes to require all schools therein to conduct courses of instruction in history, civics, and in the Constitutions of the United States and of the State "for the purpose of teaching, fostering and perpetuating the ideals, principles and spirit of Americanism, and increasing the knowledge of the organization and machinery of the government." Appellant Board of Education was directed, with advice of the State Superintendent of Schools, to "prescribe the courses of study covering these subjects" for public schools. The Act made it the duty of private, parochial and denominational schools to prescribe courses of study "similar to those required for the public schools."[1]

The Board of Education on January 9, 1942, adopted a resolution containing recitals taken largely from the Court's *Gobitis* opinion and ordering that the salute to the flag become "a regular part of the program of activities in the public schools," that all teachers and pupils "shall be required to participate in the salute honoring the Nation represented by the Flag; provided, however, that refusal to salute the Flag be regarded as an act of insubordination, and shall be dealt with accordingly."[2]

The resolution originally required the "commonly accepted salute to the Flag" which it defined. Objections to the salute as "being too much like Hitler's" were raised by the Parent and Teachers Association, the Boy and Girl Scouts, the Red Cross, and the Federation of Women's Clubs.[3] Some modification appears to have been made in deference to these objections, but no concession was made to Jehovah's Witnesses.[4] What is now required is the "stiff-arm" salute, the saluter to keep the right hand raised with palm turned up while the following is repeated: "I pledge allegiance to the Flag of the United States of America and to the Republic for which it stands; one Nation, indivisible; with liberty and justice for all."

Failure to conform is "insubordination" dealt with by expulsion. Readmission is denied by statute until compliance. Meanwhile the expelled child is "unlawfully absent"[5] and may be proceeded against as a delinquent.[6] His parents or guardians are liable to prosecution,[7] and if convicted are subject to fine not exceeding $50 and jail term not exceeding thirty days.[8]

Appellees, citizens of the United States and of West Virginia, brought suit in the United States District Court for themselves and others similarly situated asking its injunction to restrain enforcement of these laws and regulations against Jehovah's Witnesses. The Witnesses are an unincorporated body teaching that the obligation imposed by law of God is superior to that of laws enacted by temporal government. Their religious beliefs include a literal version of Exodus, Chapter 20, verses 4 and 5, which says: "Thou shalt not make unto thee any graven image, or any likeness of anything that is in heaven above, or that is in the earth beneath, or that is in the water under the earth; thou shalt not bow down thyself to them nor serve them." They consider that the flag is an "image" within this command. For this reason they refuse to salute it.

Children of this faith have been expelled from school and are threatened with exclusion for no other cause. Officials threaten to send them to reformatories maintained for criminally inclined juveniles. Parents of such children have been prosecuted and are threatened with prosecutions for causing delinquency.

The Board of Education moved to dismiss the complaint setting forth these facts and alleging that the law and regulations are an unconstitutional denial of religious freedom, and of freedom of speech, and are invalid under the "due process" and "equal protection" clauses of the Fourteenth Amendment to the Federal Constitution. The cause was submitted on the pleadings to a District Court of three judges. It restrained enforcement as to the plaintiffs and those of that class. The Board of Education brought the case here by direct appeal.[9]

This case calls upon us to reconsider a precedent decision, as the Court throughout its history often has been required to do.[10] Before turning to the *Gobitis* case, however, it is desirable to notice certain characteristics by which this controversy is distinguished.

The freedom asserted by these appellees does not bring them into collision with rights asserted by any other individual. It is such conflicts which most frequently require intervention of the State to determine where the rights of one end and those of another begin. But the refusal of these persons to participate in the ceremony does not interfere with or deny rights of others to do so. Nor is there any question in this case that their behavior is peaceable and orderly. The sole conflict is between authority and rights of the individual. The State asserts power to condition access to public education on making a prescribed sign and profession and at the same time to coerce attendance by punishing both parent and child. The latter stand on a right of self-determination in matters that touch individual opinion and personal attitude.

As the present CHIEF JUSTICE said in dissent in the *Gobitis* case, the State may "require teaching by instruction and study of all in our history and in the structure and organization of our government, including the guaranties of civil liberty, which tend to inspire patriotism and love of country." 310 U.S. at 604. Here, however, we are dealing with a compulsion of students to declare a belief. They are not merely made acquainted with the flag salute so that they may be informed as to what it is or even what it means. The issue here is whether this slow and easily neglected route to aroused loyalties constitutionally may be shortcut by substituting a compulsory salute and slogan.[12] This issue is not prejudiced by the Court's previous holding that where a State, without compelling attendance, extends college facilities to pupils who voluntarily enroll, it may prescribe military training as part of the course without offense to the Constitution. It was held that those who take advantage of its opportunities may not on ground of conscience refuse compliance with such conditions. *Hamilton* v. *Regents*, 293 U.S. 245. In the present case attendance is not optional. That case is also to be distinguished from the present one because, independently of college privileges or requirements, the State has power to raise militia and impose the duties of service therein upon its citizens.

There is no doubt that, in connection with the pledges, the flag salute is a form of utterance. Symbolism is a primitive but effective way of communicating ideas. The use of an emblem or flag to symbolize some system, idea, institution, or personality, is a short cut from mind to mind. Causes and nations, political parties, lodges and ecclesiastical groups seek to knit the loyalty of their followings to a flag or banner, a color or design. The State announces rank, function, and authority through crowns and maces, uniforms and black robes; the church speaks through the Cross, the Crucifix, the altar and shrine, and clerical raiment. Symbols of State often convey political ideas just as religious symbols come to convey theological ones. Associated with many of these symbols are appropriate gestures of acceptance or respect: a salute, a bowed or bared head, a bended knee. A person gets from a symbol the meaning he puts into it, and what is one man's comfort and inspiration is another's jest and scorn.

Over a decade ago Chief Justice Hughes led this Court in holding that the display of a red flag as a symbol of opposition by peaceful and legal means to organized government was protected by the free speech guaranties of the Constitution. *Stromberg* v. *California*, 283 U.S. 359. Here it is the State that employs a flag as a symbol of adherence to government as presently organized. It requires the individual to communicate by word and sign his acceptance of the political ideas it thus bespeaks. Objection to this form of communication when coerced is an old one, well known to the framers of the Bill of Rights.[13]

It is also to be noted that the compulsory flag salute and pledge requires affirmation of a belief and an attitude of mind. It is not clear whether the regulation contemplates that pupils forego any contrary convictions of their own and become unwilling converts to the prescribed ceremony or whether it will be acceptable if they simulate assent by words without belief and by a gesture barren of meaning. It is now a commonplace that censorship or suppression of expression of opinion is tolerated by our Constitution only when the expression presents a clear and present danger of action of a kind the State is empowered to prevent and punish. It would seem that involuntary affirmation could be commanded only on even more immediate and urgent grounds than silence. But here the power of compulsion is invoked without any allegation that remaining passive during a flag salute ritual creates a clear and present danger that would justify an effort even to muffle expression. To sustain the compulsory flag salute we are required to say that a Bill of Rights which guards the individual's right to speak his own mind, left it open to public authorities to compel him to utter what is not in his mind.

Whether the First Amendment to the Constitution will permit officials to order observance of ritual of this nature does not depend upon whether as a voluntary exercise we would think it to be good, bad or merely innocuous. Any credo of nationalism is likely to include what some disapprove or to omit what others think essential, and to give off different overtones as it takes on different accents or interpretations.[14] If official power exists to coerce acceptance of any patriotic creed, what it shall contain cannot be decided by courts, but must be largely discretionary with the ordaining authority, whose power to prescribe would no doubt include power to amend. Hence validity of the asserted power to force an American citizen publicly to profess any statement of belief or to engage in any ceremony of assent to one, presents questions of power that must be considered independently of any idea we may have as to the utility of the ceremony in question.

Nor does the issue as we see it turn on one's possession of particular religious views or the sincerity with which they are held. While religion supplies appellees' motive for enduring the discomforts of making the issue in this case, many citizens who do not share these religious views hold such a compulsory rite to infringe constitutional liberty of the individual.[15] It is not necessary to inquire whether non-conformist beliefs will exempt from the duty to salute unless we first find

power to make the salute a legal duty.

The *Gobitis* decision, however, *assumed,* as did the argument in that case and in this, that power exists in the State to impose the flag salute discipline upon school children in general. The Court only examined and rejected a claim based on religious beliefs of immunity from an unquestioned general rule.[16] The question which underlies the flag salute controversy is whether such a ceremony so touching matters of opinion and political attitude may be imposed upon the individual by official authority under powers committed to any political organization under our Constitution. We examine rather than assume existence of this power and, against this broader definition of issues in this case, reexamine specific grounds assigned for the *Gobitis* decision.

1. It was said that the flag-salute controversy confronted the Court with "the problem which Lincoln cast in memorable dilemma: 'Must a government of necessity be too *strong* for the liberties of its people, or too *weak* to maintain its own existence?'" and that the answer must be in favor of strength. *Minersville School District* v. *Gobitis, supra,* at 596.

We think these issues may be examined free of pressure or restraint growing out of such considerations.

It may be doubted whether Mr. Lincoln would have thought that the strength of government to maintain itself would be impressively vindicated by our confirming power of the State to expel a handful of children from school. Such oversimplification, so handy in political debate, often lacks the precision necessary to postulates of judicial reasoning. If validly applied to this problem, the utterance cited would resolve every issue of power in favor of those in authority and would require us to override every liberty thought to weaken or delay execution of their policies.

Government of limited power need not be anemic government. Assurance that rights are secure tends to diminish fear and jealousy of strong government, and by making us feel safe to live under it makes for its better support. Without promise of a limiting Bill of Rights it is doubtful if our Constitution could have mustered enough strength to enable its ratification. To enforce those rights today is not to choose weak government over strong government. It is only to adhere as a means of strength to individual freedom of mind in preference to officially disciplined uniformity for which history indicates a disappointing and disastrous end.

The subject now before us exemplifies this principle. Free public education, if faithful to the ideal of secular instruction and political neutrality, will not be partisan or enemy of any class, creed, party, or faction. If it is to impose any ideological discipline, however, each party or denomination must seek to control, or failing that, to weaken the influence of the educational system. Observance of the limitations of the Constitution will not weaken government in the field appropriate for its exercise.

2.   It was also considered in the *Gobitis* case that functions of educational officers in States, counties and school districts were such that to interfere with their authority "would in effect make us the school board for the country." *Id.* at 598.

The Fourteenth Amendment, as now applied to the States, protects the citizen against the State itself and all of its creatures—Boards of Education not excepted. These have, of course, important, delicate, and highly discretionary functions, but none that they may not perform within the limits of the Bill of Rights. That they are educating the young for citizenship is reason for scrupulous protection of Constitutional freedoms of the individual, if we are not to strangle the free mind at its source and teach youth to discount important principles of our government as mere platitudes.

Such Boards are numerous and their territorial jurisdiction often small. But small and local authority may feel less sense of responsibility to the Constitution, and agencies of publicity may be less vigilant in calling it to account. The action of Congress in making flag observance voluntary[17] and respecting the conscience of the objector in a matter so vital as raising the Army[18] contrasts sharply with these local regulations in matters relatively trivial to the welfare of the nation. There are village tyrants as well as village Hampdens, but none who acts under color of law is beyond reach of the Constitution.

3.   The *Gobitis* opinion reasoned that this is a field "where courts possess no marked and certainly no controlling competence," that it is committed to the legislatures as well as the courts to guard cherished liberties and that it is constitutionally appropriate to "fight out the wise use of legislative authority in the forum of public opinion and before legislative assemblies rather than to transfer such a contest to the judicial arena," since all the "effective means of inducing political changes are left free." *Id.* at 597-598, 600.

The very purpose of a Bill of Rights was to withdraw certain subjects from the vicissitudes of political controversy, to place them beyond the reach of majorities and officials and to establish them as legal principles to be applied by the courts. One's right to life, liberty, and property, to free speech, a free press, freedom of worship and assembly, and other fundamental rights may not be submitted to vote; they depend on the outcome of no elections.

In weighing arguments of the parties it is important to distinguish between the due process clause of the Fourteenth Amendment as an instrument for transmitting the principles of the First Amendment and those cases in which it is applied for its own sake.

The test of legislation which collides with the Fourteenth Amendment, because it also collides with the principles of the First, is much more definite than the test when only the Fourteenth is involved. Much of the vagueness of the due process clause disappears when the specific prohibitions of the First become its standard. The right of a State to regulate, for example, a public utility may well include, so far as the due process test is concerned, power to impose all of the restrictions which a legislature may have a "rational basis" for adopting. But freedoms of speech and of press, of assembly, and of worship may not be infringed on such slender grounds. They are susceptible of restriction only to prevent grave and immediate danger to interests which the State may lawfully protect. It is important to note that while it is the Fourteenth Amendment which bears directly upon the State it is the more specific limiting principles of the First Amendment that finally govern this case.

Nor does our duty to apply the Bill of Rights to assertions of official authority depend upon our possession of marked competence in the field where the invasion of rights occurs. True, the task of translating the majestic generalities of the Bill of Rights, conceived as part of the pattern of liberal government in the eighteenth century, into concrete restraints on officials dealing with the problems of the twentieth century, is one to disturb self-confidence. These principles grew in soil which also produced a philosophy that the individual was the center of society, that his liberty was attainable through mere absence of governmental restraints, and that government should be entrusted with few controls and only the mildest supervision over men's affairs. We must transplant these rights to a soil in which the *laissez-faire* concept or principle of non-interference has withered at least as to economic affairs, and social advancements are increasingly sought through closer integration of society and through expanded and strengthened governmental controls. These changed conditions often deprive precedents of reliability and cast us more than we would choose upon our own judgment. But we act in these matters not by authority of our competence but by force of our commissions. We cannot, because of modest estimates of our competence in such specialties as public education, withhold the judgment that history authenticates as the function of this Court when liberty is infringed.

4.   Lastly, and this is the very heart of the *Gobitis* opinion, it reasons that "National unity is the basis of national security," that the authorities have "the right to select appropriate means for its attainment," and hence reaches the conclusion that such compulsory measures toward "national unity" are constitutional. *Id.* at 595. Upon the verity of this assumption depends our answer in this case.

National unity as an end which officials may foster by persuasion and example is not in question. The problem is whether under our Constitution compulsion as here employed is a permissible means for its achievement.

Struggles to coerce uniformity of sentiment in support of some end thought essential to their time and country have been waged by many good as well as by evil men. Nationalism is a relatively recent phenomenon but at other times and places the ends have been racial or territorial security, support of a dynasty or regime, and particular plans for saving souls. As first and moderate methods to attain unity have failed, those bent on its accomplishment must resort to an ever-increasing severity. As governmental pressure toward unity becomes greater, so strife becomes more bitter as to whose unity it shall be. Probably no deeper division of our people could proceed from any provocation than from finding it necessary to choose what doctrine and whose program public education officials shall compel youth to unite in embracing. Ultimate futility of such attempts to compel coherence is the lesson of every such effort from the Roman drive to stamp out Christianity as a disturber of its pagan unity, the Inquisition, as a means to religious and dynastic unity, the Siberian exiles as a means to Russian unity, down to the fast failing efforts of our present totalitarian enemies. Those who begin coercive elimination of dissent soon find themselves exterminating dissenters. Compulsory unification of opinion achieves only the unanimity of the graveyard.

It seems trite but necessary to say that the First Amendment to our Constitution was designed to avoid these ends by avoiding these beginnings. There is no mysticism in the American concept of the State or of the nature or origin of its authority. We set up government by consent of the governed, and the Bill of Rights denies those in power any legal opportunity to coerce that consent. Authority here is to be controlled by public opinion, not public opinion by authority.

The case is made difficult not because the principles of its decision are obscure but because the flag involved is our own. Nevertheless, we apply the limitations of the Constitution with no fear that freedom to be intellectually and spiritually diverse or even contrary will disintegrate the social organization. To believe that patriotism will not flourish if patriotic ceremonies are voluntary and spontaneous instead of a compulsory routine is to make an unflattering estimate of the appeal of our institutions to free minds. We can have intellectual individualism and the rich cultural diversities that we owe to exceptional minds only at the price of occasional eccentricity and abnormal attitudes. When they are so harmless to others or to the State as those we deal with here, the price is not too great. But freedom to differ is not limited to things that do not matter much. That would be a mere shadow of freedom. The test of its substance is the right to differ as to things that touch the heart of the existing order.

If there is any fixed star in our constitutional constellation, it is that no official, high or petty, can prescribe what shall be orthodox in politics, nationalism, religion, or other matters of opinion or force citizens to confess by word or act their faith therein. If there are any circumstances which permit an exception, they do not now occur to us.[19]

We think the action of the local authorities in compelling the flag salute and pledge transcends constitutional limitations on their power and invades the sphere of intellect and spirit which it is the purpose of the First Amendment to our Constitution to reserve from all official control.

The decision of this Court in *Minersville School District* v. *Gobitis* and the holdings of those few *per curiam* decisions which preceded and foreshadowed it are overruled, and judgment enjoining enforcement of the West Virginia Regulation is

Affirmed.

NOTES

1. § 1734, West Virginia Code (1941 Supp.): "In all public, private, parochial and denominational schools located within this state there shall be given regular courses of instruction in history of the United States, in civics, and in the constitutions of the United States and of the State of West Virginia, for the purpose of teaching, fostering and perpetuating the ideals, principles and spirit of Americanism, and increasing the knowledge of the organization and machinery of the government of the United States and of the state of West Virginia. The state board of education shall, with the advice of the state superintendent of schools, prescribe the courses of study covering these subjects for the public elementary and grammar schools, public high schools and state normal schools. It shall be the duty of the officials or boards having authority over the respective private, parochial and denominational schools to prescribe courses of study for the schools under their control and supervision similar to those required for the public schools."

2. The text is as follows: "WHEREAS, The West Virginia State Board of Education holds in highest regard those rights and privileges guaranteed by the Bill of Rights in the Constitution of the United States of America and in the Constitution of West Virginia, specifically, the first amendment to the Constitution of the United States as restated in the fourteenth amendment to the same document and in the guarantee of religious freedom in Article III of the Constitution of this State, and

   "WHEREAS, The West Virginia State Board of Education honors the broad principle that one's convictions about the ultimate mystery of the universe and man's relation to it is placed beyond the reach of law; that the propagation of belief is protected whether in church or chapel, mosque or synagogue, tabernacle or meeting house; that the Constitutions of the United

States and of the State of West Virginia assure generous immunity to the individual from imposition of penalty for offending, in the course of his own religious activities, the religious views of others, be they a minority or those who are dominant in the government, but

"WHEREAS, The West Virginia State Board of Education recognizes that the manifold character of man's relations may bring his conception of religious duty into conflict with the secular interests of his fellowman; that conscientious scruples have not in the course of the long struggle for religious toleration relieved the individual from obedience to the general law not aimed at the promotion or restriction of the religious beliefs; that the mere possession of convictions which contradict the relevant concerns of political society does not relieve the citizen from the discharge of political responsibility, and

"WHEREAS, The West Virginia State Board of Education holds that national unity is the basis of national security; that the flag of our Nation is the symbol of our National Unity transcending all internal differences, however large within the framework of the Constitution; that the Flag is the symbol of the Nation's power; that emblem of freedom in its truest, best sense; that it signifies government resting on the consent of the governed, liberty regulated by law, protection of the weak against the strong, security against the exercise of arbitrary power, and absolute safety for free institutions against foreign aggression, and

"WHEREAS, The West Virginia State Board of Education maintains that the public schools, established by the legislature of the State of West Virginia under the authority of the Constitution of the State of West Virginia and supported by taxes imposed by legally constituted measures, are dealing with the formative period in the development in citizenship that the Flag is an allowable portion of the program of schools thus publicly supported.

"Therefore, be it RESOLVED, That the West Virginia Board of Education does hereby recognize and order that the commonly accepted salute to the Flag of the United States—the right hand is placed upon the breast and following pledge repeated in unison: 'I pledge allegiance to the Flag of the United States of America and to the Republic for which it stands; one Nation, indivisible, with liberty and justice for all'—now becomes a regular part of the program of activities in the public schools, supported in whole or in part by public funds, and that all teachers as defined by law in West Virginia and pupils in such schools shall be required to participate in the salute, honoring the Nation represented by the Flag; provided, however, that refusal to salute the Flag be regarded as an act of insubordination, and shall be dealt with accordingly."

3. The National Headquarters of the United States Flag Association takes the position that the extension of the right arm in this salute to the flag is not the Nazi-Fascist salute, "although quite similar to it. In the Pledge to the Flag the right arm is extended and raised, palm UPWARD, whereas the Nazis extend the arm practically *straight to the front* (the finger tips being about even with the eyes), *palm DOWNWARD*, and the Fascists do the same except they raise the arm slightly higher." James A. Moss, The Flag of the United States: Its History and Symbolism (1914) 108.

4. They have offered in lieu of participating in the flag

salute ceremony "periodically and publicly" to give the following pledge:

"I have pledged my unqualified allegiance and devotion to Jehovah, the Almighty God, and to His Kingdom, for which Jesus commands all Christians to pray.

"I respect the flag of the United States and acknowledge it as a symbol of freedom [and] justice to all.

"I pledge allegiance and obedience to all the laws of the United States that are consistent with God's law, as set forth in the Bible."

5. § 1851 (1), West Virginia Code (1941 Supp.): "If a child be dismissed, suspended, or expelled from school because of refusal of such child to meet legal and lawful requirements of the school and the established regulations of the county and/or state board of education, further admission of the child to school shall be refused until such requirements and regulations be complied with. Any such child shall be treated as being unlawfully absent from school during the time he refuses to comply with such requirements and regulations, and any person having legal or actual control of such child shall be liable to prosecution under the provisions of this article for the absence of such child from school."

6. § 4904 (4), West Virginia Code (1941 Supp.).

7. See Note 5, *supra*.

8. §§ 1847, 1851, West Virginia Code (1941 Supp.).

9. § 266 of the Judicial Code, 28 U.S.C. § 380.

10. See authorities cited in *Helvering* v. *Griffiths*, 318 U.S. 371, 401, note 52.

11. See the nation-wide survey of the study of American history conducted by the New York Times, the results of which are published in the issue of June 21, 1942, and are there summarized on p. 1, col. 1, as follows:

"82 percent of the institutions of higher learning in the United States do not require the study of United States history for the undergraduate degree. Eighteen percent of the colleges and universities require such history courses before a degree is awarded. It was found that many students complete their four years in college without taking any history courses dealing with this country.

"Seventy-two percent of the colleges and universities do not require United States history for admission, while 28 percent require it. As a result, the survey revealed, many students go through high school, college and then to the professional or graduate institution without having explored courses in the history of their country.

"Less than 10 percent of the total undergraduate body was enrolled in United States history classes during the Spring semester just ended. Only 8 percent of the freshman class took courses in the United States history, although 30 percent was enrolled in European or world history courses."

12. The Resolution of the Board of Education did not adopt the flag salute because it was claimed to have educational value. It seems to have been concerned with promotion of national unity (see footnote 2), which justification is considered later in this opinion. No information as to its educational aspect is called to our attention except Olander, Children's Knowledge of the Flag Salute, 35 Journal of Educational Research 300, 305, which sets forth a study of the ability of a large and

representative number of children to remember and state the meaning of the flag salute which they recited each day in school. His conclusion was that it revealed "a rather pathetic picture of our attempts to teach children not only the words but the meaning of our Flag Salute."

13. Early Christians were frequently persecuted for their refusal to participate in ceremonies before the statue of the emperor or other symbol of imperial authority. The story of William Tell's sentence to shoot an apple off his son's head for refusal to salute a bailiff's hat is an ancient one. 21 Encyclopedia Britannica (14th ed.) 911-912. The Quakers, William Penn included, suffered punishment rather than uncover their heads in deference to any civil authority. Braithwaite, The Beginnings of Quakerism (1912) 200, 229-230, 232-233, 447, 451; Fox, Quakers Courageous (1941) 113.

14. For example: Use of "Republic," if rendered to distinguish our government from a "democracy," or the words "one Nation," if intended to distinguish it from a "federation," open up old and bitter controversies in our political history; "liberty and justice for all," if it must be accepted as descriptive of the present order rather than an ideal, might to some seem an overstatement.

15. Cushman, Constitutional Law in 1939-1940, 35 American Political Science Review 250, 271, observes: "All of the eloquence by which the majority extol the ceremony of flag saluting as a free expression of patriotism turns sour when used to describe the brutal compulsion which requires a sensitive and conscientious child to stultify himself in public." For further criticism of the opinion in the *Gobitis* case by persons who do not share the faith of the Witnesses see: Powell, Conscience and the Constitution, in Democracy and National Unity (University of Chicago Press, 1941) 1; Wilkinson, Some Aspects of the Constitutional Guarantees of Civil Liberty, 11 Fordham Law Review 50; Fennell, The "Reconstructed Court" and Religious Freedom: The Gobitis Case in Retrospect, 19 New York University Law Quarterly Review 31; Green, Liberty under the Fourteenth Amendment, 27 Washington University Law Quarterly 497; 9 International Juridi-

cal Association Bulletin 1; 39 Michigan Law Review 149; 15 St. John's Law Review 95.

16. The opinion says "That the flag-salute is an allowable portion of a school program *for those who do not invoke conscientious scruples* is *surely not debatable.* But for us to insist that, *though the ceremony may be required, exceptional immunity must be given to dissidents,* is to maintain that there is no basis for a legislative judgment that such an exemption might introduce elements of difficulty into the school discipline, might cast doubts in the minds of the other children which would themselves weaken the effect of the exercise." (Italics ours.) 310 U.S. at 599-600. And elsewhere the question under consideration was stated, "When does the constitutional guarantee *compel exemption* from doing what society thinks necessary for the promotion of some great common end, or from a penalty for conduct which appears dangerous to the general good?" (Italics ours.) *Id.* at 593. And again, "...whether school children, like the Gobitis children, must be *excused from conduct required of all the other children* in the promotion of national cohesion...." (Italics ours.) *Id.* at 595.

17. Section 7 of House Joint Resolution 359, approved December 22, 1942, 56 Stat. 1074, 36 U.S.C. (1942 Supp.) § 172, prescribes no penalties for nonconformity but provides:

"That the pledge of allegiance to the flag, 'I pledge allegiance to the flag of the United States of America and to the Republic for which it stands, one Nation indivisible, with liberty and justice for all,' be rendered by standing with the right hand over the heart. However, civilians will always show full respect to the flag when the pledge is given by merely standing at attention, men removing the headdress...."

18. § 5 (a) of the Selective Training and Service Act of 1940, 50 U.S.C. (App.) § 307 (g).

19. The Nation may raise armies and compel citizens to give military service. *Selective Draft Law Cases,* 245 U.S. 366. It follows, of course, that those subject to military discipline are under many duties and may not claim many freedoms that we hold inviolable as to those in civilian life.

$\mathbb{A}$ United States District Court in Arizona decides for students of the Jehovah's Witness faith who had been expelled from Pinetop Elementary School solely because of their refusal to stand while other pupils sang "The Star Spangled Banner." In deciding for the students, the Court declared: "The sole justification offered by the defendants here is the opinion of the school authorities that to tolerate refusal of these plaintiffs to stand for the National Anthem would create a disciplinary problem. Evidence as to this is speculative at best and pales altogether when balanced against the 'preferred position' of First Amendment rights. . . . Indeed, there is much to be said for the view that, rather than creating a disciplinary problem, acceptance of the refusal of a few pupils to stand while the remainder stand and sing of their devotion to flag and country might well be turned into a fine lesson in American government for the entire class." The Court concluded: "Since it appears that the conduct of the pupils involved here was not disorderly and did not materially disrupt the conduct and discipline of the school, and since there is a lack of substantial evidence that it will do so in the future, a writ of injunction will issue permanently restraining the Board of Trustees of Pinetop Elementary School from excluding the plaintiffs from attendance at the school solely because they silently refuse to rise and stand for the playing or singing of the National Anthem."

Sheldon v. *Fannin*, 221 F. Supp. 766 (1963)

MATHES, District Judge:

This is a suit for injunctive relief, brought pursuant to the Civil Rights Act of 1871. [42 U.S.C. §§ 1983, 1985(3) and 1988.] Jurisdiction of this Court is invoked under 28 U.S.C. § 1343(3).

Plaintiffs Sheldon are the parents of Daniel Mark Sheldon. Plaintiffs Wingo are the parents of Merle William Wingo and Jere Bruce Wingo. All are Jehovah's Witnesses. These plaintiffs, suing only as parents, have no standing to sue in their own right [cf. People of State of Ill. ex rel. McCullom v. Board of Education, 333 U.S. 203, 68 S.Ct. 461, 92 L.Ed. 649 (1948)], since their claim based on an interest in the education of their children does not present a substantial Federal question [cf. Adler v. Board of Education, 342 U.S. 485, 502-503, 72 S.Ct. 380, 96 L.Ed. 517 (1952) (Frankfurter J., dissenting)]. However, inasmuch as they also sue on behalf of their children, they are deemed to appear as guardians *ad litem*. For the purposes of this opinion, therefore, the children will be considered to be the plaintiffs, since they are the real parties in interest as to the claims here asserted.

It should be noted in passing that the parents also purport to bring this as a class action "for all other of

Jehovah's Witnesses and their children of compulsory school age throughout the entire State of Arizona." In this respect they must fail because, as more fully appears below, the only acts as to which redress may be obtained in this case are the acts of the local school board. That board is not threatening the other parties which plaintiffs at bar purport to represent. [See Fed. R.Civ.P. 23(a) (3), 28 U.S.C.A.]

The defendants are the Arizona State Board of Education, the individual members thereof, the Superintendent of Public Instruction of the State of Arizona, the Board of Trustees of Pinetop Elementary School, a public grade school of Pinetop, Arizona, and the individual members thereof.

The facts are without controversy, and may be briefly stated. On September 29, 1961, the plaintiffs were suspended from Pinetop Elementary School for insubordination, because of their refusal to stand for the singing of the National Anthem. This refusal to participate, even to the extent of standing, without singing, is said to have been dictated by their religious beliefs as Jehovah's Witnesses, requiring their literal acceptance of the Bible as the Word of Almighty God Jehovah. Both precedent and authority for their refusal to stand is claimed to be found in the refusal of the three Hebrew children Shadrach, Meshach and Abednego, to bow down at the sound of musical instruments playing patriotic-religious music throughout the land at the order of King Nebuchadnezzar of ancient Babylon. [Daniel 3:13-28.] For a similar reason, members of the Jehovah's Witnesses sect refuse to recite the Pledge of Allegiance to the Flag of the United States, viewing this patriotic ceremony to be the worship of a graven image. [Exodus 20:4-5.] However, by some process of reasoning we need not tarry to explore, they are willing to stand during the Pledge of Allegiance, out of respect for the Flag as a symbol of the religious freedom they enjoy. [See West Virginia State Board of Education v. Barnette, 319 U.S. 624, 63 S.Ct. 1178, 87 L.Ed. 1628 (1943).]

The plaintiffs were expelled from Pinetop Elementary School solely because of their refusal to stand for the National Anthem. They were not accused of any other misconduct of any kind, and were in no scholastic difficulty. They have since continued their education at home, and are therefore subject to a charge of truancy and delinquency under Arizona law for failing to attend school until they have passed the compulsory education age. Their parents too face possible prosecution for a violation of Arizona's school laws.

For these reasons and because they have not the financial means to obtain an adequate education otherwise than in the public schools of the State, the plaintiffs allege irreparable damage and the lack of an adequate remedy at law, and hence seek the injunctive relief of this Federal court of equity against continued refusal of the defendant trustees to readmit them to Pinetop Elementary School, asserting that such action of the trustees infringes First Amendment rights protected against State action by the Fourteenth Amendment.

The plaintiffs also allege that their conduct does not present any clear or present danger to the orderly operation of the school, which the State has the Constitutional power to prevent, and they deny that their refusal to stand while other pupils sing the Star Spangled Banner is conduct which is in anywise contrary to morals, health, safety or welfare of the public, the State, or the Nation.

The plaintiffs further allege that they have exhausted administrative remedies by appealing to the Board of Trustees of Pinetop Elementary School for an order exempting them from participation in the National Anthem ceremony; that such relief has been denied them, and that further appeal to the State Board of Education, or to the Superintendent of Public Instruction, would be futile, because it must be presumed that those officials would enforce the State statutes here involved, which make no provision for any exemption from the ceremony.

The plaintiffs pray that the State statutes in question be declared invalid, both on their face, and as applied by the administrative officials of the State. Because of this prayer, a three-judge District Court was convened pursuant to 28 U.S.C. § 2281. However, after hearing argument as to whether or not this case falls within the purview of § 2281, the three judges entered an order disempanelling the multi-judge court, and returned the case to a single judge. The Supreme Court dismissed the plaintiffs' appeal from that order [Sheldon v. Fannin, 372 U.S. 228, 83 S.Ct. 679, 9 L.Ed.2d 714 (1963)], and also denied the motion of the plaintiffs for leave to file a petition for writ of mandamus to challenge the correctness of the order [Sheldon v. Merrill, 372 U.S. 904, 83 S.Ct. 744, 9 L.Ed.2d 730 (1963)].

Before proceeding to a trial of the merits, I requested the parties to consider whether the order of the three judge court, and the rulings of the Supreme Court with respect thereto, amounted to an adjudication that the action of the defendant trustees here sought to be enjoined is not "State action" within the scope of 28 U.S.C. § 1343 (3), and hence in legal effect a holding that this District Court does not have subject-matter jurisdiction of the claim to equitable relief which the plaintiffs here assert.

The complaint, as several times amended, draws in question various sections of the Arizona Revised Statutes. Section 15–102, which prescribes the duties of the State Board of Education, provides in part that:

"The state board of education shall:

*   *   *

"14. Exercise general supervision over and regulate the conduct of the public school system.

"15. Prescribe and enforce a course of study in the common schools.

"16. Prescribe the subjects to be taught in all common schools.

*   *   *

"18. Prescribe textbooks for the common schools, and shall prepare a list of three textbooks for each grade and each subject taught in the common schools for the selection by the school district of one book from such list for each student.* * *" [Ariz.Rev.Stat. § 15-102.]

Authority for the Board of Trustees of each school district to make rules and regulations for the conduct of children attending school is granted by § 15-441, which declares that:

"A. The board of trustees shall prescribe and enforce rules for the government of the schools, not inconsistent with law or rules prescribed by the state board of education." [Ariz.Rev.Stat. § 15-441.]

Duties of the local Board of Trustees are prescribed in § 15-442, which provides in part that:

"A. The board of trustees shall:

* * *

"2. Enforce the courses of study and select all textbooks used in the schools from the multiple lists determined and authorized by the state board of education * * *." [Ariz.Rev.Stat. § 15-442.]

Section 15-1031, providing for the display of the flag and the holding of certain patriotic exercises, reads in part:

"B. The state superintendent of public instruction shall prepare for use in the public schools a program providing for a salute to the flag and other patriotic exercises, as meet the requirements of the different grades. * * *" [Ariz.Rev.Stat. § 15-1031.]

The plaintiffs allege that, pursuant to the authority conferred by the above-quoted provisions of § 15-102, the State Board of Education prescribed a course of study in music for all children in rural elementary schools, of which Pinetop Elementary School was one, and issued music and song books to be used by the students therein whenever the principals or teachers called for school music assembly; that these song books contain the National Anthem and, as part of this course of study, the pupils are required to stand for the singing or playing of the National Anthem. The plaintiffs argue that the prescription of the music study and issuance of music books by the State Board was a declaration of policy by that body equivalent to a regulation, although no formal regulation was issued, and that the Pinetop trustees were required by § 15-442, supra, to adopt and implement this policy, even though not embodied in a formal regulation.

The plaintiffs also allege that the defendant Dick, acting in his dual capacity as State Superintendent of Public Instruction, and as chief executive officer of the State Board of Education, did "prepare for use in the public schools a program providing for * * * other patriotic exercises * * *," within the meaning of § 15-1031(B), supra, by distributing to all county superintendents of education Opinion No. 61-21 of the Arizona Attorney General, in which the Attorney General expressed his concurrence in an earlier opinion of Coconino County Attorney to the effect that the school officials of Arizona may compel children of Jehovah's Witnesses to stand for the National Anthem, without violating their freedom of religion.

Finally, the plaintiffs allege that, acting pursuant to the general policy above-described, the Pinetop Board of Trustees instituted a musical program for general assemblies which included the playing of the National Anthem; that pupils were required to stand during the singing of the National Anthem by the assembled group; that it was at one of these assemblies that the plaintiffs refused to stand and were ordered by the principal to leave school; that this order was specifically authorized by the Pinetop Board of Trustees with full knowledge of the plaintiffs' conscientious objection; and that following expulsion of the children and refusal of the principal to readmit them, the defendant Dick, acting in his dual capacity, made a special visit to the Pinetop school and ratified the actions of the principal and the trustees.

The plaintiffs urge that all of the above-described action was authorized by, done pursuant to, and amounted to "enforcement" of, the State statutes in question, within the meaning of 28 U.S.C. § 2281.

In their answer the defendants admit that the State Board prescribed the course of music study, but specifically allege that it was suggestive and not mandatory upon local school districts. The defendants argue, moreover, that none of the cited statutes require the plaintiffs to stand while the National Anthem is sung or played; that in all events no rule or regulation can be validly promulgated by an agency such as the State Board of Education, otherwise than by following the provisions of §§ 41-1001 to 41-1006 of the Arizona Revised Statutes, which require certification and filing in the office of the Secretary of State; and that the certificate of the Secretary of State declares no such rule or regulation has ever been filed.

The defendants also point out that the opinion of the Attorney General circulated by defendant Dick was that of a County Attorney addressed to a school board of his county, and was concurred in by the Attorney General as required by law [Ariz.Rev.Stat. § 15-122(B)], solely to protect the members of the local school board from personal liability for acts done in reliance upon the opinion of the County Attorney. [See Ariz.Rev.Stat. § 15-436(B).]—And as to the course of study prescribed by the State Board of Education and followed by the Pinetop Board of Trustees, the Arizona Director of Elementary Education states that such courses of study are suggestive only and do not require standing for the National Anthem or expulsion for failure to stand.

It was the conclusion of the three-judge court, as a result of that court's inquiry into jurisdiction [see Land v. Dollar, 330 U.S. 731, 735, n. 4, 67 S.Ct. 1009, 91 L.Ed. 1209 (1947)], that the requirement the plaintiffs stand during the National Anthem "was not imposed by statute or by administrative action of any state agency or officer other than the local school board itself, and had no application to any other school district." On the basis of this conclusion, the three-judge court held that it had no jurisdiction under 28 U.S.C. § 2281, which provides:

"An * * * injunction restraining the enforcement, operation or execution of any State statute * * or of an order made by an administrative board or commission acting under State statutes, shall not be granted by any district court or judge thereof upon the ground of the unconstitutionality of such statute unless the application therefor is heard and determined by a district court of three judges under section 2284 of this title." [28 U.S.C. § 2281.]

In support of that decision the three-judge court cited: City of Cleveland v. United States, 323 U.S. 329, 65 S.Ct. 280, 89 L.Ed. 274 (1945); Ex parte Bransford, 310 U.S. 354, 60 S.Ct. 947, 84 L.Ed. 1249 (1940); Wilentz v. Sovereign Camp, 306 U.S. 573, 59 S.Ct. 709, 83 L.Ed. 994 (1939); Ex parte Public National Bank, 278 U.S. 101, 49 S.Ct. 43, 73 L.Ed. 202 (1928); Ex parte Collins, 277 U.S. 565, 48 S.Ct. 585, 72 L.Ed. 990 (1928).

In view of the very circumscribed definition of State action which the cited cases delineate as being within the ambit of § 2281, it is clear that the order of the three-judge court does not preclude subject-matter jurisdiction under 28 U.S.C. § 1343 (3), which, repeating the essential substantive language of the Civil Rights Acts [42 U.S.C. § 1983], declares that:

"The district courts shall have original jurisdiction of any civil action authorized by law to be commenced by any person: * * *

"(3) To redress the deprivation, under color of any State *law,* statute, *ordinance,* regulation, *custom* or *usage,* of any right, privilege or immunity secured by the Constitution of the United States. * * *." [Emphasis added, 28 U.S.C. § 1343(3)].

The emphasized words from § 1343(3)—words which do not appear in § 2281—indicate that some forms of State action, although alleged to violate constitutional rights, may only be considered by a single-judge District Court. The Congress appears to have felt that a constitutional attack upon the conduct of State subdivisions or individuals acting, not as direct representatives of the State, but merely "under color of state law," does not question the very sovereignty of the State to the same degree as a constitutional attack directed against enforcement of State statutes and the administrative orders of State officials.

Two recent opinions of the Court of Appeals for the Ninth Circuit give support to this view. In Hatfield v. Bailleaux [290, F.2d 632 (9th Cir. 1961), cert. denied, 368 U.S. 862, 82 S.Ct. 105, 7 L.Ed.2d 59 (1961)], State prisoners, invoking Federal jurisdiction under 28 U.S.C. § 1343(3), sought to enjoin State officials from enforcing certain prison regulations and certain customs and usages which, plaintiffs contended, unconstitutionally limited their research on and preparation of legal papers within the purview of 42 U.S.C. § 1983. On appeal it was held that a three-judge District Court was unnecessary, but at the same time the Court found jurisdiction under 28 U.S.C. § 1343(3). The second case, Marshall v. Sawyer [301 F.2d 639 (9th Cir. 1962)], was a Civil-Rights-Act suit [42 U.S.C. § 1983] for damages and an injunction against Nevada officials allegedly responsible, through their publication of a "Black Book," for plaintiff's ouster from a casino. The Court held that this "Black Book" was not a State administrative order within 28 U.S.C. § 2281, and hence that a three-judge District Court was not required. Reversing the District Court's dismissal under the abstention doctrine, and remanding, the Court stated in dictum:

"The defendants' conduct was engaged in under color of state law if they were clothed with the authority of the state and were purporting to act thereunder, whether or not the conduct complained of was authorized or, indeed, if it was proscribed by state law." [301 F.2d at 646.]

Furthermore, the recent case of Monroe v. Pape (365 U.S. 167, 81 S.Ct. 473, 5 L.Ed.2d 492 (1961)] has made it clear that only the most tenuous connection of the defendant with the State is necessary to constitute "State action" within the ambit of 28 U.S.C. § 1343(3). The Supreme Court there held, relying on United States v. Classic, 313 U.S. 299, 61 S.Ct. 1031, 85 L.Ed. 1368 (1941) and Screws v. United States, 325 U.S. 91, 65 S.Ct. 1031, 89 L.Ed. 1495 (1945), that the phrase "under color of any statute, ordinance, regulation, custom or usage, of any State * * *" included conduct of city police officers who could show no authority whatever under State law, custom or usage therefor; conduct which, in fact, actually violated the State constitution and laws. The Court there declared that 42 U.S.C. § 1983 was "meant to give a remedy to parties deprived of constitutional rights, privileges and immunities by an official's abuse of his position." [365 U.S. at 172, 81 S.Ct. at 476, 5 L.Ed.2d 492.] The rule of Monroe v. Pape has been applied recently by the Court of Appeals for the Ninth Circuit in two actions under 42 U.S.C. § 1983 against police officers seeking redress for illegal searches and seizures which are contrary to State law and in defiance of State policy and State authority. [See: Smith v. Cremins, 308 F.2d 187 (9th Cir. 1962); Cohen v. Norris, 300 F.2d 24 (9th Cir. 1962); see also: Maryland v. Heyse, 315 F.2d 312 (10th Cir. 1963); Hardwick v. Hurley, 289 F.2d 529 (7th Cir. 1961); Selico v. Jackson, 201 F. Supp. 475 (S.D.Cal. 1962).]

However reluctantly, all of the inferior courts in the Federal judicial hierarchy must follow the holding of Monroe v. Pape. Accordingly, I must hold that the action of the Board of Trustees of Pinetop School, which, as the three-judge court found, is the only action responsible for any of the plaintiffs' claimed injuries, constitutes "State action" within the jurisdictional provisions of 28 U.S.C. § 1343(3).

Turning now to the merits, I like to recall that the founding fathers inscribed upon the Great Seal of the

United States the Latin phrase *novus ordo seclorum*—"a new order of the ages." This proud boast proclaimed their pride and their faith in the new nation they had founded here—a nation where everyone from the highest official to the most humble citizen must act under and in accordance with the law.

The keystone of this "new order" has always been freedom of expression—the widest practicable individual freedom to believe, to speak, to act.

Our forebears realized that ideas for preservation and improvement of a free society must come, not from the government, but from the people, and must compete for acceptance by the people, just as goods and services compete for acceptance in our free-enterprise economy. They realized too that in order to compete for acceptance, these ideas must be freely expressed by act and deed; that only in this way can the truth prevail; that only in this way can an idea despised today win the acceptance of reason tomorrow, or be thoroughly discredited; and that only by protecting the freedom of the smallest minority to express unpopular ideas by word or deed can the majority insure freedom to believe and express its own ideas, and to dispute and criticize those of others. [See Abrams v. United States, 250 U.S. 616, 630, 40 S.Ct. 17, 22, 63 L.Ed. 1173 (1919) (Holmes J., dissenting).]

This principle of freedom of belief and expression was so esteemed by the founding fathers that it was embodied in the First Amendment to the Constitution of the United States with the unqualified declaration that: "Congress shall make no law respecting an establishment of religion, or prohibiting the free exercise thereof; or abridging the freedom of speech, or of the press; or the right of the people peaceably to assemble, and petition the Government for a redress of grievances." And these freedoms have since been held protected against State action by the Fourteenth Amendment. [See, e.g., Cantwell v. Connecticut, 310 U.S. 296, 60 S.Ct. 900, 84 L.Ed. 1213 (1940).]

However, the unqualified declaration of the first Amendment has never been literally enforced. [See: Konigsburg v. State Bar, 366 U.S. 36, 50, 81 S.Ct. 997, 6 L.Ed.2d 105 (1961); Breard v. Alexandrie, 341 U.S. 622, 642 n. 33, 71 S.Ct. 920, 95 L.Ed. 1233 (1951); Robertson v. Baldwin, 165 U.S. 275, 281, 17 S.Ct. 326, 41 L.Ed. 715 (1897); Gompers v. United States, 233 U.S. 604, 610, 34 S.Ct. 693, 58 L.Ed. 1115 (1914).] The right to believe, to speak, to act, in the exercise of freedom of expression, like all legal rights under our common-law system of justice, presupposes the correlative legal duty always to do whatever is reasonable, and to refrain from doing whatever is unreasonable, under the circumstances; and hence these fundamental rights are ever subject to such abridgements or restraints as are dictated by reason. [See: Speiser v. Randall, 357 U.S. 513, 521, 78 S.Ct. 1332, 2 L.Ed.2d 1460 (1958); Pound, The Spirit of the Common Law, 182-183 (1921).]

But we so prize freedom of expression—deem it so essential to the maintenance of "a government of laws and not of men"—that the bounds of restraint upon First Amendment rights which will be tolerated as reasonable are narrow in the extreme.

"If there is any fixed star in our constitutional constellation, it is that no official, high or petty, can prescribe what shall be orthodox in politics, nationalism, religion, or other matters of opinion or force citizens to confess by word or act their faith therein." [West Virginia State Board of Education v. Barnette, 319 U.S. 624, 642, 63 S.Ct. 1178, 1187, 87 L.Ed. 1628 (1943).]

It was in Schenck v. United States [249 U.S. 47, 52, 39 S.Ct. 247, 249, 63 L.Ed. 470 (1919)]—a prosecution under the Espionage Act of 1917 [40 Stat. 217 (1917)]—that the criteria of permissible restraint upon freedom of expression were stated by Mr. Justice Holmes: "The question in every case is whether the words used are used in such circumstances and are of such a nature as to create a clear and present danger that they will bring about the substantive evils that Congress has a right to prevent. It is a question of proximity and degree."

"This is a rule of reason," Mr. Justice Brandeis later wrote, adding: "Correctly applied, it will preserve the right of free speech both from suppression by tyrannous, well-meaning majorities and from abuse by irresponsible, fanatical minorities. * * * [I]t can be applied correctly only by the exercise of good judgment; and to the exercise of good judgment, calmness is, in times of deep feeling and on subjects which excite passion, as essential as fearlessness and honesty." [Schaefer v. United States, 251 U.S. 466, 482-483, 40 S.Ct. 259, 264, 265, 64 L.Ed. 360 (1920).]

It is, of course, within the bounds of reasonable abridgement of freedom of expression, as Mr. Chief Justice Hughes pointed out in Near v. Minnesota [283 U.S. 697, 716, 51 S.Ct. 625, 631, 75 L.Ed. 1357 (1931)], that: "The security of the community life may be protected against incitements to acts of violence and the overthrow by force of orderly government." [See also: Whitney v. California, 274 U.S. 357, 373, 47 S.Ct. 641, 71 L.Ed. 1095 (1927); Chafee, Free Speech in the United States, 129-135 (1941); Richardson, Freedom of Expression and the Function of Courts, 65 Har.L.Rev. 1 (1951).]

The standard of permissible restraint upon freedom of speech applies as well to freedom of religion. Thus, although the State may not establish a religion, it may curtail religious expressions by word or deed which create a clear and present danger of impairing the public health or safety, or of offending widely accepted moral codes, or of resulting in a more-than-negligible breach of the peace. [Cf. Roth v. United States, 354 U.S. 476, 484, 77 S.Ct. 1304, 1 L.Ed.2d 1498 (1957); Feiner v. New York, 340 U.S. 315, 320, 71 S.Ct. 303, 95 L.Ed. 267 (1951); Chaplinsky v. New Hampshire, 315 U.S. 568, 571-572, 62 S.Ct. 766, 86 L.Ed. 1031 (1942).]

Notwithstanding offense to certain religious beliefs, the State may declare a uniform day of rest for its citizens [Braunfeld v. Brown, 366 U.S. 599, 81 S.Ct. 1144, 6 L.Ed.2d 563 (1961); Gallagher v. Crown Kosher Super Market, 366 U.S. 617, 81 S.Ct. 1122, 6 L.Ed.2d 536 (1961)]; regulate the practice of polygamy [Cleveland v. United States, 329 U.S. 14, 67 S.Ct. 13, 91 L.Ed. 12 (1946); Reynolds v. United States, 98 U.S. 145, 25 L.Ed. 244 (1878)]; regulate child labor [Prince v. Massachusetts, 321 U.S. 158, 64 S.Ct. 438, 88 L.Ed. 645 (1944)]; and require military training upon attendance at non-compulsory schools [Hamilton v. Regents, 293 U.S. 245, 55 S.Ct. 197, 79 L.Ed. 343 (1934)].

Where, however, a particular application of a general law not protective of some fundamental State concern materially abridges free expression or practice of religious belief, then the law must give way to the exercise of religion. Thus a State may not deny unemployment compensation to a Sabbatarian unwilling to accept Saturday employment. [Sherbert v. Verner, 374 U.S. 398, 83 S.Ct. 1790, 10 L.Ed.2d 965 (1963).] Nor may it prohibit door-to-door solicitation of funds by colporteurs of religious tracts [Martin v. City of Struthers, 319 U.S. 141, 63 S.Ct. 862, 87 L.Ed. 1313 (1943)], or even require them to pay a general license tax [Murdock v. Pennsylvania, 319 U.S. 105, 63 S.Ct. 870, 87 L.Ed. 1292 (1943)]. And while a State may regulate the time, place and manner of solicitation upon public streets, it may not condition issuance of a permit therefor upon administrative determination of an applicant's religious status. [Cantwell v. Connecticut, 310 U.S. 296, 60 S.Ct. 900, 84 L.Ed. 1213 (1940).]

Clearly, then, if the refusal to participate in the ceremony attendant upon the singing or playing of the National Anthem had not occurred in a public-school classroom, but in some other public or private place, there would be not the slightest doubt that the plaintiffs were free to participate or not as they choose. Every citizen is free to stand or sit, sing or remain silent, when the Star Spangled Banner is played.

But the case at bar involves refusal to participate in a public-school-classroom ceremony. Relying upon the recent "school-prayer" decisions [School District of Abington v. Schempp, 374 U.S. 203, 83 S.Ct. 1560, 10 L.Ed.2d 844 (1963); Engel v. Vitale, 370 U.S. 421, 82 S.Ct. 1261, 8 L.Ed.2d 601 (1962)], the plaintiffs first argue that the National Anthem contains words of prayer, adoration and reverence for the Deity, and

that a State's prescription of participation therein amounts to a prohibited "establishment of religion." This contention must be rejected. The singing of the National Anthem is not a religious but a patriotic ceremony, intended to inspire devotion to and love of country. Any religious references therein are incidental and expressive only of the faith which as a matter of historical fact has inspired the growth of the nation. [Cf., Engel v. Vitale, 370 U.S. 421, at 435, n. 21, 82 S.Ct. at 1269, 8 L.Ed.2d 601 (1962).] The Star Spangled Banner may be freely sung in the public schools, without fear of having the ceremony characterized as an "establishment of religion" which violates the First Amendment.

The plaintiffs next urge that coercing their participation, even to the extent of requiring them on pain of expulsion merely to stand while the other pupils sing the Star Spangled Banner, unreasonably abridges their rights to the free exercise of religion under the First Amendment. In considering this contention, it should be observed that lack of violation of the "establishment clause" does not *ipso facto* preclude violation of the "free-exercise clause." For the former looks to the majority's concept of the term religion, the latter the minority's.

In view of the plaintiffs' avowed willingness to stand for the Pledge of Allegiance to the Flag, it may strain credulity that their claim of religious objection to standing as well for the National Anthem is bona fide or sincere. But all who live under the protection of our Flag are free to believe whatever they may choose to believe and to express that belief, within the limits of free expression, no matter how unfounded or even ludicrous the professed belief may seem to others. While implicitly demanding that all freedom of expression be exercised reasonably under the circumstances, the Constitution fortunately does not require that the beliefs or thoughts expressed be reasonable, or wise, or even sensible. The First Amendment thus guarantees to the plaintiffs the right to claim that their objection to standing is based upon religious belief, and the sincerity or reasonableness of this claim may not be examined by this or any other Court. [United States v. Ballard, 322 U.S. 78, 86-88, 64 S.Ct. 882, 88 L.Ed. 1148 (1944); Cantwell v. Connecticut, 310 U.S. 296, 306-307, 60 S.Ct. 900, 84 L.Ed. 1213 (1940); and see Reynolds v. United States, 98 U.S. 145, 25 L.Ed. 244 (1878).]

Accepting, then, the plaintiffs' characterization of their conduct as religiously inspired, this case is ruled by West Virginia State Board of Education v. Barnette, 319 U.S. 624, 63 S.Ct. 1178, 87 L.Ed. 1628 (1943), where the Supreme Court held unconstitutional the expulsion of Jehovah's Witnesses from a public school for refusal to recite the Pledge of Allegiance to the Flag. The decision there rested not merely upon the "free-exercise clause," but also upon the principle inherent in the entire First Amendment: that governmental authority may not directly coerce the unwilling expression of any belief, even in the name of "national unity" in time of war.

Manifestly, the State's interest was much stronger in Barnette than in the case at bar. The sole justification offered by the defendants here is the opinion of the school authorities that to tolerate refusal of these plaintiffs to stand for the National Anthem would create a disciplinary problem. Evidence as to this is speculative at best and pales altogether when balanced against the "preferred position" of First Amendment rights. [Murdock v. Pennsylvania, 319 U.S. 105, 115, 63 S.Ct. 870, 87 L.Ed. 1292 (1943).] Indeed, there is much to be said for the view that, rather than creating a disciplinary problem, acceptance of the refusal of a few pupils to stand while the remainder stand and sing of their devotion to flag and country might well be turned into a fine lesson in American Government for the entire class.

This is not to suggest, however, that freedom of expression permits any unruly or boisterous conduct of word or deed which is in fact disruptive of order or discipline in the classroom or the school, or to suggest that the school must award a passing mark or grade to a student who refuses or fails to do required school work.

Since it appears that the conduct of the pupils involved here was not disorderly and did not materially disrupt the conduct and discipline of the school, and since there is a lack of substantial evidence that it will do so in the future, a writ of injunction will issue permanently restraining the Board of Trustees of Pinetop Elementary School from excluding the plaintiffs from attendance at the school solely because they silently refuse to rise and stand for the playing or singing of the National Anthem. The injunction will run against the defendant members of the Board of Trustees only since, as the three-judge panel found, it is their action alone which brought about the expulsion. All parties will bear their own costs.

This memorandum of decision will serve as the findings of fact and conclusions of law in this action. [Fed.R.Civ.P. 52(a), 28 U.S.C.A.] The plaintiffs' attorneys will serve and lodge with the Clerk, within ten days, a form of proposed judgment pursuant to Fed.R.Civ.P. 58. [28 U.S.C.A.]

T HE United States Court of Appeals, Fifth Circuit, holds that a Mississippi high school regulation prohibiting students from wearing to school freedom buttons containing the wording "one man one vote" and "SNCC" was an infringement of the students' First Amendment right of freedom of expression. In deciding against the school officials, the Court said: "The regulation which is before us now prohibits the wearing of 'freedom buttons' on school property. The record indicates only a showing of mild curiosity on the part of the other school children over the presence of some 30 or 40 children wearing such insignia. Even the principal testified that the children were expelled not for causing a commotion or disrupting classes but for violating the school regulation. Thus it appears that the presence of 'freedom buttons' did not hamper the school in carrying on its regular schedule of activities; nor would it seem likely that the simple wearing of buttons unaccompanied by improper conduct would ever do so. . . . Therefore, we conclude after carefully examining all the evidence presented that the regulation forbidding the wearing of 'freedom buttons' on school grounds is arbitrary and unreasonable, and an unnecessary infringement on the students' protected right of free expression in the circumstances revealed by the record."

Burnside v. *Byars,* 363 F.2d 744 (1966)

GEWIN, Circuit Judge:

Plaintiffs brought a civil rights action under 42 U.S.C. § 1983 for a preliminary injunction pursuant to 28 U.S.C. § 1343 against officials of the Booker T. Washington High School of Philadelphia, Mississippi. It was alleged that plaintiffs' children's rights under the First and Fourteenth Amendments of the United States Constitution were breached by school officials in that they denied to the children the right to wear "freedom buttons" while attending school.[1] Plaintiffs appeal from the order of the United States District Court for the Southern District of Mississippi denying a preliminary injunction.

Several days prior to September 21, 1964, Mr. Montgomery Moore, Principal of the Booker T. Washington High School of Philadelphia, Mississippi, learned that a number of his students were wearing "freedom buttons" obtained from the headquarters of the COFO[1a] organization which had been established in Philadelphia, Mississippi. The buttons were circular, approximately 1½ inches in diameter, containing the wording "One Man One Vote" around the perimeter with "SNCC" inscribed in the center. Thereupon he announced to the entire student body that they were not permitted to wear such buttons in the school house or in their various classes. Mr. Moore testified that this disciplinary regulation[2] was prom-

ulgated because the buttons "didn't have any bearing on their education," "would cause commotion," and would be disturbing [to] the school program by taking up time trying to get order, passing them around and discussing them in the classroom and explaining to the next child why they are wearing them." Despite Mr. Moore's announcement, on September 21, 1964, three or four children appeared at school wearing the buttons. All were given an opportunity to remove the buttons and remain in school but three of the children elected to keep them and return home. The following day all the children returned to school without their buttons. On the morning of September 24, 1964, Mr. Moore was summoned to the school by one of the teachers who reported that 30 or 40 children were displaying the buttons and that it was causing a commotion.[3] Mr. Moore then assembled the children in his office, reminded them of his previous announcement, and gave them the choice of removing their buttons or being sent home. The great majority elected to return home and Mr. Moore thereupon suspended them for a period of one week. Mr. Moore then delivered a letter[4] to each parent concerning the suspension, and all parents agreed to cooperate in the matter except Mrs. Burnside, Mrs. English and Mrs. Morris, whereupon injunctive proceedings were instituted against the school officials to enjoin them from enforcing the regulation.

Appellants contend that the school regulation forbidding "freedom buttons" on school property is an unreasonable rule which abridges their children's First and Fourteenth Amendment freedom of speech. It is the contention of the appellees that the regulation imposed by the principal is reasonable in maintaining proper discipline in the school and the District Court did not abuse its discretion in declining to issue a preliminary injunction.

The Negro school children who attended an all Negro high school wore the "freedom buttons" as a means of silently communicating an idea and to encourage the members of their community to exercise their civil rights.[5] The right to communicate a matter of vital public concern is embraced in the First Amendment right to freedom of speech and therefore is clearly protected against infringement by state officials. Thornhill v. State of Alabama, 310 U.S. 88, 101, 60 S.Ct. 736, 84 L.Ed. 1093, 1102. Particularly, the Fourteenth Amendment protects the First Amendment rights of school children against unreasonable rules and regulations imposed by school authorities.

"The Fourteenth Amendment, as now applied to the States, protects the citizen against the State itself and all of its creatures—Boards of Education not excepted."

West Virginia State Board of Education v. Barnette, 319 U.S. 624, 637, 63 S.Ct. 1178, 1185, 87 L.Ed. 1628, 1637.

But the liberty of expression guaranteed by the First Amendment can be abridged by state officials if their protection of legitimate state interests necessitates an invasion of free speech. Dennis v. United States, 341 U.S. 494, 510, 71 S.Ct. 857, 95 L.Ed. 1137, 1153; Whitney v. People of State of California, 274 U.S. 357, 376, 47 S.Ct. 641, 71 L.Ed. 1095, 1106. The interest of the state in maintaining an educational system is a compelling one, giving rise to a balancing of First Amendment rights with the duty of the state to further and protect the public school system. The establishment of an educational program requires the formulation of rules and regulations necessary for the maintenance of an orderly program of classroom learning. In formulating regulations, including those pertaining to the discipline of school children, school officials have a wide latitude of discretion. But the school is always bound by the requirement that the rules and regulations must be reasonable. It is not for us to consider whether such rules are wise or expedient but merely whether they are a reasonable exercise of the power and discretion of the school authorities.

Regulations which are essential in maintaining order and discipline on school property are reasonable. Thus school rules which assign students to a particular class, forbid unnecessary discussion in the classroom and prohibit the exchange of conversation between students are reasonable even though these regulations infringe on such basic rights as freedom of speech and association, because they are necessary for the orderly presentation of classroom activities. Therefore, a reasonable regulation is one which measurably contributes to the maintenance of order and decorum within the educational system.

The regulation which is before us now prohibits the wearing of "freedom buttons" on school property. The record indicates only a showing of mild curiosity on the part of the other school children over the presence of some 30 or 40 children wearing such insignia. Even the principal testified that the children were expelled not for causing a commotion or disrupting classes but for violating the school regulation. Thus it appears that the presence of "freedom buttons" did not hamper the school in carrying on its regular schedule of activities; nor would it seem likely that the simple wearing of buttons unaccompanied by improper conduct would ever do so. Wearing buttons on collars or shirt fronts is certainly not in the class of those activities which inherently distract students and break down the regimentation of the classroom such as carrying banners, scattering leaflets, and speechmaking, all of which are protected methods of expressions, but all of which have no place in an orderly classroom. If the decorum had been so disturbed by the presence of the "freedom buttons," the principal would have been acting within his authority and the regulation forbidding the presence of buttons on school grounds would have been reasonable. But the affidavits and testimony before the District Court reveal no interference with educational activity and do *not* support a conclusion that there was a commotion or that the buttons tended to distract the minds of the students away from their teachers. Nor do we think that the mere presence of "freedom buttons" is calculated to cause a disturbance sufficient to warrant their exclusion from school premises unless there is some student misconduct involved. Therefore, we conclude after carefully examining all the evidence presented that the regulation forbidding the wearing of "freedom buttons" on school grounds is arbitrary and unreasonable, and an unnecessary infringement on the students' protected right of free expression in the circumstances revealed by the record.

We are well aware of the rule that the granting or denial of an application for preliminary injunction is within the sound judicial discretion of the court to which application is made; and we have not failed to give full consideration to that sound principle of law. Under the facts and in the circumstances of this case, however, we are impelled to the conclusion that there was an abuse of discretion in refusing to grant the application. See Yakus v. United States, 321 U.S. 414, 440, 64 S.Ct. 660, 88 L.Ed. 834; Brewer v. Huger, 358

F.2d 739 (5 Cir. 1966); Joseph Brancroft & Sons Co. v. Shelly Knitting Mills, 268 F.2d 569 (3 Cir. 1959); Burton v. Matanuska Valley Lines, 244 F.2d 647 (9 Cir. 1957).

We wish to make it quite clear that we do not applaud any attempt to undermine the authority of the school. We support all efforts made by the school to fashion reasonable regulations for the conduct of their students and enforcement of the punishment incurred when such regulations are violated. Obedience to duly constituted authority is a valuable tool, and respect for those in authority must be instilled in our young people.

But, with all of this in mind, we must also emphasize that school officials cannot ignore expressions of feelings with which they do not wish to contend. They cannot infringe on their students' right to free and unrestricted expression as guaranteed to them under the First Amendment to the Constitution, where the exercise of such rights in the school buildings and schoolrooms do not materially and substantially interfere with the requirements of appropriate discipline in the operation of the school.

The order entered by the District Court denying the preliminary injunction sought is hereby vacated, the judgment is reversed and the cause is remanded with directions to the District Court to grant a preliminary injunction enjoining the officials of the Booker T. Washington High School from the enforcement of the disciplinary regulation forbidding their students from wearing "freedom buttons" on the school premises. Although there was a full evidentiary hearing in which the facts were rather fully developed, such judgment and order by the District Court shall be without prejudice to the making of a further order and judgment if additional, different or more complete facts are developed upon final hearing which would authorize the entry of such additional judgment.

Reversed and remanded with directions.

NOTES

1. In the original pleadings plaintiffs alleged that the children were expelled from school for advocating the lawful and peaceful abolition of racial segregation in Mississippi, which is protected by the First, Fifth, Thirteenth, Fourteenth and Fifteenth Amendments to the United States Constitution, 42 U.S.C. § 1983 et seq. under the Civil Rights Act of 1964; that the acts of the school officials violated plaintiffs' children's rights under the First, Fifth, and Fourteenth Amendments to the Federal Constitution to due process of law, equal protection of law and the privileges and immunities of the law; and that the acts of the school officials constituted a conspiracy to deprive the children of their rights to the equal protection of the laws and of equal privileges and immunities under the laws in violation of the First, Fifth and Fourteenth Amendments to the Federal Constitution as protected by Title 42 U.S.C. § 1985(3). These allegations were not raised in the District Court and are not in issue on appeal.

1a. Council of Federated Organizations.

2. Authority for the issuance of such disciplinary regulation was based on The Student Handbook, 1962-1963, which provides in paragraph G:

"Regulations for Student Conduct: Discipline is looked upon by the administration as a means to accomplish two primary purposes: (a) to insure students and teachers against annoying, distracting or disorderly conduct which results in the loss of valuable time and learning opportunities; (b) to help develop within each student the capacity for enlightened self control."

The wearing of buttons in the school was not unusual. On former occasions students had worn what they described as "Beatle buttons" and buttons containing initials of students, and the words "His" and "Hers." The wearing of buttons had not been proscribed on these prior occasions.

3. "Mr. Wells: When you got there what was reported to you by Mr. Murdy?

"Mr. Moore: That it had disturbed the class as students wanted to see them. And, of course, they had been passing them around the hall before they went into class."

4. The letter stated:

"Dear Parent: This is to inform you that your child has been suspended from school until you can come and have a talk with me. It is against the school policy for anything to be brought into the school that is not educational."

5. "Mr. Aronson: What were you trying to do with these buttons?

"Miss English (age 14): The reason we were wearing them is for our rights.

"Mr. Aronson: What rights were you concerned with?

"Miss English: Our rights to speech and to do the things we would like to do.

"Mr. Aronson: What kind of things would you like to do?

"Miss English: Go uptown and sit in the drugstores and wherever we buy things uptown we can sit down and won't have to walk right out at the time we get it.

"Mr. Aronson: What else?

"Miss English: And to register and vote without being beat up and killed."

* * *

"Mr. Aronson: It says 'One Man One Vote.' What does that mean to you?

"Miss Jordon (age 16): I wanted to try to help the people to make them understand, why I wore this pin, because I wanted them to go up to the court house and register to vote.

"Mr. Aronson: What people?

"Miss Jordon: The colored people in our community.

"Mr. Aronson: Do they vote in Philadelphia?

"Miss Jordon: No, Sir."

THE United States Court of Appeals, Fifth Circuit, on the same day it decided in *Burnside* that the regulation prohibiting students from wearing to school "freedom buttons" was arbitrary and unreasonable, decides that a similar prohibition at another Mississippi high school was reasonable where the wearing of the buttons led to confusion, disruption of class instruction, and a breakdown of orderly discipline. In deciding for the board of education, the Court said: "In the instant case, as distinguished from the facts in *Burnside*, there was more than a mild curiosity on the part of those who were wearing, distributing, discussing and promoting the wearing of buttons. There was an unusual degree of commotion, boisterous conduct, a collision with the rights of others, an undermining of authority, and a lack of order, discipline and decorum. The proper operation of public school systems is one of the highest and most fundamental responsibilities of the State. The school authorities in the instant case had a legitimate and substantial interest in the orderly conduct of the school and a duty to protect such substantial interests in the school's operation. Again we emphasize the difference in the conduct here involved and that involved in *Burnside*. In this case the reprehensible conduct described above was so inexorably tied to the wearing of the buttons that the two are not separable. In these circumstances we consider the rule of the school authorities reasonable."

Blackwell v. *Issaquena County Bd. of Education,* 363 F.2d 749 (1966)

GEWIN, Circuit Judge.

The appellants filed a civil rights action under 42 U.S.C. § 1983 to enjoin pursuant to 28 U.S.C. § 1343 school officials from enforcing a regulation forbidding school children from wearing "freedom buttons" as a denial of First and Fourteenth Amendment rights under the United States Constitution.[1] The United States District Court for the Southern District of Mississippi refused to grant a preliminary injunction.

On Friday, January 29, 1965, approximately 30 pupils at the all-Negro Henry Weathers High School wore "freedom buttons" to class. The buttons were about an inch in diameter depicting a black and white hand joined together with "SNCC" inscribed in the margin. It was reported to the principal, Mr. O.E. Jordan, that some of these students were creating a disturbance by noisily talking in the hall when they were scheduled to be in class and three students were brought to the principal's office where they were told that no one could be permitted to create a disturbance and that they would have to remove their buttons.

The following Monday, February 1, 1965, approximately 150 pupils came to school wearing the buttons.

These students distributed buttons to students in the corridor of the school building and accosted other students by pinning the buttons on them even though they did not ask for one.[2] One of the students tried to put a button on a younger child who began crying. This activity created a state of confusion, disrupted class instruction, and resulted in a general breakdown of orderly discipline, causing the principal to assemble the students in the cafeteria and inform them that they were forbidden to wear the buttons at school. At the assembly and also during conferences with the students immediately thereafter, several students conducted themselves discourteously and displayed an attitude of hostility.[3]

The next day, February 2, 1965, close to 200 students appeared wearing buttons. The students were assembled in the gymnasium where they were told that the rule forbidding them from wearing freedom buttons was necessary in order to maintain decorum and to keep from disturbing classrooms and other students; and if they returned to school again wearing buttons, they would be suspended.

The following day, February 3, 1965, the students

returned to school wearing the buttons whereupon the principal immediately sent them home. As the students gathered their books to go home, classes were generally disturbed by students' comments inviting others to join them. One of the suspended students entered a classroom while class was in session, ignored the teacher and without permission importuned another student to leave class.[4] Before the students left, a bus driver, Charles Cole, entered the school building with a cardboard box full of buttons, and began distributing them and even entered a classroom without permission, offering buttons to the students. Also, some students after boarding the busses, re-entered the school building with buttons, trying to pin them on anyone walking in the hall, and some threw buttons into the building through the windows.[5]

More children were suspended during the week for button wearing. Parents of the suspended children met several times with the Superintendent, Mr. H.G. Fenton, and Mr. Jordan but no agreement was ever reached. Those children who continued to remain at home after a period of 20 days, approximately 300 from various elementary and high schools in the school district, were suspended for the balance of the school year.

On April 1, 1965, a mandatory preliminary injunction was sought to compel school officials to re-admit the suspended pupils and to allow them to wear freedom buttons so long as no disturbance resulted therefrom. The motion for preliminary injunction was noticed for hearing on April 23, but the hearing was not conducted until May 10 because the District Judge was engaged in holding court elsewhere. Relief was denied on May 17. It is asserted in appellees' brief that the school term was scheduled to end the latter part of May or the early part of June.

The issue presented on this appeal, whether the school regulation forbidding the wearing of "freedom buttons" is a reasonable rule necessary for the maintenance of school discipline or an unreasonable rule which infringes on the students' right to freedom of speech guaranteed by the First Amendment of the United States Constitution, is identical to that in Burnside et al. v. Byars et al., 363 F.2d 744 (5 Cir. 1966), decided simultaneously with this case. In that case we recognized that the right of students to express and communicate an idea, by wearing a freedom button inscribed with "One Man One Vote," was protected by the First Amendment guarantee of freedom of speech; but we also recognized that reasonable regulations, necessary for keeping orderly conduct during school session, could infringe upon such First Amendment rights. We held in Burnside that a school regulation forbidding the wearing of freedom buttons was unreasonable in that the presence of such buttons on school grounds did not cause a disturbance of class-room activities nor was such a rule necessary for the maintenance of order and discipline within the school under the facts and in the circumstances of that case. Therefore, we found such regulation to be an infringement upon students' protected right of free expression.

In the case now before us, the affidavits and testimony from the District Court present quite a different picture from the record in Burnside where no disruption of classes or school routine appeared in the evidence. Here, the District Court was presented with evidence of numerous instances, which have been set out in the statement of facts, where students conducted themselves in a disorderly manner, disrupted classroom procedure, interfered with the proper decorum and discipline of the school and disturbed other students who did not wish to participate in the wearing of the buttons. Despite the factual differences in the two cases, the question we must decide remains the same. Is the regulation forbidding the wearing of freedom buttons by school children reasonable? A reasonable regulation is one which is "essential in maintaining order and discipline on school property" and "which measurably contributes to the maintenance of order and decorum within the educational system." Burnside v. Byars et al., 363 F.2d 744 (5 Cir. 1966).

The facts demonstrate that during the time students wore freedom buttons to school, much disturbance was created by these students. Their actions in the school building are indeed reprehensible and the school officials certainly have the authority to mete out punishment as they deem appropriate for their discourteous behavior toward school authorities, their disregard for the orderly progression of classroom instruction, and their complete disregard for the rights of their fellow students. The record clearly indicates that these actions by the students in distributing buttons, pinning them on others, and throwing them through windows constituted a complete breakdown in school discipline. It is necessary to prohibit students from using buttons or any other means of disrupting school routine in order to maintain discipline, therefore regulations against the distribution, pinning, and throwing of buttons as well as regulations prohibiting discourteous remarks to school personnel, the deliberate absence of a student from class without permission and loud conversation in halls and corridors which can be heard in classrooms are necessary if the school is to continue to properly instruct its students.

It is always within the province of school authorities to provide by regulation the prohibition and punishment of acts calculated to undermine the school routine. This is not only proper in our opinion but is necessary.

Cases of this nature, which involve regulations

limiting freedom of expression and the communication of an idea which are protected by the First Amendment, present serious constitutional questions. A valuable constitutional right is involved and decisions must be made on a case by case basis,[6] keeping in mind always the fundamental constitutional rights of those being affected. Courts are required to "weigh the circumstances" and "appraise the substantiality of the reasons advanced" which are asserted to have given rise to the regulations in the first instance. Thornhill v. State of Alabama, 310 U.S. 88, 60 S.Ct. 736, 84 L.Ed. 1093 (1940). The constitutional guarantee of freedom of speech "does not confer an absolute right to speak" and the law recognizes that there can be an abuse of such freedom. The Constitution does not confer "unrestricted and unbridled license giving immunity for every possible use of language and preventing the punishment of those who abuse this freedom." Whitney v. People of State of California, 274 U.S. 357, 47 S.Ct. 641, 71 L.Ed. 1095 (1927). The interests which the regulation seeks to protect must be fundamental and substantial if there is to be a restriction of speech. In Dennis v. United States, 341 U.S. 494, 71 S.Ct. 857, 95 L.Ed. 1137 (1951), the Supreme Court approved the following statement of the rule by Chief Judge Learned Hand:

> "In each case [courts] must ask whether the gravity of the 'evil,' discounted by its improbability, justifies such invasion of free speech as is necessary to avoid the danger."

In West Virginia State Bd. of Educ. v. Barnette, 319 U.S. 624, 63 S.Ct. 1178, 87 L.Ed. 1628 (1943), involving a school board regulation requiring a "salute to the flag" and a pledge of allegiance, the Court was careful to note that the refusal of the students to participate in the ceremony did not interfere with or deny rights of others to do so and the behavior involved was "peaceable and orderly."

In the instant case, as distinguished from the facts in *Burnside*, there was more than a mild curiosity on the part of those who were wearing, distributing, discussing and promoting the wearing of buttons. There was an unusual degree of commotion, boisterous conduct, a collision with the rights of others, an undermining of authority, and a lack of order, discipline and decorum. The proper operation of public school systems is one of the highest and most fundamental responsibilities of the state. The school authorities in the instant case had a legitimate and substantial interest in the orderly conduct of the school and a duty to protect such substantial interests in the school's operation. Again we emphasize the difference in the conduct here involved and that involved in *Burnside*. In this case the reprehensible conduct described above was so inexorably tied to the wearing of the buttons that the two are not separable. In these circumstances we consider the rule of the school authorities reasonable. As we said in *Burnside*, "It is not for us to consider whether such rules are wise or expedient but merely whether they are a reasonable exercise of the power and discretion of the school authorities." There was an abundance of clear, convincing and unequivocal testimony which supported the action of the District Court in refusing to grant the requested preliminary injunction. We are unable to find an abuse of discretion.

The judgment is affirmed but without prejudice to the right of the appellants to relief upon final hearing if the facts justify such relief, emphasizing as we do the importance of the right of freedom of expression and communication as protected by the First Amendment, and the fundamental requirement that school officials should be careful in their monitoring of student expression in circumstances in which such expression does not substantially interfere with the operation of the school.

The judgment is affirmed.

NOTES

1. Plaintiffs also filed suit under 42 U.S.C. § 1983 to enjoin the defendant school authorities from operating compulsory racially segregated school. This request for a preliminary injunction pursuant to 28 U.S.C. § 1343 was granted by the United States District Court for the Southern District of Mississippi.

2. In an affidavit signed by all members of the Board of Trustees and the District Superintendent of one of the school districts is the following statement:

    > "A full hearing was given these parents, and the entire problem involved was explained to them. They were advised at that time that prior to the suspension of these students, *a general state of confusion existed in the classrooms and school buildings.* Many of these children were accosting other students in the corridors and halls of the buildings and *placing these pins on the clothing of children whether they wanted them or not,* and generally tried to persuade all of the students to wear and exhibit these buttons. The result was *a state of confusion, a disruption of class instruction and a general breakdown of orderly discipline.*" (Emphasis added)

3. The state of affairs which developed may be illustrated by the following excerpts from the affidavit of Principal O. E. Jordan:

    > "On February 1, 1965, more than one hundred students came to school wearing these buttons. Hazel Lamb, a teacher, reported to me that *students were going up and down the corridor passing out buttons* to those who did not have them and pinning buttons on other students who did not do so voluntarily. I investigated the matter and found this to be true. *This activity on their part* had created a state of confusion and had disrupted the orderly procedure at the school. I assembled all the students wearing buttons at the cafeteria and requested that they remove the buttons *so that some order of discipline* could be restored. Two students were particularly hostile to my

request and displayed a nasty attitude. I told the students that since they were *creating such confusion* in the classrooms and in the corridor with the buttons, that they were forbidden to wear the buttons at school." (Emphasis added.)

* * *

"At this time some of the students *had on as many as three buttons varying in size*. At this meeting, several of the students present took over from their leader and one boy, Dan White, went so far as to call me an 'Uncle Tom.' I dismissed them courteously with a statement that they could not attend school wearing buttons and *creating a disturbance* unless the Superintendent or the School Board overruled me." (Emphasis added.)

* * *

"During this session a boy by the name of Morganfield became intolerably obnoxious. I dismissed the group and informed them that if they returned Wednesday wearing buttons that I would send them home."

4. One of the teachers in her affidavit described this incident as follows:

    "On Wednesday, February 3, 1965, the day the children were suspended, I was trying to teach typing during the first period of classes. One of the children that had been suspended *came into my classroom, without permission and ignoring me and the classroom procedure,* and went over to one of my students, Recilla Rogers, and tried to get her to leave my class and get on the bus. She refused, saying that she was staying in school.

    "As the students were leaving to go home some got on the buses and then came back into the building with buttons *trying to pin them on any that were just walking in the hall,* and some threw buttons back in the building through the windows. *All of this took place while the classes were going on.* This caused a general disturbance." (Emphasis added.)

5. The following additional statement from the affidavit of Principal Jordan illustrates conditions at this time:

    "Before the students left, a bus driver by the name of Charles Cole brought a cardboard box full of buttons and started distributing them down the Junior High wing of the school, as reported to me by a teacher. By the time I had gotten down there he had disappeared.

    "Before the school buses left, some of the parents came in and wanted to know why were the children being sent home. I stated that they were continually causing *disturbances with the buttons and their actions.* I explained to them that *students who did not want the buttons nor knew anything about them were being subjected to harassment by the ones that had them, and teachers were prevented from carrying on in the normal way."* (Emphasis added.)

6. In Dennis v. United States, 341 U.S. 494, 508, 71 S.Ct. 857, 95 L.Ed. 1137, 1152 (1951), Mr. Chief Justice Vinson in commenting upon the earlier case of American Communications Asso. v. Douds, 339 U.S. 382, 70 S.Ct. 674, 94 L.Ed. 925, asserted the following:

    "But we further suggested that neither Justice Holmes nor Justice Brandeis ever envisioned that a shorthand phrase should be crystallized into a rigid rule to be applied inflexibly without regard to the circumstances of each case."

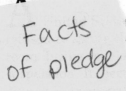
Facts of pledge

...s District Court in New York decides for students who ...e flag and at the same time refused to leave the class- ...g salute ritual; their behavior was possible grounds for ...ling for the students, the Court stated: "Pedagogical ...to courtesy, are also inadequate grounds for coercive ...nendment expressions. Certainly, the fact that others ...ntiffs [students] in sitting out the Pledge is no justi- ...; plaintiffs' protests. The First Amendment protects ...well as ineffective protests."

Frain v. Baro...   (1969)

JUDD, Distri...
Memorandum and Order

These civil rights actions are significant because they pit popular ideas of patriotism and the authority of school administrators against students' rights of free expression. The particular controversy is minor, involving the refusal of three students to leave their "homerooms" during the daily Pledge of Allegiance, as a condition for exercising their undoubted constitutional right not to participate in the Pledge. The resulting collision is serious, because it involves suspension from school as one alternative, and a court injunction against the school authorities as the other.

The facts and legal authorities must be reviewed in the light of the principle that:

"It is now beyond dispute that the constitution goes to school with the student and that the state may not interfere with the student's enjoyment of its presence." Denno, Mary Beth Tinker Takes the Constitution to School, 38 Fordham L. Rev. (1969) 35, 56.

Facts

The Pledge of Allegiance was written by Frances Bellamy, a Baptist minister, to be used at the Chicago World's Fair Grounds in October, 1892, on the four hundredth anniversary of the discovery of America. Its present form, as set forth in Regulations of the New York Commissioner of Education (Art. XVI, § 150, ¶ 5) and in the United States Code (36 U.S.C. § 172) is:

"I pledge allegiance to the flag of the United States of America and to the Republic for which it stands, one Nation under God, indivisible, with liberty and justice for all."

The words "under God" were added in 1954 (Pub. L. 83-297). The Corporation Counsel has recognized in an earlier case that anyone may be excused from repeating these two words. See Matter of Superintendent of Schools v. Seymour Jacobs, a Regular Teacher of French, Report of Bethuel L. Webster as Trial Examiner, p. 5 (1968).

The Commissioner of Education is required by statute to prepare a program for a daily salute and pledge of allegiance to the flag. Education Law § 802, McKinney's Consol.Laws, c. 16, subd. 1. The By-Laws of the New York City Board of Education require a salute to the flag only once a week (Sec. 90, subd. 31), but a Circular from the Superintendent of Schools in 1963 directed that:

"at the commencement of each school day, the Pledge of Allegiance to the Flag be followed by the singing in unison of a patriotic song."

The purpose of the ceremony is to encourage patriotism and loyalty to democratic institutions.

Plaintiffs Mary Frain and Susan Keller are twelve-year old white girls attending Junior High School 217Q, in an accelerated class which does three years' work in two years.

Plaintiff Raymond Miller is a black boy, a senior at Jamaica High School.

All three plaintiffs refused to recite the Pledge of Allegiance, because of a belief that the words "with liberty and justice for all" are not true in America today. One is an atheist, who also objected to the words "under God."

They refused to stand during the Pledge, because that would constitute participation in what they considered a lie. They also refused to leave the room, and stand in the hall outside their homerooms until the conclusion of the ceremony, because they considered exclusion from the room to be a punishment for their exercise of constitutional rights.

It does not appear whether any plaintiff joined in the required patriotic song, or whether they were required to stay in the hall during the singing as well as the Pledge.

Plaintiff Miller was required to submit to the Assistant Principal for Guidance a written statement of his reasons for not saluting. His typewritten statement, in one page, expresses the belief that "America is perhaps the greatest country in the world," but that it must undergo certain basic changes, and provide true equality, freedom and justice for all, end oppression of minorities, and give black people a greater opportunity to advance. He concluded that:

"As for the pledge: I believe it is untrue ('Liberty and justice for all') and I refuse to swear to a lie."

Mary Frain and Susan Keller are the remnant of a larger group who previously sat in silence during the Pledge of Allegiance. The others, after being summoned to the Principal's office to discuss their conduct, accepted one of the alternatives, of standing silently or going outside their classrooms during the Pledge. The papers do not show what supervision, if any, is provided in the halls while the non-participating students are excluded from class.

The policy of requiring a non-participating student to leave the area in which the flag salute is taking place was adopted by the Superintendent of Schools in March, 1969, in granting a petition from the student at Jamaica High School to be excused from taking part. The Superintendent stated:

"This decision is based on rulings by the United States Supreme Court and more recently by a Trial Examiner designated by the Board of Education, that both pupils and teachers have a right, as a matter of conscience, to refuse to salute the flag and recite the Pledge of Allegiance. I believe that no pupil should be permitted to sit during such a ceremony, since to do so might create disorder."

Raymond Miller asserts that he was nevertheless permitted to remain seated from March to October, when the publicity about the Frain suit called attention to the matter. Defendants assert that he stood silently during this time, and was not observed to remain seated until October 17, 1969, when his conduct resulted in suspension. This minor dispute of fact does not require decision at this time.

Between October 10, when the Frain and Miller girls were returned to school under this court's temporary restraining order, and November 10, when the City's reply papers were submitted, fifty other students in Junior High School 217Q have also sat silently during the Pledge of Allegiance, on one or more occasions. There is no showing that this has caused any disorder.

For two months in 1967 a teacher in Far Rockaway High School remained seated during the Pledge of Allegiance and did not recite the Pledge. A special Trial Examiner for the Board of Education, in ruling on charges against the teacher, found that his conduct did not cause disorder in the classroom. Matter of Superintendent of Schools v. Jacobs, *supra* at p. 8.

The principal of Jamaica High School asserts in an affidavit filed in this case that permitting a student to remain seated during the Pledge could be "a real and present threat to the maintenance of discipline" and would be "pedagogically foolhardy." Other school administrators echo these words. For the purpose of the pending motions, these conclusory assertions are insufficient to support a finding of serious harm to defendants from the granting of an injunction.

Both suits are brought as class actions. The court finds that the questions of law presented are common to a substantial number of students in public junior and senior high schools who wish to remain in their seats in silence during the Pledge of Allegiance; that the plaintiffs will fairly and adequately protect the interests of the class; and that defendants have acted on grounds generally applicable to the entire class. F.R. Civ.P. Rule 23(b) (2).

Legal Authorities

The thrust of recent decisions of the Supreme Court and lower federal courts has been toward increasing judicial concern with the clash between student expression and school authorities. This increasing concern has been accompanied by a shift in focus, well illustrated by comparing the Supreme Court's decision in West Virginia State Board of Education v. Barnette, 319 U.S. 624, 63 S.Ct. 1178, 87 L.Ed. 1628 (1943), overruling Minersville School District v. Gobitis, 310 U.S. 586, 60 S.Ct. 1010, 84 L.Ed. 1375 (1940), with the recent decision in Tinker v. Des Moines Independent Community School District, 393 U.S. 503, 89 S.Ct. 733, 21 L.Ed.2d 731 (1969). The original concern with limitation of the state's power to compel a student to act contrary to his beliefs has shifted to a concern for affirmative protection of the student's right to express his beliefs. The present case is novel in that the context, school patriotic exercises, is one in which courts have previously intervened to limit coerced participation, while these plaintiffs are urging not only a right of non-participation but a right of silent protest by remaining seated.

Barnette established the right of students to refrain from participation in a legislatively mandated flag ceremony. Rejecting compulsory participation as a proper vehicle for instilling patriotism, Mr. Justice Jackson stated (319 U.S. at 642, 63 S.Ct. at 1187):

"If there is any fixed star in our constitutional constellation, it is that no official, high or petty, can prescribe what shall be orthodox in politics, nationalism, religion, or other matters of opinion or force citizens to confess by word or act their faith therein."

Of pertinence to the present case, the opinion recognized that "The freedom asserted by these appellees does not bring them into collision with rights asserted by any other individual." 319 U.S. at 630, 63 S.Ct. at 1181. Justice Jackson also foreshadowed the present case by commenting that "liberty and justice for all," unless accepted merely as an ideal, "might to some seem an overstatement." 319 U.S. at 634, n. 14, 63 S.Ct. at 1183, n. 14.

Under the authority of *Barnette,* a federal district court held that a refusal to stand during the singing of the National Anthem did not justify exclusion from school. Sheldon v. Fannin, 221 F.Supp. 766 (D.Ariz. 1963). However, *Barnette,* standing alone, might not be decisive of the present case. While Mr. Justice Jackson's opinion expressly disclaimed reliance on the religious beliefs of the plaintiffs, who were Jehovah's Witnesses, two of the six majority justices concurred on that basis. The plaintiffs in *Sheldon* were also Jehovah's Witnesses. In addition, neither *Barnette* nor *Sheldon* involved the alternative to participation of waiting outside the room; the choice was participation or exclusion from school.

The Supreme Court's decision in *Tinker* makes it unnecessary to explore further the differences between *Barnette* and the present case. *Tinker* held that public school students could not be suspended for wearing black arm-bands to protest American involvement in Vietnam, a form of silent expression in the classroom. While *Tinker* did not involve a refusal to participate in patriotic exercises in school, the Supreme Court did not tie its opinion to a particular set of facts, but enunciated a rule of general applicability. Mr. Justice Fortas stated (393 U.S. 509, 89 S.Ct. at 738):

"In order for the State in the person of school officials to justify prohibition of a particular expression of opinion, it must be able to show that its action was caused by something more than a mere desire to avoid the discomfort and unpleasantness that always accompany an unpopular viewpoint. Certainly where there is no finding and no showing that the exercise of the forbidden right would *materially and substantially interfere with the requirements of appropriate discipline* in the operation of the school,' the prohibition cannot be sustained. Burnside v. Byars, *supra,* 363 F.2d at 749." (Emphasis supplied.)

Emphasizing that no disorders had in fact occurred, Mr. Justice Fortas concluded (393 U.S. 514, 89 S.Ct. at 740-741):

"These petitioners merely went about their ordained rounds in school. Their deviation consisted only in wearing on their sleeve a band of black cloth, not more than two inches wide. They wore it to exhibit their disapproval of the Vietnam hostilities and their advocacy of a truce, to make their views known, and by their example, to influence others to

adopt them. They neither interrupted school activities nor sought to intrude in the school affairs or the lives of others. They caused discussion outside of the classrooms, but no interference with work and no disorder. In the circumstances, our Constitution does not permit officials of the State to deny their form of expression."

Tinker thus places on the school authorities the burden of justifying a particular restriction on student expression. The student is free to select his form of expression, so long as he does not materially infringe the rights of other students or disrupt school activities.

The first quotation from the *Tinker* opinion is based upon Burnside v. Byars, 363 F.2d 744 (5th Cir. 1966). That case sustained the right of students to wear "freedom buttons" where no disruption or commotion resulted. Also consistent with *Tinker* is the decision in Matter of Superintendent of Schools v. Jacobs, *supra,* which upheld the right of a public school teacher to remain seated and not participate in the Pledge of Allegiance. The teacher who raised the issue expressed sentiments like the plaintiffs' in this case, that liberty and justice do not yet exist for all Americans. The learned Trial Examiner, Bethuel M. Webster, former President of the Association of the Bar of the City of New York, stated that:

"the Board is required under *Shelton* [Shelton v. Tucker, 364 U.S. 479 [81 S.Ct. 247, 5 L.Ed.2d 231] (1960)] and other cases to adopt means for promoting student patriotism that do not impair the personal liberties of teachers." Report, at p. 11.

Respondent advances no persuasive reason why the approach of *Tinker* should not be used here. Accordingly, it is not incumbent upon plaintiffs to convince the court that the offered alternative of leaving the room during the Pledge of Allegiance constituted punishment. Rather, respondent must convince the court that the particular expression of protest chosen by plaintiffs, remaining seated, materially infringed the rights of other students or caused disruption.

Supreme Court decisions involving the exercise of First Amendment rights in non-school contexts support plaintiffs' position here. In Brown v. Louisiana, 383 U.S. 131, 86 S.Ct. 719, 15 L.Ed.2d 637 (1966), involving a sit-in in a segregated public library, the court stated that the right of free speech is not confined to verbal expression but includes

"the right in a peaceable and orderly manner to protest by silent and reproachful presence, *in a place where the protestant has every right to be.*" (Emphasis added.)

In Street v. New York, 394 U.S. 576, 89 S.Ct. 1354, 1366, 22 L.Ed.2d 572 (1969), Mr. Justice Harlan, one of the dissenters in *Tinker,* stated that the First

Amendment provides "freedom to express publicly one's opinions about our flag, including those opinions which are defiant or contemptuous."

The draft-card burning case on which the City relies (United States v. Miller, 367 F.2d 72 [2d Cir. 1966]) is not comparable. Destruction of even trivial property is more than free speech. Of some similarity to the present case is a recent decision in another Circuit sustaining a mild penalty for a spectator's refusal to stand at the beginning of a court session. United States ex rel. Robson v. Malone, 412 F.2d 848 (7th Cir. 1969). The decision is not binding here and, in any event, is distinguished by the fact that a spectator's attendance in the courtroom is voluntary, while attendance in a public high school is compulsory.

Fear of disorder, which the City cites to justify its policy, has been ruled out as a ground for limiting peaceful exercise of First Amendment rights. Edwards v. South Carolina, 372 U.S. 229, 83 S.Ct. 680, 9 L.Ed.2d 697 (1963). The Supreme Court dealt with this argument again in Tinker, saying (393 U.S. at 508, 89 S.Ct. at 737):

"The District Court concluded that the action of the school authorities was reasonable because it was based upon their fear of a disturbance from the wearing of the armbands. But, in our system, undifferentiated fear or apprehension of disturbance is not enough to overcome the right to freedom of expression. Any departure from absolute regimentation may cause trouble. Any variation from the majority's opinion may inspire fear. Any word spoken, in class, in the lunchroom, or on the campus, that deviates from the views of another person, may start an argument or cause a disturbance. But our Constitution says we must take that risk * * *."

See also Tuttle, J., dissenting, in Ferrell v. Dallas Independent School District, 392 F.2d 697, 705-706 (5th Cir. 1968); In re Peck, 38 L.W. 2285 (N.Y. App. Div. 4th Dept., Oct. 30, 1969) (holding that judge cannot forbid female attorney to wear miniskirt because of fear of distraction or disruption).

Pedagogical opinions, or appeals to courtesy, are also inadequate grounds for coercive responses to First Amendment expressions.

Certainly, the fact that others have joined the plaintiffs in sitting out the Pledge is no justification for impeding plaintiffs' protests. The First Amendment protects successful dissent as well as ineffective protests.

This does not mean that the court has created an open season for students to defy authority. The same panel of the same court which upheld the wearing of "freedom buttons" in Burnside, supra, 363 F.2d 744, also held that the right to wear the buttons was forfeited where the button-wearers harassed other students and created a disturbance. Blackwell v. Issaquena County Board of Education, 363 F.2d 749 (5th Cir. 1966).

Madera v. Board of Education, 386 F.2d 778 (2d Cir. 1967), which defendants cite, dealt with the right to counsel at a guidance conference, and has no bearing on the present case.

President Harold C. Martin of Union College recently called attention to the emotions which are aroused by a case like this:

"The refusal of some religious sects today to swear an oath of allegiance to the flag infuriates many citizens who find themselves unable to consent to a set of principles different from the one they hold." The Meaning of "Law and Order," 74 Case & Comment, Nov.-Dec., 1969, p. 45 at p. 46.

The policy of the New York City Board of Education is a sincere attempt to prevent disorders which may develop as the reaction of infuriated members of the majority to the silent dissent expressed by plaintiffs. The flaw in the policy is that the constitution does not recognize fears of a disorderly reaction as ground for restricting peaceful expression of views. As the court said in Tinker:

"Freedom of expression would not truly exist if the right could be exercised only in an area that a benevolent government has provided as a safe haven for crackpots." (393 U.S. at 513, 89 S.Ct. at 740).

Preliminary Injunction

On the basis of the facts and legal authorities, the court is satisfied that plaintiffs have a strong possibility of ultimate success on the merits, that the grant of a preliminary injunction will cause no appreciable harm to defendants, and that denial of an injunction would be prejudicial to plaintiffs.

New rules adopted by the Board of Education since the argument of these motions would limit the Board's power of suspension, but do not affect the court's jurisdiction of this action.

It is therefore ordered:

(1) That the two cases be consolidated under the caption of 69 Civil 1250;

(2) That the consolidated case may be maintained as a class action under F.R.Civ.P. 23(b)(2);

(3) That defendants' motions to dismiss be denied, with leave to answer pursuant to F.R.Civ.P. 12(a); and

(4) That defendants be enjoined during the pendency of this action from excluding plaintiffs from their classrooms during the Pledge of Allegiance, or from treating any student who refuses for reasons of

conscience to participate in the Pledge in any different way from those who participate.

After defendants' answer is filed, any party may apply to the court for a prompt hearing on the merits.

Any party may apply for a more detailed injunction order, on notice, if deemed desirable.

T HE United States Supreme Court gives First Amendment protection to public school students who had been suspended from school for wearing black armbands to school to publicize their "objections to the hostilities in Vietnam and their support for a truce." Delivering the opinion of the Court, Justice Fortas stated: "First Amendment rights, applied in light of the special characteristics of the school environment, are available to teachers and students. It can hardly be argued that either students or teachers shed their constitutional rights to freedom of speech or expression at the schoolhouse gate. This has been the unmistakable holding of this Court for almost 50 years. . . . In our system, state-operated schools may not be enclaves of totalitarianism. School officials do not possess absolute authority over their students. Students in school as well as out of school are 'persons' under our Constitution. They are possessed of fundamental rights which the State must respect, just as they themselves must respect their obligations to the State. In our system, students may not be regarded as closed-circuit recipients of only that which the State chooses to communicate. They may not be confined to the expression of those sentiments that are officially approved."

Tinker v. *Des Moines School District,* 393 U.S. 503 (1969)

MR. JUSTICE FORTAS delivered the opinion of the Court.

Petitioner John F. Tinker, 15 years old, and petitioner Christopher Eckhardt, 16 years old, attended high schools in Des Moines, Iowa. Petitioner Mary Beth Tinker, John's sister, was a 13-year-old student in junior high school.

In December 1965, a group of adults and students in Des Moines held a meeting at the Eckhardt home. The group determined to publicize their objections to the hostilities in Vietnam and their support for a truce by wearing black armbands during the holiday season and by fasting on December 16 and New Year's Eve. Petitioners and their parents had previously engaged in similar activities, and they decided to participate in the program.

The principals of the Des Moines schools became aware of the plan to wear armbands. On December 14, 1965, they met and adopted a policy that any student wearing an armband to school would be asked to remove it, and if he refused he would be suspended until he returned without the armband. Petitioners were aware of the regulation that the school authorities adopted.

On December 16, Mary Beth and Christopher wore black armbands to their schools. John Tinker wore his armband the next day. They were all sent home and suspended from school until they would come back without their armbands. They did not return to school until after the planned period for wearing armbands had expired—that is, until after New Year's Day.

This complaint was filed in the United States District Court by petitioners, through their fathers, under § 1983 of Title 42 of the United States Code. It prayed for an injunction restraining the respondent school officials and the respondent members of the board of directors of the school district from disciplining the petitioners, and it sought nominal damages. After an evidentiary hearing the District Court dismissed the complaint. It upheld the constitutionality of the school authorities' action on the ground that it was reasonable in order to prevent disturbance of school discipline. 258 F. Supp. 971 (1966). The court referred to but expressly declined to follow the Fifth Circuit's holding in a similar case that the wearing of symbols like the armbands cannot be prohibited unless it "materially and substantially interfere[s] with the requirements of appropriate discipline in the operation of the school." *Burnside* v. *Byars,* 363 F. 2d 744, 749 (1966).[1]

On appeal, the Court of Appeals for the Eighth Circuit considered the case *en banc.* The court was equally divided, and the District Court's decision was accordingly affirmed, without opinion. 383 F. 2d 988 (1967). We granted certiorari. 390 U.S. 942 (1968).

I.

The District Court recognized that the wearing of an armband for the purpose of expressing certain views is the type of symbolic act that is within the Free Speech Clause of the First Amendment. See *West Virginia* v. *Barnette,* 319 U.S. 624 (1943); *Stromberg* v. *California,* 283 U.S. 359 (1931). Cf. *Thornhill* v. *Alabama,* 310 U.S. 88 (1940); *Edwards* v. *South Carolina,* 372 U.S. 229 (1963); *Brown* v. *Louisiana,* 383 U.S. 131 (1966). As we shall discuss, the wearing of armbands in the circumstances of this case was entirely divorced from actually or potentially disruptive conduct by those participating in it. It was closely akin to "pure speech" which, we have repeatedly held, is entitled to comprehensive protection under the First Amendment. Cf. *Cox* v. *Louisiana,* 379 U.S. 536, 555 (1965); *Adderley* v. *Florida,* 385 U.S. 39 (1966).

First Amendment rights, applied in light of the special characteristics of the school environment, are available to teachers and students. It can hardly be argued that either students or teachers shed their constitutional rights to freedom of speech or expression at the schoolhouse gate. This has been the unmistakable holding of this Court for almost 50 years. In *Meyer* v. *Nebraska,* 262 U.S. 390 (1923), and *Bartels* v. *Iowa,* 262 U.S. 404 (1923), this Court, in opinions by Mr. Justice McReynolds, held that the Due Process Clause of the Fourteenth Amendment prevents States from forbidding the teaching a foreign language to young students. Statutes to this effect, the Court held, unconstitutionally interfere with the liberty of teacher, student and parent.[2] See also *Pierce* v. *Society of Sisters,* 268 U.S. 510 (1925); *West Virginia* v. *Barnette,* 319 U.S. 624 (1943); *McCollum* v. *Board of Education,* 333 U.S. 203 (1948); *Wieman* v. *Updegraff,* 344 U.S. 183, 195 (1952) (concurring opinion); *Sweezy* v. *New Hampshire,* 354 U.S. 234 (1957); *Shelton* v. *Tucker,* 364 U.S. 479, 487 (1960); *Engel* v. *Vitale,* 370 U.S. 421 (1962); *Keyishian* v. *Board of Regents,* 385 U.S. 589, 603 (1967); *Epperson* v. *Arkansas, ante,* p. 97 (1968).

In *West Virginia* v. *Barnette, supra,* this Court held that under the First Amendment, the student in public school may not be compelled to salute the flag. Speaking through Mr. Justice Jackson, the Court said:

> "The Fourteenth Amendment, as now applied to the States, protects the citizen against the State itself and all of its creatures—Boards of Education not excepted. These have, of course, important, delicate, and highly discretionary functions, but none that they may not perform within the limits of the Bill of Rights. That they are educating the young for citizenship is reason for scrupulous protection of Constitutional freedoms of the individual, if

we are not to strangle the free mind at its source and teach youth to discount important principles of our government as mere platitudes." 319 U.S., at 637. On the other hand, the Court has repeatedly emphasized the need for affirming the comprehensive authority of the States and of school officials, consistent with fundamental constitutional safeguards, to prescribe and control conduct in the schools. See *Epperson* v. *Arkansas, supra,* at 104; *Meyer* v. *Nebraska, supra,* at 402. Our problem lies in the area where students in the exercise of First Amendment rights collide with the rules of the school authorities.

II.

The problem posed by the present case does not relate to regulation of the length of skirts or the type of clothing, to hair style, or deportment. Cf. *Ferrell* v. *Dallas Independent School District,* 392 F. 2d 697 (1968); *Pugsley* v. *Sellmeyer,* 158 Ark. 247, 250 S.W. 538 (1923). It does not concern aggressive, disruptive action or even group demonstrations. Our problem involves direct, primary First Amendment rights akin to "pure speech."

The school officials banned and sought to punish petitioners for a silent, passive expression of opinion, unaccompanied by any disorder or disturbance on the part of petitioners. There is here no evidence whatever of petitioners' interference, actual or nascent, with the schools' work or of collision with the rights of other students to be secure and to be let alone. Accordingly, this case does not concern speech or action that intrudes upon the work of the schools or the rights of other students.

Only a few of the 18,000 students in the school system wore the black armbands. Only five students were suspended for wearing them. There is no indication that the work of the schools or any class was disrupted. Outside the classrooms, a few students made hostile remarks to the children wearing armbands, but there were no threats or acts of violence on school premises.

The District Court concluded that the action of the school authorities was reasonable because it was based upon their fear of a disturbance from the wearing of the armbands. But, in our system, undifferentiated fear or apprehension of disturbance is not enough to overcome the right to freedom of expression. Any departure from absolute regimentation may cause trouble. Any variation from the majority's opinion may inspire fear. Any word spoken, in class, in the lunchroom, or on the campus, that deviates from the views of another person may start an argument or cause a disturbance. But our Constitution says we must take this risk, *Terminiello* v. *Chicago,* 337 U. S. 1 (1949); and our history says that it is this sort of hazardous freedom—this kind of openness—that is the basis of our national strength and of the independence and vigor of Americans who grow up and live in this relatively permissive, often disputatious, society.

In order for the State in the person of school officials to justify prohibition of a particular expression of opinion, it must be able to show that its action was caused by something more than a mere desire to avoid the discomfort and unpleasantness that always accompany an unpopular viewpoint. Certainly where there is no finding and no showing that engaging in the forbidden conduct would "materially and substantially interfere with the requirements of appropriate discipline in the operation of the school," the prohibition cannot be sustained. *Burnside* v. *Byars, supra,* at 749.

In the present case, the District Court made no such finding, and our independent examination of the record fails to yield evidence that the school authorities had reason to anticipate that the wearing of the armbands would substantially interfere with the work of the school or impinge upon the rights of other students. Even an official memorandum prepared after the suspension that listed the reasons for the ban on wearing the armbands made no reference to the anticipation of such disruption.[3]

On the contrary, the action of the school authorities appears to have been based upon an urgent wish to avoid the controversy which might result from the expression, even by the silent symbol of armbands, of opposition to this Nation's part in the conflagration in Vietnam.[4] It is revealing, in this respect, that the meeting at which the school principals decided to issue the contested regulation was called in response to a student's statement to the journalism teacher in one of the schools that he wanted to write an article on Vietnam and have it published in the school paper. (The student was dissuaded.[5])

It is also relevant that the school authorities did not purport to prohibit the wearing of all symbols of political or controversial significance. The record shows that students in some of the schools wore buttons relating to national political campaigns, and some even wore the Iron Cross, traditionally a symbol of Nazism. The order prohibiting the wearing of armbands did not extend to these. Instead, a particular symbol—black armbands worn to exhibit opposition to this Nation's involvement in Vietnam—was singled out for prohibition. Clearly, the prohibition of expression of one particular opinion, at least without evidence that it is necessary to avoid material and substantial interference with schoolwork or discipline, is not constitutionally permissible.

In our system, state-operated schools may not be enclaves of totalitarianism. School officials do not possess absolute authority over their students. Students in school as well as out of school are "persons" under our Constitution. They are possessed of fundamental rights which the State must respect, just as they themselves must respect their obligations to the State. In our system, students may not be regarded as closed-circuit recipients of only that which the State chooses to communicate. They may not be confined to the expression of those sentiments that are officially approved. In the absence of a specific showing of constitutionally valid reasons to regulate their speech, students are entitled to freedom of expression of their views. As Judge Gewin, speaking for the Fifth Circuit, said, school officials cannot suppress "expressions of feelings with which they do not wish to contend." *Burnside* v. *Byars, supra,* at 749.

In *Meyer* v. *Nebraska, supra,* at 402, Mr. Justice McReynolds expressed this Nation's repudiation of the principle that a State might so conduct its schools as to "foster a homogeneous people." He said:

"In order to submerge the individual and develop ideal citizens, Sparta assembled the males at seven into barracks and intrusted their subsequent education and training to official guardians. Although such measures have been deliberately approved by men of great genius, their ideas touching the relation between individual and State were wholly different from those upon which our institutions rest; and it hardly will be affirmed that any legislature could impose such restrictions upon the people of a State without doing violence to both letter and spirit of the Constitution."

This principle has been repeated by this Court on numerous occasions during the intervening years. In *Keyishian* v. *Board of Regents,* 385 U.S. 589, 603, MR. JUSTICE BRENNAN, speaking for the Court, said:

" 'The vigilant protection of constitutional freedoms is nowhere more vital than in the community of American schools.' *Shelton* v. *Tucker,* [364 U.S. 479,] at 487. The classroom is peculiarly the 'marketplace of ideas.' The Nation's future depends upon leaders trained through wide exposure to that robust exchange of ideas which discovers truth 'out of a multitude of tongues, [rather] than through any kind of authoritative selection.' "

The principle of these cases is not confined to the supervised and ordained discussion which takes place in the classroom. The principal use to which the schools are dedicated is to accommodate students during prescribed hours for the purpose of certain types of activities. Among those activities is personal intercommunication among the students.[6] This is not only an inevitable part of the process of attending school; it is also an important part of the educational process. A student's rights, therefore, do not embrace merely the classroom hours. When he is in the cafeteria, or on the playing field, or on the campus during the authorized hours, he may express his opinions, even on controversial subjects like the conflict in Vietnam, if he does so without "materially and substantially interfer[ing] with the requirements of appropriate discipline in the operation of the school" and without colliding with the rights of others. *Burnside* v. *Byars, supra,* at 749. But conduct by the student, in class or out of it, which for any reason—whether it stems from time, place, or type of behavior—materially disrupts classwork or involves substantial disorder or invasion of the rights of others is, of course, not immunized by the constitutional guarantee of freedom of speech. Cf. *Blackwell* v. *Issaquena County Board of Education,* 363 F. 2d 749 (C. A. 5th Cir. 1966).

Under our Constitution, free speech is not a right that is given only to be so circumscribed that it exists in principle but not in fact. Freedom of expression would not truly exist if the right could be exercised only in an area that a benevolent government has provided as a safe haven for crackpots. The Constitution says that Congress (and the States) may not abridge the right to free speech. This provision means what it says. We properly read it to permit reasonable regulation of speech-connected activities in carefully restricted circumstances. But we do not confine the permissible exercise of First Amendment rights to a telephone booth or the four corners of a pamphlet, or to supervised and ordained discussion in a school classroom.

If a regulation were adopted by school officials forbidding discussion of the Vietnam conflict, or the expression by any student of opposition to it anywhere on school property except as part of a prescribed classroom exercise, it would be obvious that the regulation would violate the constitutional rights of students, at least if it could not be justified by a showing that the students' activities would materially and substantially disrupt the work and discipline of the school.

Cf. *Hammond* v. *South Carolina State College,* 272 F. Supp. 947 (D. C. S. C. 1967) (orderly protest meeting on state college campus); *Dickey* v. *Alabama State Board of Education,* 273 F. Supp. 613 (D. C. M. D. Ala. 1967) (expulsion of student editor of college newspaper). In the circumstances of the present case, the prohibition of the silent, passive "witness of the armbands," as one of the children called it, is no less offensive to the Constitution's guarantees.

As we have discussed, the record does not demonstrate any facts which might reasonably have led school authorities to forecast substantial disruption of or material interference with school activities, and no disturbances or disorders on the school premises in fact occurred. These petitioners merely went about their ordained rounds in school. Their deviation consisted only in wearing on their sleeve a band of black

cloth, not more than two inches wide. They wore it to exhibit their disapproval of the Vietnam hostilities and their advocacy of a truce, to make their views known, and, by their example, to influence others to adopt them. They neither interrupted school activities nor sought to intrude in the school affairs or the lives of others. They caused discussion outside of the classrooms, but no interference with work and no disorder. In the circumstances, our Constitution does not permit officials of the State to deny their form of expression.

We express no opinion as to the form of relief which should be granted, this being a matter for the lower courts to determine. We reverse and remand for further proceedings consistent with this opinion.

Reversed and remanded.

NOTES

1. In *Burnside,* the Fifth Circuit ordered that high school authorities be enjoined from enforcing a regulation forbidding students to wear "freedom buttons." It is instructive that in *Blackwell* v. *Issaquena County Board of Education,* 363 F. 2d 749 (1966), the same panel on the same day reached the opposite result on different facts. It declined to enjoin enforcement of such a regulation in another high school where the students wearing freedom buttons harassed students who did not wear them and created much disturbance.

2. *Hamilton* v. *Regents of Univ. of Cal.,* 293 U.S. 245 (1934), is sometimes cited for the broad proposition that the State may attach conditions to attendance at a state university that require individuals to violate their religious convictions. The case involved dismissal of members of a religious denomination from a land grant college for refusal to participate in military training. Narrowly viewed, the case turns upon the Court's conclusion that merely requiring a student to participate in school training in military "science" could not conflict with his constitutionally protected freedom of conscience. The decision cannot be taken as establishing that the State may impose and enforce any conditions that it chooses upon attendance at public institutions of learning, however violative they may be of fundamental constitutional guarantees. See, e.g., *West Virginia* v. *Barnette,* 319 U.S. 624 (1943); *Dixon* v. *Alabama State Board of Education,* 294 F. 2d 150 (C. A. 5th Cir. 1961); *Knight* v. *State Board of Education,* 200 F. Supp. 174 (D. C. M. D. Tenn. 1961); *Dickey* v. *Alabama State Board of Education,* 273 F. Supp. 613 (D. C. M. D. Ala. 1967). See also Note, Unconstitutional Conditions, 73 Harv. L. Rev. 1595 (1960); Note, Academic Freedom, 81 Harv. L. Rev. 1045 (1968).

3. The only suggestions of fear of disorder in the report are these:

"A former student of one of our high schools was killed in Viet Nam. Some of his friends are still in school and it was felt that if any kind of a demonstration existed, it might evolve into something which would be difficult to control."

"Students at one of the high schools were heard to say that they would wear arm bands of other colors if the black bands prevailed."

"Moreover, the testimony of school authorities at trial indicates that it was not fear of disruption that motivated the regulation prohibiting the armbands; the regulation was directed against "the principle of the demonstration" itself. School authorities simply felt that "the schools are no place for demonstrations," and if the students "didn't like the way our elected officials were handling things, it should be handled with the ballot box and not in the halls of our public schools."

4. The District Court found that the school authorities, in prohibiting black armbands, were influenced by the fact that "[t]he Viet Nam war and the involvement of the United States therein has been the subject of a major controversy for some time. When the arm band regulation involved herein was promulgated, debate over the Viet Nam war had become vehement in many localities. A protest march against the war had been recently held in Washington, D.C. A wave of draft card burning incidents protesting the war had swept the country. At that time two highly publicized draft card burning cases were pending in this Court. Both individuals supporting the war and those opposing it were quite vocal in expressing their views." 258 F. Supp., at 972-973.

5. After the principals' meeting, the director of secondary education and the principal of the high school informed the student that the principals were opposed to publication of his article. They reported that "we felt that it was a very friendly conversation, although we did not feel that we had convinced the student that our decision was a just one."

6. In *Hammond* v. *South Carolina State College,* 272 F. Supp. 947 (D. C. S. C. 1967), District Judge Hemphill had before him a case involving a meeting on campus of 300 students to express their views on school practices. He pointed out that a school is not like a hospital or a jail enclosure. Cf. *Cox* v. *Louisiana,* 379 U.S. 536 (1965); *Adderley* v. *Florida,* 385 U.S. 39 (1966). It is a public place, and its dedication to specific uses does not imply that the constitutional rights of persons entitled to be there are to be gauged as if the premises were purely private property. Cf. *Edwards* v. *South Carolina,* 372 U.S. 229 (1963); *Brown* v. *Louisiana,* 383 U.S. 131 (1966).

A United States District Court in Texas decides for several students of Mexican-American descent who had been suspended for wearing brown armbands to express their dissatisfaction with certain educational policies and practices within the Tahoka, Texas, school system. In deciding for the students, the Court stated: "The facts as here found put this case on all fours with that decided by the United States Supreme Court in *Tinker* v. *Des Moines Community School District....* Therefore, the law as announced in that decision controls here. This Court concludes that the controlling law from *Tinker* is as follows: 'the wearing of an armband for the purpose of expressing certain views is the type of symbolic act that is within the Free Speech clause of the First Amendment.' The logic of such a conclusion is obvious when the symbol, the armband, is translated back into the expression which it symbolizes—'I support those in the community who advocate certain changes in the educational system'—and of that expression it is asked, 'Is it within the protection of the First Amendment?' No room for doubt exists."

Aguirre v. *Tahoka Ind. School Dist.,* 311 F. Supp. 664 (1970)

WOODWARD, District Judge.

This is an action filed by the next friends of five minor children, individually and as a class, all of whom are students at Tahoka Junior High School and Tahoka High School, Tahoka, Texas. By this suit plaintiffs seek to enjoin the Tahoka Independent School District and its officials from enforcing the school district's regulation prohibiting students from wearing "apparel decoration that is disruptive, distracting, or provocative." The decorative apparel specifically involved in this suit are brown armbands. This opinion is concerned only with plaintiffs' prayer for temporary injunction against enforcement of said regulation pending final determination of the case.

From the testimony and evidence introduced in a hearing in open Court on March 2nd and 3rd, 1970, at which all parties and their attorneys were in attendance and presented arguments and authorities, the Court found the following pertinent facts:

The parents of plaintiffs and many other local people, mostly of Mexican-American descent, had become dissatisfied with certain educational policies and practices within the Tahoka school system. A group of these people known as "Concerned Mexican American Parents," had attempted to have these matters corrected by means of written correspondence and meetings with various school officials and attorneys advising the school. In a further effort to obtain redress of their grievances, these plaintiffs had also instituted a suit in this Court, Civil Action No. 5-675, alleging violation of their Civil Rights by the school policies and practices which were the subject of correspondence and meetings.

In expression and support of their view that the substance of their grievances was justified and worthy of corrective action by school officials, plaintiffs and other students wore brown armbands to school; the first such wearing being on February 12, 1970.

As of that date there were no dress regulations in effect within the Tahoka school system which would have been violated by armbands such as these. Immediately, however, the Board of Education met and promulgated a Supplement to the existing Student Handbook in which it was announced that "any act, unusual dress, coercion of other students, passing out literature, buttons, etc., or *apparel decoration that is disruptive,* distracting, or provocative so as to incite students of other ethnic groups will not be permitted" (emphasis added). The date of said Supplement was February 13, 1970.

Further implementation of this "dress" regulation was achieved by Board of Education approval of a new procedure under which students could be temporarily suspended from school on the ground of "incorrigibility" for violation of the new dress regulation. This new disciplinary procedure was also dated February 13, 1970.

This Court found as a fact that although neither the dress regulation nor the disciplinary procedure specifically mentioned armbands and neither were limited to armbands or similar devices, both actions by the Board of Education were precipitated by and directed at the wearing of brown armbands by students as well as other activities not involved in this suit.

The dress regulation and disciplinary procedures were made known to students and their parents, including plaintiffs and their next friends. Despite the knowledge that suspension was a likely consequence, plaintiffs and other students continued to wear armbands. At the date of hearing a total of seventeen students, plaintiffs included, had been temporarily suspended after having been given an opportunity to remove their armbands. The only condition required for reinstatement or lifting of suspension was the removal of the armbands.

A thorough and deliberate examination of the testimony of witnesses revealed to the Court that only isolated incidents of unrest or apprehension were attributable to the wearing of the brown armbands. A brief summary of these incidents follows:

A young girl testified that on one occasion in the gym several other girls attempted to force her to wear an armband, but did not persist when she refused. She was not harmed in any way, nor, by her own testimony, was she even frightened. Possible loss of friendship was the only disturbing outgrowth of this incident. A female gym-teacher, who was implied by defendants' counsel to have been connected with this incident, was called by the Court only to disclose that she had no personal knowledge of the incident or the seriousness of it.

On another occasion a female student called her mother to come to school to get her because she was afraid of something. It was never quite clear what was the cause for fright, if there was any actual fright. It could easily have been fear of being suspended from school for wearing armbands or a fear of someone wanting her to wear armbands. In any event, there was no evidence of force, threats, violence, nor harm to the girl.

Children of another family were kept home from school by their father because he was afraid of some unspecified trouble at school. As far as could be determined, these children did not wear armbands, were never forced to, nor were they involved in any disturbance related to armbands.

Finally, after both sides had rested, defendants' attorney, while presenting his closing argument, referred to a march or demonstration as further indication of school disruption. The hearing was recessed until the next day in order for defendants to produce competent evidence concerning this march or demonstration as the Court felt that such evidence was relevant and therefore should be presented. However, only one witness was called in this regard the next day and that

witness was wholly unable to enlighten the Court on the march or demonstration. In any event, school activities were not disrupted by any march, demonstration, or rumors thereof.

These, then, represent the only actual indications of disruption. Of course, several of the school officials offered their conclusions or opinions that wearing of the armbands in violation of school policy was a disruption in and of itself. This Court does not so find.

As announced in open court at the conclusion of the hearing, this Court finds as a fact that there has been no showing that the wearing of the armbands by plaintiffs and the class they represent would materially and substantially interfere with the requirements of appropriate discipline or be disruptive of normal educational functions.

The facts as here found put this case on all fours with that decided by the United States Supreme Court in Tinker v. Des Moines Community School District, 393 U.S. 503, 89 S.Ct. 733, 21 L.Ed.2d 731 (1969). Therefore, the law as announced in that decision controls here. This Court concludes that the controlling law from *Tinker* is as follows:

"The wearing of an armband for the purpose of expressing certain views is the type of symbolic act that is within the Free Speech Clause of the First Amendment." *Tinker, supra* at 505, 89 S.Ct. at 736. The logic of such a conclusion is obvious when the symbol, the armband, is translated back into the expression which it symbolizes—"I support those in the community who advocate certain changes in the educational system"—and of that expression it is asked, "Is it within the protection of the First Amendment?" No room for doubt exists.

The public school setting for the exercise of First Amendment rights by students is permissible but there must be a careful consideration of the special circumstances involved. Such consideration has led the Supreme Court to conclude:

Certainly where there is no finding and no showing that engaging in the forbidden conduct would "materially and substantially interfere with the requirements of appropriate discipline in the operation of the school," the prohibition cannot be sustained. Burnside v. Byars, 363 F.2d 744, 749 (5th Cir. 1966). *Tinker* at 509, 89 S.Ct. at 738.

Here, there has been no such finding as would justify prohibition under this rule. Therefore, plaintiffs are entitled to temporary injunctive relief pending final determination of this cause. The other relief prayed for by plaintiffs will also be determined at that time.

Another matter deserving of comment is the fact that this Court is determined to pay more than lip service to the oft-quoted phrase that nothing done by the

Court is intended to undermine the authority of school officials. Nothing in this opinion nor in the order of this Court is to be construed as in any way to limit or take away the authority of proper officials to regulate, administer and operate the Tahoka Independent School District and its schools. For that reason this Court retains continuing jurisdiction of this cause and will promptly hear and decide any alleged future disturbances and if it should appear that the facts and the laws justify such action, the temporary injunction here ordered will be revoked.

The final matter for those who may critically read this opinion is the observation that this holding is not contrary to that announced by Judge Taylor in Butts v. Dallas Independent School District, 306 F.Supp. 488 (N.D. Tex. 1969). As previously stated, the facts in this cause are in line with those of *Tinker, supra,* while Judge Taylor found that "[t]he facts here [in Butts] show a more aggravated situation than Justice Fortas described in the Tinker case." *Id.* at 490. The instant case is distinguishable on its facts from *Butts* and a different result is to be expected.

Judgment has been entered in accordance with this memorandum opinion.

The Clerk will furnish a copy hereof to the attorneys for all parties in this case.

A United States District Court in Florida declares unconstitutional a Florida regulation requiring students to recite the Pledge of Allegiance to the flag or to stand quietly while others in class participated in the flag salute ceremony. The Court stated: "The right to differ and express one's opinions, to fully vent his First Amendment rights, even to the extent of exhibiting disrespect for our flag and country by refusing to stand and participate in the pledge of allegiance, cannot be suppressed by the imposition of suspensions. It is, therefore, clear that School Board Policy-Regulation 6122 [guidelines for instructions pertaining to the flag, Pledge of Allegiance, and National Anthem] is in direct conflict with the free speech and expression guarantee of the First Amendment as applied to the states through the Fourteenth Amendment to the United States Constitution."

Banks v. Board of Public Instruction of Dade County, 314 F.Supp 285 (1970)

CABOT, District Judge:

Final hearing in these consolidated cases was held on May 25, 1970, before the three-judge court convened pursuant to the provisions of 28 U.S.C. §§ 2281 and 2284. The cases all involve the common question of the facial constitutionality of Florida Statute 232.26, F.S.A.,[1] which provides for suspension of public school children for misbehavior. They also present the issue of the validity of School Board Policy-Regulation 5114[2] which was enacted under the statute, as well as other issues not common to all three cases. The backgrounds of the separate cases follow.

Banks v. Board of Public Instruction of Dade County

Plaintiff, Andrew Robert Banks, a senior at Coral Gables High School, filed his amended complaint by his guardian ad litem alleging he was suspended from school as a result of his refusal to stand during the pledge of allegiance. The complaint seeks class relief and a declaration pursuant to 28 U.S.C. §§ 2201 and 2202 that Florida Statute 232.26, F.S.A. and School Board Policy-Regulation 5114, issued thereunder, are unconstitutional on their face as being vague, overbroad, and indefinite, and for failure to provide prior notice and hearing so as to comport with procedural due process of law. The plaintiff also challenges the constitutionality of School Board Policy-Regulation 6122, entitled "Guidelines for Instruction Pertaining to the Flag, Pledge of Allegiance, and National Anthem,"[3] asserting that the regulation violates the free speech and expression guarantee of the First Amendment as applied to the states through the Fourteenth Amendment to the United State Constitution.

The constitutional application of the statute and the policy-regulations are also challenged, and in this regard the parties have stipulated that the transcript of testimony taken at the earlier hearing on the application for temporary injunction to restore plaintiff to school attendance (which was granted) may be received in evidence. Finally, at the time of final hearing, defendants' motion to dismiss the cause as a class action was pending for determination by the full court.

Mobley v. Braddock; Hill v. Board of Public Instruction of Dade County

On February 25, 1970, Robin Mobley, a student at Drew Junior High School, was suspended for walking through Drew Elementary School, a facility on the same school compound, during school hours without permission. On February 27, 1970, Michael Hill, a student at Parkway Junior High School, was suspended for possession of marbles. Both acts were contrary to established rules of which the suspended students had knowledge. The complaints in these suits were filed by the minors' legal guardians and seek a declaration pursuant to 28 U.S.C. §§ 2201 and 2202 that Florida Statute 232.26, F.S.A. and School Board Policy-Regulation 5114, issued thereunder, are unconstitutional on their face as being vague, overbroad, and indefinite, and for failure to provide prior notice and hearing so as to comport with procedural due process of law. The constitutional application of the statute and the policy-regulation are challenged in both cases, and in this regard the parties have stipulated that the transcript of testimony taken at the earlier hearings on applications for temporary injunction to restore the plaintiffs to school attendance (which were denied) may be received in evidence. At the time for final hearing no motions were pending for consideration by the court in *Hill*, but in *Mobley* there awaits for determination by this panel the defendant's motion to dismiss the cause as a class suit.

We turn now to a discussion of the issues:

Class Action Relief

The complaints in *Banks* and in *Mobley* alleged that the suits are being brought on behalf of the named plaintiffs and on behalf of all others similarly situated who have been or will be threatened with suspensions from schools in Dade County, Florida, pursuant to the authority vested in the county's school principals by Florida Statute 232.26 and Policy-Regulation 5114. Additionally, in *Banks* the class was alleged to consist of those students in the Dade County school system who are subject to the provisions of School Board Policy-Regulation 6122. The defendants in these two cases have filed motions to dismiss alleging that class relief is not appropriate to these cases.

Rule 23(a) of the Fedral Rules of Civil Procedure provides that one or more members of a class may sue or be sued as representative parties on behalf of all only if there are questions of law or fact common to the class and the remaining requirements of subsections (a) and (b) are satisfied.

In both *Mobley* and *Banks*, the complaints fail to show the existence of a question of law or fact common to the class of persons alleged to be subject to the statute and Regulation 5114.

The reasons for which students may be lawfully suspended from school are limited only by the varieties of misbehavior which their ingenuity can devise. They are so numerous as to defy listing.

If the statute is facially unconstitutional the judgment so declaring will apply throughout the state without the necessity for class relief. On the other hand, in considering the constitutionality of the statute as applied, a different set of facts surrounds each suspension. The constitutional issue, therefore, is variable, one of mixed law and fact, and precludes the finding of a question of law or fact common to the class as described. The defendants' motion striking this aspect of the class relief will be granted.

Banks, however, also challenges the constitutionality of Policy-Regulation 6122 and alleges this to be a matter appropriate for class relief, with the class consisting of all those Dade County public school students who refuse to stand during the pledge of allegiance ceremony, but merely sit in their seats, and therefore have been suspended or are subject to suspension. Thus, there is a question of law common to the members of this class.

Moreover, the court finds that the plaintiff will fairly and adequately protect the interests of the class and that the party opposing the class has acted on grounds generally applicable to the class. *See* Frain v. Baron, *infra,* for a similar result. Class relief is appropriate in *Banks* and the defendants' motion will be denied.

Facial Constitutionality of Florida Statute 232.26

Florida Statute 232.26 F.S.A. provides in pertinent part as follows:

Authority of Principal. * * * The principal may suspend a pupil for wilful disobedience, for open defiance of authority of a member of his staff, for use of profane or obscene language, for other serious misconduct, and for repeated misconduct of a less serious nature; provided, that each such suspension with the reasons therefor shall be reported immediately in writing to the parent and to the county superintendent. * * *

The plaintiffs in these consolidated cases assert that the statute is unconstitutional on its face as being vague, overbroad, and indefinite, and for its failure to provide for prior notice and hearing so as to comport with procedural due process of law.

Vagueness—Overbreadth. Plaintiffs assert that the statutory language is vague because "* * * men of common intelligence must necessarily guess at its meaning and differ as to its application." Connally v. General Construction Co., 1926, 269 U.S. 385, 46 S.Ct. 126, 70 L.Ed. 322. They point out that the "void for vagueness doctrine" applies to civil as well as criminal actions, Boutilier v. Immigration and Naturalization Serv., 1967, 387 U.S. 118, 87 S.Ct. 1563, 18 L.Ed.2d 661, and that the doctrine has been applied in reviewing both university, Soglin v. Kauffman, W.D.Wis. 1968, 295 F.Supp. 978, aff'd 7 Cir. 1969, 418 F.2d 163, and high school sanctions, Sullivan v. Houston Independent School District, S.D.Tex. 1969, 307 F. Supp. 1328. Analyzing each phrase separately, the plaintiffs have attempted to show that the language of the statute does nothing more than allow school administrators unfettered discretion in meting out suspensions. We disagree.

In order to resolve the question of whether or not the plaintiffs were denied their constitutional rights it is important to weigh and contrast the gravity of those rights with the interest of the state in maintaining discipline in the educational system. It has always been within the province of school authorities to provide by regulation for the prohibition and punishment of acts calculated to undermine the school routine. Obviously, such authority is necessary and proper. Blackwell v. Issaquena County Board of Education, 5 Cir. 1966, 363 F.2d 749, 753.

The Supreme Court has on several occasions "* * * emphasized the need for affirming the comprehensive authority of the states and of school officials, consistent with fundamental constitutional safeguards, to prescribe and control conduct in the schools." Tinker v. Des Moines Independent Community School District, 1969, 393 U.S. 503, 89 S.Ct. 733, 21 L.Ed.2d 731. In this regard it should be obvious that:

> * * * in measuring the appropriateness and reasonableness of school regulations against the constitutional protections of the First and Fourteenth Amendments the courts must give full credence *to the role and purposes of the schools and of the tools with which it is expected that they deal with their problems, and careful recognition to the differences between what are reasonable restraints in the classroom and what are reasonable restraints on the street corner.* [Emphasis added.]

Clearly, the community

> * * * expects that the requirements of order, and of protection and implementation of the educational program of the school, will be met by limited enforcement means—the force of the school establishment itself and the school related disciplines of reprimand, suspension, and expulsion—recognizing that the school room is an inappropriate place for the policeman to be either called or needed. Godbold, J., specially concurring in Ferrell v. Dallas Independent School District, 5 Cir. 1968, 392 F.2d 697.

The proper operation of the public school system is one of the highest and most fundamental responsibilities of the state. *Blackwell, supra.* In order to fulfill that responsibility, we acknowledge the power of school authorities to discipline students, but do not require that school suspension statutes satisfy the same rigorous standards as those imposed upon criminal statutes. Soglin v. Kauffman, *supra* 418 F.2d at 168; Sullivan v. Houston Independent School District, *supra* 307 F.Supp. at 1344; Buttny v. Smiley, D.Colo. 1968, 231 F.Supp. 280. What is required is that basic notions of justice and fair play be employed within the school setting to insure that the standards for acceptable conduct are easily understood. Florida Statute 232.26, F.S.A., does use broad language but the rules of conduct contained therein are not so vague as to require the court to declare them invalid. Although not all of the statutory language to which plaintiffs object is couched in specific prohibitions, it is obvious that the many and varying types of misconduct which justify a suspension are incapable of exact description and, therefore, necessitate the use of encompassing words.

The language objected to in the statute, though it might be condemned as constitutionally deficient if included in a criminal statute, does set standards which are readily determinable and easily understood within the framework of the public school system. Individual analysis of the terms is not necessary. The statute is neither vague nor overbroad but rather is necessary to the proper operation of the public school system and therefore constitutionally sound.

Finally, it should also be recognized that the right of the school board to discipline students is not solely dependent upon Florida Statute 232.26, F.S.A., Florida Statute 230.23(6) (c), F.S.A. delegates to the county school boards the power to promulgate rules and regulations for the control, discipline, and suspension of students. In like manner Florida Statute 230.22, F.S.A. empowers the county school boards to adopt such policies, rules, and regulations as are deemed necessary for the efficient operation and general improvement of the county school system. Florida Statute 232.26, F.S.A., therefore, is merely a statute specifically limiting the authority of the principal to suspend, and even without it, school authorities, by virtue of the cited statutes, as well as the powers inherent in their offices, have the power to suspend and otherwise discipline students for misbehavior.

Due Process. The plaintiffs in all of these cases have alleged that Florida Statute 232.26 F.S.A. and Policy-Regulation 5114 are unconstitutional as violative of due process of law in that they permit a school principal to suspend a student for a period up to ten days without affording him a prior notice and hearing of the charges.

The plaintiffs place heavy reliance on Dixon v. Alabama State Board of Education, 5 Cir. 1961, 294 F.2d 150. In *Dixon* the court held that due process requires notice and some opportunity for hearing before students at a tax supported college are expelled for misconduct. Since 1961 numerous cases have adopted the view expressed in *Dixon* to the extent that this holding is well established and widely acknowledged. *See, e.g.,* Woods v. Wright, 5 Cir. 1964, 334 F.2d 369, Stricklin v. Regents of Univ. of Wisconsin, W.D.Wis. 1969, 297 F.Supp. 416, Marzette v. McPhee, W.D. Wis.1968, 294 F.Supp. 562, Due v. Fla. A. & M. Univ., N.D.Fla.1963, 233 F.Supp. 396.

Florida Statute 232.26, F.S.A. provides that when a student is suspended "the reasons therefor shall be reported immediately in writing to the parent and to the county superintendent. * * *" The statute does not provide for a hearing prior to suspension. Policy-

Regulation 5114 recognizes that "suspension[s] * * * are extreme measures to be employed only when all available school resources are exhausted and school personnel are unable to cope constructively with pupil misconduct." The regulation details the authority of both the principal and the superintendent and sets forth the procedures to be employed in suspending or expelling students. It provides that when a student is to be suspended from school for up to ten days the principal shall prepare a notice of suspension, the original copy of which is to be sent to the child's parents. Form 37, the standard form notice of suspension which is provided for in the regulation, provides blanks for the student's name and the reason for the suspension, and ends with an invitation to the parents to contact the school to discuss the matter more thoroughly with the authorities. The regulation further provides that every effort shall be made to contact the parent or parents of a pupil who is being suspended in order to inform them of the reason for the suspension and that a formal notice of suspension has been sent to them in the mail. The regulation does not provide for a hearing prior to suspension.

The plaintiffs assert that before students at a public school can be suspended they must be given a hearing with notice of the charges. The requirement of a hearing, of course, is nothing more than fair play. However, it does not follow that the hearing need be prior to the suspension. The right to a hearing, when analyzed within the setting of the public school system, is necessarily subject to limitations imposed in order to insure the orderly administration of education and to preserve both decorum in the classroom and respect for teachers and administrators.

The touchstone for sustaining school regulatory and disciplinary legislation is the demonstration that it is necessary to alleviate interference with the educational process. *Tinker, supra,* Ferrell v. Dallas Independent School System, *supra* 392 F.2d at 703. Thus the plaintiffs here do not urge, nor could they successfully, that educators may not lawfully discipline students in summary fashion in a riot or other emergency. This is so because such a riot or emergency by its nature disrupts the educational process and threatens both the welfare and safety of students and the preservation of the school plant.

Providing a hearing to a student *prior* to his suspension for misconduct itself produces a disruptive effect upon the educational process. Consider, for example, misconduct which occurs during class. If the misconduct in the teacher's opinion justifies suspension, it would also seem to require that the student be immediately removed from the room as the teacher must be able to continue the teaching process without undue interference. If a hearing is to be held prior to suspension the teacher must leave the room with the student or leave a later scheduled class in order to offer testimony. Those students who were witness to the misconduct must likewise leave the room or spend class time preparing written statements to be presented at the hearing. If the teacher leaves the room the class in the meantime must be left either without supervision or under the guidance of one who is ill-prepared or needed elsewhere. In any event the likelihood is that the remaining students would suffer in their pursuit of an education.

If the misconduct should occur in a common area, such as the cafeteria, the hallways or a recreation area, it is likely that a number of staff and student witnesses must be called out of class to "testify" at such a prior hearing, thus multiplying the disruptive effect on the educational process. The parents, of course, must be notified of the hearing and told to come to the school immediately to confer with their child and help prepare his "case."

If, on the other hand, both student and teacher remain in class following the incident until a later time, perhaps the end of the school day, the authority of the teacher and the respect in which he is held will suffer. Moreover, allowing the student who has misbehaved to remain in class is certain to have a disruptive effect.

If the hearing is to be held after school, student witnesses must be kept late to testify and the "offender" will no doubt be conferring with them throughout the remainder of the day both in and out of class in order to prepare for the hearing. Of course, there is the possibility that the teacher might remain in class and just send the student to the principal to be kept in detention until the hearing. But this alternative would prevent the student from conferring with witnesses and preparing his case. It is apparent that providing public school students with hearing prior to suspension would result in a disruption of the educational process which cannot be permitted.

In reaching this conclusion we have attempted to balance the rights of public school students with the demands imposed upon the educators by the community at large. Public school children suspended for misconduct are not criminals. The legal processes due them are less exacting than that due one who is accused under a criminal statute. The procedure set forth in the statute and regulation are consistent with the constitutional guarantee of due process of law in a school setting, are educationally sound, and necessary to the proper administration of the educational process. Recognizing the objectives of our public school system and of the tools with which school administrators must deal with student disciplinary problems, it does not appear that either the statute or the regulation is facially unconstitutional.

There is a dearth of cases involving the suspension

of public school students for misconduct which occurred in the school plant. Dixon v. Alabama State Board of Education, *supra,* involving college students, is of course persuasive and this court adopts that decision insofar as it requires that notice be given, a hearing provided for, and that the hearing include the rudimentary adversary elements. Thus, the students should be given specific notice of the charges, the names of witnesses with a summary of their testimony, and should be given the opportunity to refute the charges by oral or written testimony. We do not, however, require, as *Dixon* does, that the hearing be held prior to the suspension.

There are significant factual distinctions between *Dixon* and this case—between a college suspension and a public school suspension. For example, in a college or university, teachers and students are rarely in class for more than a few hours a day, whereas in the public school system teachers and students are in class throughout the day. While public school teachers and administrators would be called upon to miss class if a prior hearng is held, the same is not usually true in colleges and universities. The disruption of the educational process that occurs as a result of a prior hearing therefore is less likely to occur in the college than it is in the public school.

Additionally, the consequences of a public school suspension are considerably less serious than those which follow from a university suspension. In fact, School Board Policy-Regulation 5114 provides, in cases of ten-day and thirty-day suspensions, that there shall be no evidence of the suspension posted on the pupil's permanent record. However, suspension or expulsion from a college or university may seriously affect a student's opportunity to obtain a graduate or postgraduate degree, or otherwise achieve professional status.

The procedures set forth in the statute and the regulation provide for immediate notice of the suspension and the reasons therefor to be sent to the parents, and for the parents to be notified of the suspension before the student can be sent home. Moreover, the notice of suspension invites the parents to contact the school if they desire to discuss the matter. This procedure, which provides for a hearing after the fact upon request of the parents, while somewhat informal when contrasted with criminal procedure, is nonetheless consistent with the dictates of due process when examined in light of the public school setting.

Accordingly, we hold that the procedures set forth in Florida Statute 232.26, F.S.A. and School Board Policy-Regulation 5114 are necessary to insure the orderly administration of the educational process and, therefore, are consistent with the due process provisions of the Fifth and Fourteenth Amendments to the United States Constitution.

Constitutional Application of Florida Statute 232.26 and Policy-Regulation 5114

Finally, the plaintiffs in these cases contend that the statute and the policy-regulations were unconstitutionally applied to them. As previously mentioned, the parties have all stipulated that the transcripts of testimony taken on the applications for temporary relief may be introduced in evidence and used for the purpose of disposing of this issue.

The testimony elicited at the hearing on the motion for temporary relief in *Banks* centered primarily upon the reason for the suspension, i.e., the plantiff's refusal to stand during the pledge of allegiance ceremony. Nothing in the record supports a finding that the statute was unconstitutionally applied. The plaintiff has simply failed to sustain his burden of proof on this issue.

The testimony taken on the motion for temporary relief in *Hill* establishes that he was not denied due process of law as a result of the application of either the statute or the regulation.

Michael Hill was suspended from school at the end of the school day on Thursday, February 26, 1970, for what he thought was the throwing of marbles, which he admitted having on his person during school hours. The notice of suspension sent to his home arrived on Saturday, February 28, 1970, and indicated that the suspension was for possession of marbles. The notice, which was sent in accordance with the mandate of the statute and the policy-regulation, invited the parents to contact the school, if they desired to discuss the matter. The record reflects that on learning of their son's suspension, the parents did not call the school themselves but rather retained an attorney who called for them, and on the principal's refusal to reinstate their son, the parents, before personally contacting the school or going there for a conference, filed suit Friday afternoon, February 27, 1970, challenging the constitutional validity of the statute. While the parents had the right to employ an attorney and seek redress of their grievance in court, the transcript reflects that of the eight boys who were suspended with the Hill child for the possession of marbles all but this plaintiff and his parents went to see the principal and discuss the matter, and all but this plaintiff were reinstated.

The Fifth Circuit, on May 26, 1970, in Stevenson v. Board of Education, Wheeler County, Georgia, 426 F.2d 1154, not yet reported, a case involving constitutional attack on a school board "good grooming rule," stated that the district court should have required that the plaintiffs be first referred to the Board of Education to insure that the action complained of was final within the institution in the sense that it was ripe for adjudication. This case demonstrates the wisdom of that rule, for it appears that the plaintiff was not deprived of due process of law by the application of the statute or the policy-regulation, but rather that both he and his parents failed to employ the informal procedures available to them under the statute and the regulation.

The record in *Mobley* indicates that she was apprehended by Board of Public Instruction security officials on the morning of February 19, 1970, at nine o'clock while walking through Drew Elementary School, a separate facility adjacent to the junior high school she was attending. The notice of suspension, hand delivered to the plaintiff's mother by a visiting teacher on the afternoon of the suspension, states the reason for the suspension, and the record indicates that plaintiff knew that junior high school students were not permitted in the elementary school during school hours. This rule of conduct was designed to prevent students from the junior high school from trespassing upon the elementary school grounds and disrupting classes therein, a problem which frequently occurred during the school year. The assistant principal, the individual charged with the investigation of this matter, testified that upon Robin's being brought to his office he heard her explanation as to why she was off school property and at the elementary school, and attempted to independently verify her explanation which he found inadequate. The record further reflects that the plaintiff was advised of the serious nature of the conduct and was told by the assistant principal that a ten day suspension would be recommended. The school principal testified that Mrs. Mobley and Robin returned to the school the day of the suspension and had a conference with him about the matter. Moreover, Mrs. Mobley was given the opportunity to and did confer with the principal on a second occasion.

The record clearly indicates that the suspension was lawful, that notice of the charges was given orally to the plaintiff and in writing to her mother, and that the informal hearings and conferences conducted with the child by the assistant principal and with the child and her mother on two occasions by the principal, were sufficient to comport with due process of law. Neither the statute nor the policy-regulations were unconstitutionally applied to this plaintiff.

Regulation 6122
*Guidelines for Instructions Pertaining
to the Flag, Pledge of Allegiance,
and National Anthem*

The facts essential to the disposition of the case are not in dispute. Andrew Robert Banks was suspended from school on January 29, 1970, for a period of ten days, and again suspended for a like term on February 9, 1970, for his refusal to stand in accordance with the procedure contained in School Board Policy-Regulation 6122 during the flag salute ceremony conducted each morning in the homeroom period. The regulation states that "students who for religious or other deep personal conviction, do not participate in the salute and pledge of allegiance to the flag will stand quietly."

The plaintiff asserts that he has the constitutional right to refuse to stand for the pledge and salute and that his suspension constituted a penalty imposed upon him for the exercise of his constitutional right of free speech and expression. The defendant has denied that the plaintiff's refusal to stand was an exercise of his constitutional right of free speech and expression and has asserted that there is a compelling governmental purpose to be served in requiring students to stand during the pledge.

In West Virginia State Board of Education v. Barnette, 1943, 319 U.S. 624, 63 S.Ct. 1178, 87 L.Ed. 1628, the Supreme Court, overruling Minersville School District v. Gobitis, 1940, 310 U.S. 586, 60 S.Ct. 1010, 84 L.Ed. 1375, held that a West Virginia State Board of Education resolution which required children, as a prerequisite to their continued attendance at public school, to salute the flag and recite the pledge, was unconstitutional as applied to children of Jehovah's Witnesses since it denied them freedom of speech and freedom of worship. In rejecting the resolution the court held that the state could not "prescribe what shall be orthodox in politics, nationalism, religion, or other matters of opinion," nor can the state "force citizens to confess by word or act their faith therein." *Barnette* at 624, 63 S.Ct. at 1187. In holding that the state could not compel obedience to its symbol at the expense of First Amendment rights, save "grave and immediate dangers to interests which the state may lawfully protect," the court observed that:

Freedom to differ is not limited to things that do not matter much. That would be a mere shadow of freedom. The test of substance is the right to differ as to things that touch the heart of the existing order. *Barnette*, at 642, 63 S.Ct. at 1187.

Without more *Barnette* would be dispositive of this matter for Andrew Banks was suspended for his refusal to act in accordance with a regulation, the operation of which prevented him from exercising his First Amendment rights. Yet, the tenor of *Barnette* is negative. It prohibits the state from compelling individuals to act in a certain manner; it is not a recognition of student's rights. On the other hand, the Supreme Court's decision in Tinker v. Des Moines Independent Community School District, 1969, 303 U.S. 503, 89 S.Ct. 733, 21 L.Ed.2d 731, speaks affirmatively. There the court held that public school students could not be suspended for wearing black armbands to protest American involvement in Vietnam, a form of silent protest and non-disruptive First Amendment expression in the classroom. In writing for the majority, Mr. Justice Fortas stated that:

First Amendment rights, applied in light of the special characteristics of the school environment, are available to teachers and students. It can hardly be argued that either teachers or students shed their constitutional rights to freedom of speech or expression at the schoolhouse gate. *Tinker* at 506, 89 S.Ct. at 736.

The court recognized that "[i]n the absence of a specific showing of constitutionally valid reasons to regulate their speech, students are entitled to freedom of expression of their views." *Tinker* at 503, 89 S.Ct. at 739. However, the court was careful to point out that:

[c]onduct by the student, in class or out of it, which for any reason—whether it stems from time, place, or type of behavior—materially disrupts classwork or involves substantial disorder or invasion of the rights of others is, of course, not immunized by the constitutional guarantee of free speech. *Tinker* at 513, 89 S.Ct. at 740.

The conduct of Andrew Banks in refusing to stand during the pledge ceremony constituted an expression of his religious beliefs and political opinions. His refusal to stand was no less a form of expression than the wearing of the black arm-band was to Mary Beth Tinker. He was exercising a right "akin to pure speech."

The plaintiff testified that the basis of his refusal to abide by the regulation was his religious beliefs. He testified that he is a Unitarian, that he believes a "Uni-world" government is necessary to world peace, that he intends to be a Unitarian minister, and further that his refusal to stand was a simple protest against black repression in the United States. A student in the plaintiff's homeroom who sits next to him testified that when the flag salute period comes, "Sometimes he [Banks] stands up and doesn't say anything and sometimes he just sits down but he doesn't cause any disturbance in class or you know, make the other kids—make it conspicuous just what he is doing." The unrefuted testimony clearly reflects that the plaintiff's refusal to stand has not caused any disruption in the educational process. While there may be some who would question the sincerity with which this plaintiff holds his religious and political views, such inquiry is not a proper consideration for a court. The First Amendment guarantees to the plaintiff the right to claim that his objection to standing during the ceremony is based upon religious and political beliefs. West Virginia State Board of Education v. Barnette, *supra* 63 S.Ct. at 1183; United States v. Ballard, 1944, 322 U.S. 78, 64 S.Ct. 882, 88 L.Ed. 1148; Cantwell v. Connecticut, 1940, 310 U.S. 296, 60 S.Ct. 900, 84 L.Ed. 1213; Sheldon v. Fannin, D.Ariz.1963, 221 F.Supp. 766.

The flag is a symbol of our government. Its colors, its stripes, and its stars represent our country and all that it is, its history and accomplishments, its hopes and aspirations. Mr. Justice Jackson, writing for the majority in *Barnette,* recognized that symbols of state, such as the crown, the mace, the altar, and even black robes, often have associated with them gestures of acceptance or respect including the salute, a bowed or bared head, or a bended knee. Likewise, standing is an integral portion of the pledge ceremony and is no less a gesture of acceptance and respect than is the salute or the utterance of the words of allegiance. Here, as in *Barnette,* the regulation required the individual to communicate, by standing, his acceptance of and respect for all that for which our flag is but a symbol.

The same conclusion has been reached on facts virtually identical to those presented in the instant case in Sheldon v. Fannin, D.Ariz.1963, 221 F.Supp. 766. There the court issued a permanent injunction restraining the state board of education from suspending for insubordination students who, because of their religious beliefs as Jehovah's Witnesses, refused to stand during the singing of the national anthem. That court, relying heavily upon West Virginia v. Barnette, recognized that the First Amendment guarantee protects even the expressions of beliefs which appear to be ludicrous and unfounded. The court stated that "[w]hile implicitly demanding that all freedom of expression be exercised reasonably under the circumstances, the Constitution fortunately does not require that the beliefs or thoughts expressed be reasonable, or wise, or even sensible."

In a recent case, Frain v. Baron, E.D.N.Y.1970, 307 F.Supp. 27, the court issued a temporary injunction enjoining the defendant administrators of the New York school system from excluding the plaintiffs from their classrooms during the pledge of allegiance. The opinion reflects that the students who refused to leave the room and stand in the hall so acted because of a mixture of religious and political beliefs. The court there also relied heavily upon *Barnette* and *Tinker* in supporting its position.

The right to differ and express one's opinions, to fully vent his First Amendment rights, even to the extent of exhibiting disrespect for our flag and country by refusing to stand and participate in the pledge of allegiance, cannot be suppressed by the imposition of suspensions. It is, therefore, clear that School Board Policy-Regulation 6122 is in direct conflict with the free speech and expression guarantee of the First Amendment as applied to the states through the Fourteenth Amendment to the United States Constitution.

This memorandum opinion shall serve as findings

of fact and conclusions of law in these cases.

Accordingly, it is ordered and adjudged that:

1. Defendants' motion to dismiss plaintiff's application for class relief in the case of Mobley v. Braddock, No. 70-241-Civ-TC, is treated as a motion to strike and as such is granted.

2. Defendants' motion to dismiss plaintiff's application for class relief in the case of Banks v. Board of Public Instruction of Dade County, Florida, No. 70-197-Civ-TC, is treated as a motion to strike and as such is denied.

3. Florida Statute 232.26, F.S.A. is hereby declared constitutional.

4. School Board Policy-Regulation 5114 is hereby declared constitutional.

5. School Board Policy-Regulation 6122 is hereby declared unconstitutional as violative of the First and Fourteenth Amendments to the United States Constitution, and the Dade County Board of Public Instruction is permanently enjoined from enforcing its provisions.

6. Neither Florida Statute 232.26, F.S.A. nor Policy-Regulation 5114 have been unconstitutionally applied to these plaintiffs.

APPENDIX I
FLORIDA STATUTE 232.26

232.26 *Authority of Principal*

Subject to law and rules and regulations of the state board and of the county board, the principal or teacher in charge of a school may delegate to any teacher or other member of the instructional staff or to any bus driver transporting pupils of the school such responsibility for the control and direction of the pupils as he may consider desirable. The principal may suspend a pupil for wilful disobedience, for open defiance of authority of a member of his staff, for use of profane or obscene language, for other serious misconduct, and for repeated misconduct of a less serious nature; provided, that each such suspension with the reasons therefor shall be reported immediately in writing to the parent and to the county superintendent; and provided, further, that no one suspension shall be for more than ten days and that no suspension shall be made a dismissal unless so ordered by the county board in a resolution adopted and spread upon its minutes. He may suspend any pupil transported to or from school at the public expense from the privilege of riding on a school bus for a period of ten days, or until such suspension is modified or made a dismissal by the county board, giving immediate notice in writing to the county superintendent and to the parent as provided above.

APPENDIX II

Elementary and Secondary

Suspension and Expulsion
Suspension and expulsion are extreme measures to be employed only when all available school resources are exhausted and school personnel are unable to cope constructively with pupil misconduct. Suspension from school may be authorized by the principal or Superintendent for a short period of time. Expulsion from school requires action of the Board to effect and rescind.

Principal's Authority
The principal shall have the authority to:
1. Suspend a pupil from school for a period of not more than 10 school days for any one suspension.
2. Recommend to the Superintendent, with the approval of the district superintendent, that a pupil (a) be suspended by the Superintendent up to an additional 30 school days or (b) be suspended by the Superintendent up to an additional 30 school days and be expelled by the Dade County School Board.

Superintendent's Authority
The Superintendent shall have the authority to:

1. Suspend a pupil up to 30 school days or assign a pupil to an individually designated program or other special placement.
2. Recommend to the Board that a pupil be dismissed permanently or for a specified period of time.
3. Recommend assignment of a pupil to be expelled from his regular school to an individually designated program or to other special placement.

Expulsion by the Dade County School Board
In recommending expulsion by the Board, the principal shall present a report on the school record of the pupil (attendance, conduct, academic progress, and suspensions) as well as contacts of school personnel with the pupil and family.

Upon recommendation of the Superintendent:
1. The Board may expel from school any pupil (a) having, using or handling substances that modify mood and/or behavior or (b) bringing to school or having in his possession a deadly weapon including but not limited to a gun, knife, razor, explosives and ice pick.

Rev. eff.: 3/26/69; 11/5/69
16"

2. The Board also may expel from school any pupil involved in a serious breach of conduct such as an assault on school personnel or on other pupils, lewd or lascivious behavior, arson or serious vandalism or misbehavior which disrupts the orderly conduct of the school.

3. The Board also may expel pupils for less serious but continuing misconduct, which may include the use of profane, obscene or abusive language, that seriously affects the school program in a negative way. In making a recommendation for this type of expulsion, the principal shall present a written report on measures taken to bring about the proper conduct of the pupil.

Procedures: Pupil Expulsion Hearings

The following procedures will be observed when the Superintendent recommends a student for expulsion.

1. Pupil May Request a Hearing

The Superintendent shall by certified mail or by hand delivery by appropriate staff member notify the pupil's parents or guardian of school record that he is recommending that their child be expelled from the Dade County schools. This letter shall set forth the charges against the pupil and advise the parent that he has seven days in which to request a hearing on those charges before a hearing committee.

Should the parent not request a hearing within the specified time, the Board will act on the Superintendent's recommendation at the first available Board meeting. Said recommendation will set forth a brief statement of the pupil's act or acts which warrant expulsion.

2. Hearing

Should the pupil's parent request a hearing, the hearing shall be conducted before one of the hearing examiners appointed by the Board and shall be conducted under the rules and procedures for administrative hearings adopted by Board Resolution 63-19. (See Regulation 4119.-5.)

Legal Reference: Florida Statues, 230.23(8) [6] (c)); 230.33(8)(c); 232.26

DADE COUNTY SCHOOL BOARD
Miami, Florida
Policy adopted: 12/7/66
Effective: 12/7/66
Rev. eff.: 3/26/69; 11/5/69
16"

Elementary and Secondary

Suspension, Expulsion, Exclusion, Juvenile Court and Protective Services Referrals

1. Suspension, 10 Days or Less

The principal has the authority to suspend a pupil from school up to 10 days for any one offense.

When a pupil is to be suspended from school up to 10 days by the principal, the principal shall prepare in triplicate Form 37; *Notice of Suspension.* The original copy is sent to the parent, a copy is sent to the district superintendent and a copy is filed in the pupil's cumulative guidance record. There shall be no evidence of the 10-day suspension posted on the pupil's permanent record other than that reflected by his attendance record. The copy filed in the pupil's cumulative guidance record may be removed later, with the approval of the principal, when the pupil's behavior becomes more acceptable.

Every effort shall be made to contact the parent of a pupil who is being suspended, the reason for the suspension stated, and the parent informed that the notice of suspension has been sent to him by U.S. mail. If the parent cannot be contacted, the pupil is NOT to be sent home during the school day.

After any suspension from school it is advisable that the principal determine the extent of follow-up procedures to be taken to assure the rehabilitation and progress of the pupil.

2. Additional 30-Day Suspension

Only the Superintendent of Schools has the authority to suspend a pupil from school for more than 10 days.

If more than a 10-day suspension is deemed necessary, the principal may request an additional 30-day suspension (total 40 school days). This request for an additional 30-day suspension shall be prepared in triplicate on Form 39: *Request for 30-Day Suspension* and the original and one copy sent to the district office for the superintendent's study, concurrence, and signature. This request must include justification for the recommended action. If approved by the district superintendent, the original copy must be sent to the Supervisor of Attendance Services, Pupil Personnel Services Department, within a 3-day period of the initial 10-day suspension in order to have time to process the request before the expiration of the initial 10-day suspension. The district superintendent and the school principal shall each retain a carbon copy of the request.

The principal has the responsibility to notify immediately the appropriate police department and the School Security Department at the time of the incident described in the request for the suspension, if this action is warranted.

Rev. eff.: 8/18/69
13"

Elementary and Secondary

Suspension, Expulsion, Exclusion, Juvenile Court and Protective Services Referrals

2. Additional 30-Day Suspension (cont.)

At the time a pupil is recommended for a 30-day suspension by the principal and the district superintendent, they shall also recommend whether or not the pupil shall have the opportunity to attend a Center for Special Instruction during the suspension period. On approval of the 30-day suspension by the Superintendent of Schools, he shall notify the parent by certified mail of the suspension and the basis for the action taken. The Superintendent's letter shall state also if the pupil's attendance at a Center for Special Instruction is approved. Copies of this letter are forwarded to the district superintendent and the principal.

At this time the school shall file in the pupil's cumulative guidance record Form 39: *Request for 30-Day Suspension* and a copy of the letter of the Superintendent of Schools to the parent. A brief narrative comment of the suspension should be noted in section 9 of the cumulative guidance record.

There shall be no evidence of the 30-day suspension posted on the pupil's permanent record except that which is reflected by the pupil's attendance record.

3. Early Termination of 30-Day Suspension

The principal, with the concurrence of the district superintendent may request an early termination of a 30-day suspension.

If there is sufficient reason to request an early termination of the 30-day suspension, the principal shall prepare in triplicate Form 39a: *Request for Termination of 30-Day Suspension,* sending the original and one copy to the district superintendent.

If the district superintendent concurs with this action, he signs the original copy of Form 39a and forwards it immediately to the Supervisor of Attendance Services for the attention of the Superintendent of Schools. If the Superintendent of Schools approves this early termination of the 30-day suspension, the parent is notified by letter, with a copy to the principal and district superintendent. The Supervisor of Attendance Services, or a delegated visiting teacher, notifies the principal immediately in order to expedite the early return of the pupil to school. The parent will also be notified by a visiting teacher, if the principal requests this service.

The copy of Form 39a and the principal's copy of the letter to the parent shall be filed in the pupil's cumulative guidance record and a notation made in section 9 on the cumulative guidance record as to the date of the early termination of the suspension.

Rev. eff.: 8/18/69
13"

4. Expulsion

Only the Board of Public Instruction, by law, has the right to expel a pupil from school.

Reasons for recommending that the Superintendent of Schools requests the Board to expel a pupil from school may be because of:

a. Having, using, or handling substances that modify mood and/or behavior;

b. Bringing to school or having in his/her possession a deadly weapon, including but not limited to a gun, knife, razor, explosives or ice pick;

c. Being involved in a serious breach of conduct such as an assault on school personnel or another pupil;

d. Lewd or lascivious behavior, arson or serious vandalism;

e. Other serious instances or misbehavior;

f. Less serious but continuing misconduct.

In making a request for expulsion, the principal shall prepare in triplicate Form 39: *Request for 30-Day Suspension* and follow the same procedure as in requesting a 30-day suspension. The principal must have issued a 10-day suspension, prior to submitting Form 39.

When a principal recommends the expulsion of a pupil from school for less serious but continuing misconduct, item f. above, in addition to the data included in Form 39, he must prepare a letter addressed to the Superintendent of Schools with detailed information about the pupil regarding:

a. Attendance, conduct and suspension;

b. Number of times the pupil has been seen by the visiting teacher, counselor, or other school resource personnel;

c. Curriculum adjustments made;

d. Number of times the parents have been involved in the pupil's adjustment problems;

e. Other measures taken by the school to bring about a change in the conduct of the pupil.

Rev. eff.: 8/18/69

13"

This letter forwarded to the Supervisor of Attendance Services will be made available to members of the hearing committee, pupil's parents, and to School Board members as part of the background information for the recommended action for expulsion.

At the time a pupil is recommended for expulsion by the principal and district superintendent, they shall also recommend whether or not the pupil shall have the opportunity to attend a Center for Special Instruction. If expelled by the Board of Public Instruction and approval is granted to attend a Center for Special Instruction, the pupil will be notified of his eligibility through a letter to the parents issued by the Supervisor of Attendance Services.

The school shall file in the pupil's cumulative guidance record Form 39: *Request for 30-Day Suspension* and the official notice of expulsion from the School Board office. A narrative comment of this action should be noted in section 9 of the cumulative guidance record.

There shall be no evidence of the expulsion posted on the pupil's permanent record except that which is reflected by the pupil's attendance record.

5. Release from Compulsory School Attendance: Exclusion

The Supervisor of Attendance Services has the responsibility for approving the joint request of the principal and the district coordinator of pupil personnel services for the withdrawal from school of a pupil of compulsory school attendance age.

Reasons for the release from compulsory school attendance may include financial, emotional, physical or other critical conditions which temporarily cause the pupil to become unable to take advantage of the school program.

If it becomes necessary to consider the withdrawal of a pupil of compulsory school attendance age from school and the parent is in agreement with this action, a request by the principal for this withdrawal shall be made to the district coordinator of pupil personnel services. This request shall include:

a. The principal's statement of the problem;

b. A copy of any psychological or medical evaluation and recommendations;

c. A written request or agreement of the parent for withdrawal;

d. A statement from any school support services or nonschool professionals familiar with the case;

e. A report on any measures taken by the school to bring about the proper conduct and school progress;

f. Suggested plans which may insure the pupil's early return to school.

Rev. eff.: 8/18/69

13"

If the pupil's withdrawal seems warranted, the district coordinator of pupil personnel services shall forward this request with an appropriate cover letter to the Supervisor of Attendance Services for approval. The Supervisor of Attendance Services shall notify the principal of the disposition of the case by letter and at the same time send a copy of the letter to the district coordinator of pupil personnel services. The principal then notifies the parent or guardian of the action taken. The letter of notification from the Supervisor of Attendance Services shall be filed in the pupil's cumulative guidance record. A narrative comment of this action should be noted in section 9 of the pupil's cumulative guidance record.

The permanent record should bear a notation of withdrawal as of a certain date.

6. Juvenile Court and Child Protective Services Referrals

The Juvenile Court has asked the office of Attendance Services, Pupil Personnel Services Department and the office of the Security Department to act as the only agents in bringing to its attention any case involving a pupil who commits a violation of law or is in conflict with the school law or regulations in that he is an incorrigible child or a persistent truant from school. Child Protective Services of Dade County also ask that the above offices be the only agents in bringing related school problems to its attention.

When a child is in violation of Florida Statutes, the Security Department should be involved immediately.

The principal or assistant principal requesting that a particular pupil be brought to the attention of the Juvenile Court or Protective Services should consult with the visiting teacher and appropriate school personnel prior to making the formal request. If a referral is requested because of a school situation, the principal of that school must write a letter to the Superintendent of Schools requesting proper agency action. The original letter and one copy is sent to the Supervisor of Attendance Services and a second copy is sent to the district coordinator of pupil personnel services. The principal's copy of the letter to the Superintendent of Schools requesting agency action is to be filed in the pupil's cumulative guidance record.

Rev. eff.: 8/18/69
13"

A court letter must include pertinent information regarding the pupil, including a description of the attitude of the pupil, general conduct, progress in his school work, the attitude and cooperation of the home, and any other information which may be of help in explaining the situation to the court. If the referral seems to be an attendance problem, the dates and reasons for the absences during the entire school year should be specified. This information is most important in presenting the case in court. A Protective Services letter must show dependency, neglect or abuse as a basis for the referral. In any case valid supporting evidence is necessary regarding proof of any statement of charges. A representative of the referring school is to be present at the hearing before the judge when requested.

7. Confidential Report on Pupils Suspended, Expelled and Excluded

A confidential listing, for school personnel only, shall be compiled and released routinely by the office of Attendance Services, giving the names of all students currently on 30-day suspension, expulsion or exclusion. A limited number of these reports will be sent to district offices, to all school centers and to certain county administrators.

Rules approved: 12/7/66
Effective: 12/7/66
Rev. eff.: 2/8/68; 8/18/69

APPENDIX III

Objectives of the Instructional Program

Guidelines for Instruction Pertaining to the Flag, Pledge of Allegiance, and National Anthem

The flag, the pledge of allegiance to the flag, and the national anthem are important symbols of the democratic heritage of the United States.

The public school system is one of the major social institutions responsible for the transmission of our democratic heritage to present and future generations. In fulfilling that responsibility, each school through its instructional programs and activities will provide a knowledge of—and encourage respect for—the important symbols of our Nation.

Board policy, Florida and federal statutes, and court decisions provide the bases for the following guidelines to be observed by each school in carrying on instructional activities in regard to the flag, pledge of allegiance, and the national anthem.

1. Teachers will direct their instructional efforts toward understanding patriotism and appreciation of freedom in our country.
2. The essentials of the United States constitution and flag education, including proper flag display and flag salute will be taught in all schools.
3. Students will stand at attention when the national anthem is played.
4. In pledging allegiance to the flag, the following pledge will be used: "I pledge allegiance to the flag of the United States of America and to the republic for which it stands, one nation under God, indivisible, with liberty and justice for all."
5. The pledge of allegiance will be rendered by standing with the right hand over the heart. Full respect to the flag will always be shown when the pledge is given by merely standing at attention, males removing the headdress.
6. Students, who for religious or other deep personal conviction, do not participate in the salute and pledge of allegiance to the flag will stand quietly.

   A. The staff will counsel with students who do not participate in the pledge and flag salute. Parents are to be contacted to determine the reason for the student's behavior. The main purpose for counseling would be to assist students in understanding our democratic heritage and in respecting the rights of all citizens.
   B. Students not participating in the pledge and salute to the flag who interfere with others doing so will be considered disrespectful. Any gestures, words or actions other than those officially prescribed above will be considered interference with the rights of others and disrespectful. In those instances where interference or disrespect occur, the school staff will take appropriate disciplinary action.

Legal Reference: Florida Statutes 233.061, 233.065, Board Policy 6121(9); U.S.Laws 1965 c. 65-239, #34, eff. July 1, 1965; West Virginia State Board of Education et al. v. Barnette et al., reported in 319 U.S. 624, 63 S. Ct. 1178, 87 L.Ed. 1628

DADE COUNTY SCHOOL BOARD
Miami, Florida

Policy adopted: 12/10/69
Effective: 12/10/69
17"

NOTES

1. See Appendix I for text.
2. See Appendix II for text.
3. See Appendix III for text.

A United States District Court in Connecticut decides for a teacher who had been suspended from her teaching duties and charged with insubordination because she refused to lead or recite the Pledge of Allegiance. The Court declared: "There is no question but that Mrs. Hanover's refusal to recite or lead recitation of the Pledge of Allegiance is a form of expression protected by the First Amendment which may not be forbidden at the risk of losing her job."

Hanover v. *Northrup,* 325 F.Supp. 170 (1970)

BLUMENFELD, District Judge.

In thousands of schools across the country, tens of thousands of teachers lead hundreds of thousands of students in the primary grades in a recital of the Pledge of Allegiance,[1] at the commencement of every school day. This case, brought under the Civil Rights Act, 42 U.S.C. § 1983, presents the question of the legal consequences to a teacher who refuses to comply with that traditional practice.

Plaintiff, Mrs. Nancy L. Hanover, has been a seventh and eighth grade school teacher at Booth Free School in Roxbury, Connecticut, since September 1968. On December 8, 1969, the defendant members of the Board of Education, at the instance of the new Superintendent of Schools, Charles Northrup, also a defendant herein, promulgated "Policy Identification 2-B" which directed: "The Salute to the Flag is to be part of each day's opening exercises in Grade K [kindergarten] through Grade 8." However, Mrs. Hanover had previously reached the conclusion that the Salute's final phrase, "with liberty and justice for all," was an untrue statement of present fact and "was not a pledge to work for something because it doesn't say that." (Tr. 27). Mrs. Hanover notified the school principal of her refusal to lead or recite the Pledge, and arranged for a student to lead the class in the Pledge, while she remained seated at her desk with her head bowed. Defendant Northrup, on December 18, 1969, and subsequently, ordered Mrs. Hanover to lead the class in the Pledge, which she refused to do. Regarding her refusal as insubordination and fortified by an official statement from the State Commissioner of Education, he suspended Mrs. Hanover from her teaching duties, with pay, on February 10, 1970. On April 14, 1970, the Board of Education held a hearing to consider the termination of plaintiff's contract on the sole ground of "insubordination" in the failure to obey defendant Northrup's order. On April 28, 1970, the Board voted to terminate the contract.

Plaintiff seeks an order enjoining defendants from terminating her contract, and requiring them to reinstate her to her teaching duties pending final disposition of this case. Her claim is that the termination of her contract deprives her of her first amendment right to free expression and her fourteenth amendment rights to due process and equal protection.

Federal jurisdiction of her claim is conferred by 28 U.S.C. § 1343(3), the jurisdictional counterpart of 42 U.S.C. § 1983. *Cf.* Eisen v. Eastman, 421 F.2d 560, 562 (2d Cir. 1969). *See* Tinker v. Des Moines Independent Community School Dist., 258 F.Supp. 971 (S.D.Iowa 1966), aff'd, 383 F.2d 988 (8th Cir. 1967), rev'd, 393 U.S. 503, 89 S.Ct. 733, 21 L.Ed.2d 731 (1969); Sheldon v. Fannin, 221 F.Supp. 766 (D.Ariz.1963).

Recent Supreme Court and lower federal court opinions reflect an increasing measure of protection for the exercise of first amendment rights in the schoolhouse. E. g., Tinker v. Des Moines Independent Community School Dist., 393 U.S. 503, 89 S.Ct. 733, 21 L.Ed.2d 731 (1969); West Virginia State Bd. of Educ. v. Barnette, 319 U.S. 624, 63 S.Ct. 1178, 87 L.Ed. 1628 (1943); Frain v. Baron, 307 F.Supp. 27 (E.D.N.Y.1969). As the Court in *Tinker* held:

"First Amendment rights, applied in light of the special characteristics of the school environment, are available to teachers and students. It can hardly be argued that either students or teachers shed their constitutional rights to freedom of speech or expression at the schoolhouse gate." 393 U.S. at 506, 89 S.Ct. at 736.

See also, Epperson v. Arkansas, 393 U.S. 97, 107, 89 S.Ct. 266, 272, 21 L.Ed.2d 228 (1968) ("It is much too late to argue that the State may impose upon the teachers in its schools any conditions that it chooses, however restrictive they may be of constitutional guarantees.").

There is no question but that Mrs. Hanover's

refusal to recite or lead recitation of the Pledge of Allegiance is a form of expression protected by the first amendment which may not be forbidden at the risk of losing her job. It does not matter that her expression took the form of silence. See Brown v. Louisiana, 383 U.S. 131, 86 S.Ct. 719, 15 L.Ed.2d 637 (1966). Nor is it relevant to inquire whether her expression is attributable to a doubtful grammatical construction of the Pledge of Allegiance or outright disagreement with it. First amendment rights of expression are fundamental to the preservation of an open, democratic society, since restriction on their exercise inhibits the debate by which society's values are set and its laws reformed to reflect prevailing opinion. See Kovacs v. Cooper, 336 U.S. 77, 89, 95-96, 69 S.Ct. 448, 93 L.Ed. 513 (1949) (concurring opinion of Mr. Justice Frankfurter).

The Court in *Tinker, supra,* 393 U.S. at 509, 89 S.Ct. 733, clearly places on school authorities the burden of justifying restrictions of expression on either students or teachers. In assessing the state's asserted justifications, reference must be made to the Court's statement in *Barnette, supra,* 319 U.S. at 639, 63 S.Ct. at 1186, that freedom of expression is "susceptible of restriction only to prevent grave and immediate danger to interests which the state may lawfully protect." Judge Judd, in a well-considered opinion in *Frain v. Baron, supra,* 307 F.Supp. 27 (upholding the right of students to stay in their classrooms rather than go into the hall during the daily Pledge of Allegiance in which they did not participate), held that conclusory assertions in the defendants' affidavits of a real and present threat to the maintenance of discipline and fear of disorder would not support a finding of serious harm to school authorities. Nor is mere fear that disorder might occur sufficient justification for restriction on expression. *Tinker, supra,* 393 U.S. at 508, 89 S.Ct. 733. *See* Edwards v. South Carolina, 372 U.S. 229, 83 S.Ct. 680, 9 L.Ed.2d 697 (1963).

In the instant case, there was no suggestion that Mrs. Hanover's behavior resulted in any disruption of school activities, or that her behavior interfered with or denied the rights of other teachers or students. *See Barnette, supra,* 319 U.S. at 630, 63 S.Ct. 1178. On the contrary, Mrs. Hanover's testimony that she directed a student to lead the class in the Pledge, and that there were no discipline problems with the students as a result of her behavior, was uncontradicted.

It does not matter whether some of her students, who also refrained from recitation of the Pledge were persuaded to do so because of the plaintiff's conduct. "The First Amendment protects successful dissent as well as ineffective protests." Frain v. Baron, *supra,* 307 F.Supp. at 33.

In short, the plaintiff in refusing to lead recitation of the Pledge of Allegiance was participating in a form of expression restriction of which cannot be justified on any of the grounds so far advanced by the state.

On the basis of the foregoing, the court is satisfied that the plaintiff has a strong possibility of ultimate success on the merits, that she will suffer irreparable injury unless the defendants are enjoined and that the grant of a preliminary injunction will cause no appreciable harm to defendants. It is, therefore,

Ordered: (1) That the defendants' motion to dismiss be denied.

(2) That the case may not proceed as a class action pursuant to Fed.R.Civ.P. 23(b) (2).

(3) That defendants be enjoined during the pendency of this action from terminating their contract with plaintiff.

(4) That defendants immediately reinstate plaintiff to her teaching duties pending final disposition of this action.

NOTES

1. The official form of the Pledge of Allegiance is set forth at 36 U.S.C. § 172:
    "I pledge allegiance to the flag of the United States of America and to the Republic for which it stands, one Nation under God, indivisible, with liberty and justice for all."

THE United States Court of Appeals, Sixth Circuit, decides against a seventeen year old Cleveland, Ohio, high school student who had been suspended from school for refusing to remove, while in classrooms and on school premises, an anti-war button which solicited participation in an anti-war demonstration in Chicago. In deciding for the school authorities who had a long-standing rule forbidding all wearing of buttons and symbols, the Court stated that the student's button was "provocative" and "in our view, the potentiality and the imminence of the admitted rebelliousness in the Shaw [high school] students support the wisdom of the no-symbol rule. Surely those charged with providing a place and atmosphere for educating young Americans should not have to fashion their disciplinary rules only after good order has been at least once demolished."

Guzick v. *Drebus*, 431 F.2d 594 (1970)

O'SULLIVAN, Senior Circuit Judge.

Plaintiff-Appellant, Thomas Guzick, Jr.,—prosecuting this action by his father and next friend, Thomas Guzick—appeals from dismissal of his complaint in the United States District Court for the Northern District of Ohio, Eastern Division. Plaintiff's complaint sought an injunction and other relief against defendant Drebus, the principal of Shaw High School in East Cleveland, Ohio, as well as against the Superintendent and Board of Education for the schools of said city. Plaintiff also asked for declaratory relief and damages.

The complaint charged that Thomas Guzick, Jr., a seventeen year old, eleventh grade student at Shaw High School, had been denied the right of free speech guaranteed to him by the United States Constitution's First Amendment. He asserted that this right had been denied him when he was suspended for refusing to remove, while in the classrooms and the school premises, a button which solicited participation in an anti-war demonstration that was to take place in Chicago on April 5. The legend of the button was:

"April 5 Chicago
GI—Civilian
Anti-War
Demonstration
Student Mobilization Committee"

With the currency of reliance on the First Amendment as support for so many and so varied claims for relief in the federal courts, it would be well to remind ourselves of that Amendment's exact language.

"ART. 1. Congress shall make no law respecting an establishment of religion, or prohibiting the free exercise thereof; or abridging the freedom of speech, or of the press; or the right of the people peaceably to assemble, and to petition the government for a redress of grievances."

On March 11, 1969, young Guzick and another student Havens, appeared at the office of defendant Drebus, principal of the high school, bringing with them a supply of pamphlets which advocated attendance at the same planned Chicago anti-war demonstration as was identified by the button. The boys were denied permission to distribute the pamphlets, and were also told to remove the buttons which both were then wearing. Guzick said that his lawyer, counsel for him in this litigation, told him that a United States Supreme Court decision entitled him to wear the button in school. Principal Drebus directed that he remove it and desist from wearing it in the school. Being told by Guzick that he would not obey, the principal suspended him and advised that such suspension would continue until Guzick obeyed. The other young man complied, and returned to school. Guzick did not, and has made no effort to return to school. This lawsuit promptly followed on March 17. The complaint prayed that the school authorities be required to allow Guzick to attend school wearing the button, that it be declared that Guzick had a constitutional right to do so, and that damages of $1,000 be assessed for each day of school missed by Guzick as a result of the principal's order.

The District Judge denied plaintiff's application for a preliminary injunction, and after a plenary evidentiary hearing, which was concluded on March 26, 1969, the complaint was dismissed. The opinion and judgment of the District Judge were filed and entered on April 2, 1969. The case is reported as Guzick v. Drebus, 305 F.Supp. 472 (N.D. Ohio 1969).

We affirm.

Plaintiff insists that the facts of this case bring it within the rule of Tinker v. Des Moines Independent

Community School District, 393 U.S. 503, 89 S.Ct. 733, 21 L.Ed.2d 731 (1969). We are at once aware that unless *Tinker* can be distinguished, reversal is required. We consider that the facts of this case clearly provide such distinction.

The rule applied to appellant Guzick was of long standing—forbidding all wearing of buttons, badges, scarves and other means whereby the wearers identify themselves as supporters of a cause or bearing messages unrelated to their education. Such things as support the high school athletic teams or advertise a school play are not forbidden. The rule had its genesis in the days when fraternities were competing for the favor of the students and it has been uniformly enforced. The rule has continued as one of universal application and usefulness. While controversial buttons appeared from time to time, they were required to be removed as soon as the school authorities could get to them.

Reciting the history of the no button or symbol rule, and the fact that the current student population of Shaw High School is 70% black and 30% white, the District Judge observed:

"The rule was created in response to a problem which Shaw has had over a period of many years. At the time high school fraternities were in vogue, the various fraternities at Shaw were a divisive and disruptive influence on the school. They carved out portions of the school cafeteria in which only members of a particular fraternity were permitted to sit. The fraternities were competitive and engaged in activities which disrupted the educational process at Shaw. There were fights between members of the individual fraternities and often strong feelings between the members.

"The same problem was encountered with the informal clubs, which replaced high school fraternities and sororities. The problem again exists as a result of the racial mixture at Shaw. Buttons, pins, and other emblems have been used as identifying 'badges.' They have portrayed and defined the divisions among students in the school. They have fostered an undesirable form of competition, division and dislike. The presence of these emblems, badges and buttons are taken to represent, define and depict the actual division of the students in various groups.

"The buttons also encourage division among the students, for they portray and identify the wearer as a member of a particular group or the advocate of a particular cause. This sets the wearer apart from other students wearing different buttons or without buttons. It magnifies the differences between students, encourages emphasis on these differences, and tends to polarize the students into separate, distinct, and unfriendly groups. In addition, there have

been instances in which students have attempted to force other students to wear a particular manner of dress or to wear their particular insignia or expressive button. For these reasons Shaw High officials have enforced the anti-button rule and have prohibited the wearing of such indicia.

"The rule has acquired a particular importance in recent years. Students have attempted to wear buttons and badges expressing inflammatory messages, which, if permitted, and as the evidence indicates, would lead to substantial racial disorders at Shaw. Students have attempted to wear buttons with the following messages inscribed thereon. 'White is right'; 'Say it loud, Black and Proud'; 'Black Power.' Other buttons have depicted a mailed black fist, commonly taken to be the symbol of black power.

"There have been occasions when the wearing of such insignia has led to disruptions at Shaw and at Kirk Junior High. A fight resulted in the cafeteria when a white student wore a button which read 'Happy Easter, Dr. King.' (Dr. Martin Luther King was assassinated in the Easter season.)" 305 F. Supp. at 476-477.

From the total evidence, including that of educators, school administrators and others having special relevant qualifications, the District Judge concluded that abrogation of the rule would inevitably result in collisions and disruptions which would seriously subvert Shaw High School as a place of education for its students, black and white.[1]

1. The Rule of *Tinker*.

Contrasting with the admitted long standing and uniform enforcement of Shaw's no symbol rule, the majority opinion in *Tinker* was careful to point out,

"It is also relevant that the school authorities [in *Tinker*] did not purport to prohibit the wearing of all symbols of political or controversial significance. The record shows that students in some of the schools wore buttons relating to national political campaigns, and some even wore the Iron Cross, traditionally a symbol of Nazism. *The order prohibiting the wearing of armbands did not extend to these.* Instead, a particular symbol—black armbands worn to exhibit opposition to this Nation's involvement in Vietnam—was singled out for prohibition." 393 U.S. at 510-511, 89 S.Ct. at 738-739.

The armband demonstration in *Tinker* was a one time affair, with a date for its ending fixed in its original plan. Plaintiff here argues that Shaw's no symbol rule should be abrogated to accommodate his wish to be relieved from obeying it. The majority in *Tinker* emphasized that it was following what had been "the unmistakable holding of this Court for almost 50 years." 393 U.S. at 506, 89 S.Ct. at 736.

Opinions of Mr. Justice McReynolds in Meyer v. Nebraska, 262 U.S. 390, 43 S.Ct. 625, 67 L.Ed. 1042 (1923) and Bartels v. Iowa, 262 U.S. 404, 43 S.Ct. 628, 67 L.Ed. 1047 (1923), were referred to as announcing the long standing rule that the United States Constitution must be respected by those who operate our public schools. West Virginia State Bd. of Education v. Barnette, 319 U.S. 624, 63 S.Ct. 1178, 87 L.Ed. 1628 (1943) was cited to emphasize the relevancy of the First Amendment in public school administration. However, *Meyer* and *Bartels* struck down state statutes which forbade the teaching of a foreign language to young students and *Barnette* held that it was constitutionally impermissible to compel young students to salute the flag. These authorities while they do confirm the presence of the Constitution in our public schools, bear no resemblance to the critical facts of the case at bar. Neither do any of the other decisions of the Supreme Court cited in *Tinker,* 393 U.S. on pages 506 and 507, 89 S.Ct. 733 of the opinion.

Further distinguishing *Tinker* from our case are their respective settings. No potential racial collisions were background to *Tinker,* whereas here the changing racial composition of Shaw High from all white to 70% black, made the no symbol rule of even greater good than had characterized its original adoption. In our view, school authorities should not be faulted for adhering to a relatively non-oppressive rule that will indeed serve our ultimate goal of meaningful integration of our public schools. Such was the command of Brown v. Board of Education, 347 U.S. 483, 74 S.Ct. 686, 98 L.Ed. 873 (1954).

2.   Shaw High School's need for its Rule.

In *Tinker* the Court concluded that a regulation forbidding expressions opposing the Vietnam conflict anywhere on school property would violate the students' constitutional rights,

"at least *if it could not be justified* by a showing that the students' activities would materially and substantially disrupt the work and discipline of the school." 393 U.S. at 513, 89 S.Ct. at 740 (Emphasis supplied.)

The Supreme Court then went on to say that the District Judge in *Tinker* made no such finding and that,

"our independent examination of the record fails to yield evidence that the school authorities had reason to anticipate that the wearing of the armbands would substantially interfere with the work of the school or impinge upon the rights of other students. Even an official memorandum prepared after the suspension that listed the reasons for the ban on wearing the armbands *made no reference to the anticipation of such disruptions.*" 393 U.S. at 509, 89 S.Ct. at 738 (Emphasis supplied.)

But in the case at bar, the District Judge, upon a valid appraisal of the evidence, did find that "if all buttons are permitted or if any buttons are permitted, a serious discipline problem will result, racial tensions will be exacerbated, and the educational process will be significantly and substantially disrupted." 305 F.Supp. at 478. Again, in *Tinker,* the majority said,

"But, in our system, undifferentiated fear or apprehension of disturbance is not enough to overcome the right of freedom of expression." 393 U.S. at 508, 89 S.Ct. at 737.

Here, the District Court, conscious of the commands of *Tinker,* said,

"Furthermore, there is in the present case *much more than an 'undifferentiated fear or apprehension'* of disturbances likely to result from the wearing of buttons at Shaw High School. The wearing of buttons and other emblems and insignia has occasioned substantial disruptive conduct in the past at Shaw High. It is likely to occasion such conduct if permitted henceforth. The wearing of buttons and other insignia will serve to exacerbate an already tense situation, to promote divisions and disputes, including physical violence among the students, and to disrupt and interfere with the normal operation of the school and with appropriate discipline by the school authorities." 305 F.Supp. at 479 (Emphasis supplied).

The District Judge was of the view that the situation at Shaw was "incendiary." The evidence justified such a view.

"The Court has concluded that if all buttons were permitted at Shaw High, many students would seek to wear buttons conveying an inflammatory or provocative message or which would be considered as an insult or affront to certain of the other students. Such buttons have been worn at Shaw High School in the past. One button of this nature, for example, contained the message 'Happy Easter, Dr. King.' This button caused a fight last year in the school cafeteria at Shaw. Other buttons, such as 'Black Power,' 'Say it loud, Black and Proud,' and buttons depicting a black mailed fist have been worn at Shaw and would likely be worn again, if permitted. These buttons would add to the already incendiary situation and would undoubtedly provoke further fighting among the students and lead to a material and substantial disruption of the educational process at Shaw High." 305 F.Supp. at 479, 480.

Further distinction from *Tinker* is provided by the long standing and *universal application* of Shaw's rule. In *Tinker* the majority said:

"The record shows that students in some of the schools wore buttons relating to national political campaigns and some even wore the Iron Cross, traditionally a symbol of Nazism. The order prohibiting the wearing of armbands *did not extend to these.* Instead, a particular symbol—black armbands worn to exhibit opposition to the Nation's involvement in Vietnam—was singled out for prohibition." 393 U.S. at 510, 511, 89 S.Ct. at 739. (Emphasis supplied.)

The District Judge here points out that for school authorities to allow some buttons and not others would create an unbearable burden of selection and enforcement. He said:

"In addition, any rule which attempts to permit the wearing of some buttons, but not others, would be virtually impossible to administer. It would involve school officials in a continuous search of the halls for students wearing the prohibited type of buttons. It would occasion ad hoc and inconsistent application. It would make the determination of permissible versus impermissible buttons difficult, if not impossible. It would make it difficult for the school officials to give both the substance and appearance of fairness, and would deprive the school officials of their present position of neutrality." 305 F.Supp. at 477-478.

We believe that the Supreme Court has commanded that, when dealing with questions of constitutional magnitude, we are not at liberty to accept the fact trier's findings merely because we consider them not "clearly erroneous" as that term is employed in Rule 52(a) F.R.Civ.P. We must make our own examination of the material from which decision is made. Feiner v. New York, 340 U.S. 315, 322-325, 71 S.Ct 303, 95 L.Ed. 267 (1951) (Black, dissenting); Edwards v. South Carolina, 372 U.S. 229, 235, 83 S.Ct. 680, 9 L.Ed.2d 697 (1963); Jacobellis v. Ohio, 378 U.S. 184, 189, 84 S.Ct. 1676, 12 L.Ed.2d 793 (1964).

Obedient to that rule, we have made our own examination of the record before us and are persuaded that the factual findings of the District Judge are fully supported by the evidence and we agree with them.

The majority opinion in *Tinker* discusses the Fifth Circuit's decisions of Burnside v. Byars, 363 F.2d 744 (5th Cir. 1966) and Blackwell v. Issaquena County Bd. of Educ., 363 F.2d 749 (5th Cir. 1966). At first view, these cases appear to be "on all fours" with the case at bar. In the *Burnside* case, students were held, as an exercise of free speech, to be entitled to wear buttons with the legend "One Man, One Vote" around the perimeter and "SNCC" inscribed in the center, notwithstanding the school authorities' order to take them off. In that case, however, there had been no previous rule of general application prohibiting the wearing of all buttons. Neither did the wearing of such buttons cause any disturbance at the time involved, nor had button wearing caused any past disturbances. In

holding that the school authorities were required to allow the buttons, the Court said,

"Thus, it appears that the presence of 'freedom buttons' did not hamper the school in carrying on its regular schedule or activities; *nor would it seem likely that the simple wearing of buttons unaccompanied by improper conduct would ever do so.* Wearing buttons on collars or shirt fronts is certainly not in the class of those activities which inherently distract students and break down the regimentation of the classroom such as carrying banners, scattering leaflets, and speechmaking, all of which are protected methods of expressions, *but all of which have no place in an orderly classroom.* If the decorum had been so disturbed by the presence of the 'freedom buttons,' the principal would have been acting within his authority and the regulation forbidding the presence of buttons on school grounds would have been reasonable." 363 F.2d at 748 (emphasis supplied).

In the *Blackwell* case, buttons were forbidden which evidently came from the same source as those in *Burnside,* but their legends consisted of the marginal position of SNCC and the depicting of a black and a white hand joined together. We find this legend not provocative, but its original appearance in the school and its wearing by many after the School Board had forbidden it caused quite serious commotion, in fact, "all hell broke loose." Students were suspended and they and their parents sought to have the school authorities enjoined from forbidding the wearing of the button. Here the Fifth Circuit sustained District Court denial of the injunction, notwithstanding its *Burnside* decision, announced the same day. It did so because the proofs showed that the *Blackwell* button caused trouble and the *Burnside* button did not. That the button was the cause of trouble in *Blackwell* is made clear by the Court's assertion, "In this case the reprehensible conduct described above was so inexorably tied to the wearing of the buttons that the two are not separable." 363 F.2d at 754. We can imagine no more cogent argument for Shaw's long standing and all-inclusive "no button" rule than the facts of *Burnside* and *Blackwell.*

The button in *Blackwell* was an invitation to friendship between the blacks and whites. What more non-controversial message could there be? But it caused serious trouble. Certainly the message of the *Guzick* button, supportive of a divisive demonstration, was more provocative than the *Blackwell* button's reach for friendship. Counsel for plaintiff's brief candidly asserts:

"There is rebelliousness among Shaw students. In January of 1969 a planned walkout of black students was aborted only when Drebus called in the police.

In the aftermath Drebus and his staff interrogated three hundred black students. The denouement was a public statement issued by Drebus in which he said:

'We will take every positive action necessary to make sure that no organization or group of organizations, no teacher or group of teachers, no parents or group of parents, and no students or group of students hinder Shaw High pupils in their quest to obtain their purposeful goals and future opportunities.'"

In our view, the potentiality and the imminence of the admitted rebelliousness in the Shaw students support the wisdom of the no-symbol rule. Surely those charged with providing a place and atmosphere for educating young Americans should not have to fashion their disciplinary rules only after good order has been at least once demolished.

3. Conclusion.

We will not attempt extensive review of the many great decisions which have forbidden abridgment of free speech. We have been thrilled by their beautiful and impassioned language. They are part of our American heritage. None of these masterpieces, however, were composed or uttered to support the wearing of buttons in high school classrooms. We are not persuaded that enforcement of such a rule as Shaw High School's no-symbol proscription would have excited like judicial classics. Denying Shaw High School the right to enforce this small disciplinary rule could, and most likely would, impair the rights of its students to an education and the rights of its teachers to fulfill their responsibilities.

Mr. Justice Douglas spoke for a majority of the Court in Terminiello v. Chicago, 337 U.S. 1, 69 S.Ct. 894, 93 L.Ed. 1131 (1949) which had to do with utterances made at a public meeting in a Chicago auditorium. Describing the nature of free speech, he said:

"[A] function of free speech under our system of government is to invite dispute. It may indeed best serve its high purpose when it induces a condition of unrest, creates dissatisfaction with conditions as they are, or even stirs people to anger. Speech is often provocative and challenging. It may strike at prejudices and preconceptions and have profound unsettling effects as it presses for acceptance of an idea." 337 U.S. at 4, 69 S.Ct. at 896.

However correct such language when applied to an open public protest meeting, we doubt the propriety of protecting in a high school classroom such aggressive and colorful use of free speech. We must be aware in these contentious times that America's classrooms and their environs will lose their usefulness as places in which to educate our young people if pupils come to school wearing the badges of their respective disagreements, and provoke confrontations with their fellows and their teachers. The buttons are claimed to be a form of free speech. Unless they have some relevance to what is being considered or taught, a school classroom is no place for the untrammeled exercise of such right.

All Courts and constitutional writers have emphasized the need for proper balancing in the exercise of the guarantees of the Constitution. In *Burnside, supra,* the Fifth Circuit observed:

"The interest of the state in maintaining an educational system is a compelling one, giving rise to a *balancing of First Amendment rights* with the duty of the state to further and protect the public school system." 363 F.2d at 748 (Emphasis supplied).

In his monograph "The Supreme Court and the Meiklejohn Interpretation of the First Amendment," Mr. Justice William Brennan emphasized the propriety of this balancing:

"The 'redeeming social value,' 'clear and present danger,' and 'balancing' tests recognize *some governmental power to inhibit speech,* but it must also be said that none of these limitations has been given an across-the-board application. Each has been primarily utilized to sustain governmental regulation in particular contexts: 'the redeeming social value' test primarily in obscenity cases; the 'clear and present danger' test primarily in regulation of subversive activity and of the publication of matter thought to obstruct justice; *and the 'balancing' test primarily in the case of regulations not intended directly to condemn the content of speech but incidentally limiting its exercise.*" 79 Harv. L.Rev. 1, 11 (1965). (Emphasis supplied.)

The complaint's contention that Guzick was denied equal protection of the law is not argued to this Court; neither is it now asserted that he was denied due process of law in the method by which the relevant discipline was imposed.

Judgment affirmed.

McALLISTER, Senior Circuit Judge (dissenting).

When a few students noticed the button which appellant was wearing, and asked him "what it said," appellant's explanation resulted only in a casual reaction; and there was no indication that the wearing of the button would disrupt the work and discipline of the school.

I am of the opinion that the judgment of the district court should be reversed and the case dismissed upon the authority of Tinker v. Des Moines Independent School District, 393 U.S. 503, 89 S.Ct. 733, 21 L.Ed.2d 731 (1969).

NOTE

1. He concluded that this was so even though he did not find the message of the particular button inflammatory, per se, "Although there was evidence that the message conveyed in this particular button might be such as to inflame some of the students at Shaw High, the Court does not feel that such a result is likely." 305 F.Supp. at 479.

T̲HE Court of Appeals of Maryland declares unconstitutional Maryland's 1970 flag salute statute which had required "all students and teachers in charge to stand and face the flag and while so standing render an approved salute, and recite in unison the Pledge of Allegiance. . . . " In deciding for the teacher and student (father and son) who had challenged the constitutionality of the statute, the Court stated: "Entertaining no doubt that there is ample authority to punish students or teachers who materially disrupt proper school activities, including the voluntary patriotic programs, we are far from convinced that the mere refusal to participate in any phase of the Pledge of Allegiance ritual is punishable. To reach a contrary conclusion would allow the schools to discipline such refusal as 'an act of disrespect,' even though they may not compel this ceremony in the first place."

State v. *Lundquist,* 278 A.2d 263 (1971)

DIGGES, Judge.

More than a quarter of a century has passed since June 14—Flag Day—1943, when the Supreme Court ruled in West Virginia State Board of Education v. Barnette, 319 U.S. 624, 63 S.Ct. 1178, 87 L.Ed. 1628, that a state may not compel unwilling school children to salute and pledge allegiance to the flag of the United States. On September 18, 1970 the Circuit Court for Anne Arundel County (Evans, J.) issued a declaratory decree invalidating the key provisions of the recently enacted "Flag Salute" statute, Chapter 737, Laws of Maryland 1970,[1] as violative of the First Amendment (applicable to the states through the Fourteenth Amendment) of the Federal Constitution which provides: "Congress shall make no law * * * abridging the freedom of speech." Basing his decision squarely on the holding in *Barnette,* Judge Evans enjoined the appellants, the State of Maryland and the Anne Arundel County Board of Education, from enforcing the quotidian schoolroom requirement that all students and teachers, except those who object for "religious reasons," must stand, salute the flag and recite in unison the pledge of allegiance. He also prohibited enforcement of the disciplinary provision of Ch. 737 which directed that any person "who may commit an act of disrespect, either by word or action, shall be considered to be in violation of the intent of this act." Agreeing with the trial judge that *Barnette* fully controls the case before us we shall affirm the decree.

The oath of loyalty is no recent phenomenon in Western civilization. Described as a potent social bond in classical Greek and Roman society, and mentioned as a pledge of fealty to the king in feudal times, it had become deeply embedded in the common law of England long before its importation to America. See, Maitland, The Constitutional History of England, 364-66 (1931) and other authorities noted by Chief Justice Vanderbilt in Imbrie v. Marsh, 3 N.J. 578, 71 A.2d 352, 18 A.L.R. 2d 241 (1950), aff'g, 5 N.J.Super. 239, 68 A.2d 761 (1949). Oaths to uphold the United States Constitution are required of all our executive, legislative and judicial officeholders on both the state and national levels by Art. II, § 1 and Art. VI of that document itself, and oaths requiring claims of loyalty or disclaimers of subversive intent by teachers, civil servants and a multitude of citizens have been the subject of endless judicial review. In determining the validity of oaths, courts have inquired into the narrowness with which they are drawn, the specific governmental interest they are designed to protect and their effect on free speech as well as due process rights. See generally Whitehill v. Elkins, 389 U.S. 54, 88 S.Ct. 184, 19 L.Ed.2d 228 (1967) and Annot. thereto contained in 19 L.Ed.2d 1333 (1968); Note, Loyalty Oaths, 77 Yale L.J. 739 (1968); Annot. Imbrie v. Marsh, *supra,* contained in 18 A.L.R.2d 268 (1951) and extensive later case service to date. Thus, as recently as February 1971 the United States Supreme Court upheld an oath of loyalty to the Constitution required by the rules for admission to the New York Bar as sufficiently narrow in scope, directly related to the important governmental interest of regulating the legal profession and not employed in such a manner as to penalize political beliefs. Law Students Civil Rights Research Council v. Wadmond, 401 U.S. 154, 161-164, 91 S.Ct. 720, 27 L.Ed.2d 749 (1971).

As a peculiar sub-species of loyalty oaths, the pledge of allegiance to the flag was not conceived until

1892, but then only as a voluntary and recommended patriotic exercise for the quadricentennial celebration of Columbus Day. New York was the first state to make the pledge of allegiance an obligatory requirement of education law in 1898, one day after the Spanish-American War began. Although other states quickly followed suit by enacting similar or identical statutes, it was not until World War I that Maryland made the pledge of allegiance a required schoolroom exercise. Ch. 75, Laws of 1918. *See,* Weig and Appleman, The History of the United States Flag, *passim* (1961). These statutes were to become the target of considerable litigation, but over the strident religious objections of the Jehovah's Witnesses during the 1930's the mandatory salute was upheld in a series of cases in state and federal courts, all culminating in Minersville School District v. Gobitis, 310 U.S. 586, 60 S.Ct. 1010, 84 L.Ed. 1375 (1940).[2] Only three years later the Supreme Court abruptly reversed this holding in West Virginia State Board of Education v. Barnette, *supra.* The Maryland pledge of allegiance statute, most recently codified as § 77 of Art. 77, (Code 1957, 1969 Repl. Vol.), remained unchanged until it was repealed and re-enacted by Ch. 737 of the Laws of 1970.

The plaintiffs who have challenged the new statute in their own behalf and in behalf of others similarly situated are August Luther Lundquist and his son Eric. The father teaches social sciences at Brooklyn Park High School and his fifteen year old son attends Andover High School. Both schools are located in the Baltimore metropolitan area just within the boundaries of Anne Arundel County. At the hearing before Judge Evans only Mr. Lundquist appeared as a witness. His testimony consisted of a statement read into the record (see appendix) and cross-examination. He claimed that he would refuse to engage in a mandatory flag salute ceremony, not for religious reasons but because he could not "in good conscience" force patriotism upon his classes. He voluntarily if not eagerly instructed his world history classes in patriotic and democratic ideals and he had no objection to teaching courses, such as civics, which made instruction in democracy a required part of the curriculum. Mr. Lundquist also objected strongly to being forced to salute the flag because he believed such a requirement eliminated his right to freely express his own loyalty to the United States. He indicated, without objection, that his son shared these views and would similarly refuse to engage in the flag salute.

Judge Evans determined that under the Uniform Declaratory Judgment Act, Art. 31A, § 16, (Code 1957, 1971 Repl.Vol.) both the teacher's and the student's First Amendment rights were affected by the statute and they possessed requisite standing to challenge Ch. 737. The Attorney General has not questioned this rul-

ing on appeal. Although the new act has no explicit provision outlining the consequences for refusing to salute the flag, it is quite clear that such recalcitrant students and teachers can be disciplined under other sections of the public education laws, specifically §§ 75 and 114, Art. 77 (Code 1957, 1969 Repl.Vol.). Finally, if there should be any doubt about the immediacy of the threat to the appellants, aside from the obvious chilling effect on their First Amendment rights, *see* Dombrowski v. Pfister, 380 U.S. 479, 486–87, 85 S.Ct. 1116, 14 L.Ed.2d 22 (1965), the Attorney General has admitted in the answer to the Lundquists' amended complaint that a program of enforcement is in preparation and awaits only the outcome of this case. See Grimm v. Co. Com'rs of Wash. Co., 252 Md. 626, 632-633, 250 A.2d 866 (1969); *compare* Hitchcock v. Kloman, 196 Md. 351, 355-356, 76 A.2d 582 (1950); *cf.* Bruce v. Director, Dept. of Chesapeake Bay Affairs, Md., 276 A.2d 200 (1971).

The Attorney General claims that *Barnette* was decided on religious grounds, and since Ch. 737 provides for a religious exemption, the constitutionality of this act is not controlled by *Barnette*. Rejecting this contention, Judge Evans' very thoughtful memorandum opinion rested on the assumption that *Barnette* was decided primarily on freedom of speech grounds and was therefore completely controlling. To support this conclusion he relied on Justice Harlan's statement for the Court in Street v. New York, 394 U.S. 576, 593, 89 S.Ct. 1354, 1366, 22 L.Ed.2d 572 (1969):

"* * * [i]n West Virginia State Board of Educ. v. Barnette * * * this court held that to require unwilling school-children to salute the flag would violate *rights of free expression* assured by the Fourteenth Amendment." (Emphasis added.)

The Attorney General claims that this is gratuitous dictum and offers the following explanation, as we understand it from his brief and his oral argument, to demonstrate why *Barnette* does not control this case:

He first asserts it has been traditionally understood that *Barnette* was decided on religious grounds, having been cited as a freedom of religion precedent in Frain v. Baron, 307 F.Supp. 27 (E.D.N.Y. 1969) and Lewis v. Allen, 5 Misc.2d 68, 159 N.Y.S.2d 807, aff'd, 11 A.D.2d 447, 207 N.Y.S.2d 862 (1960), though he may well have added Prince v. Massachusetts, 321 U.S. 158, 165-166, 64 S.Ct. 438, 88 L.Ed. 645 (1944). Moreover, *Barnette* affirmed an injunction granted at the instance of religious plaintiffs and "those similarly situated" who sought to be relieved from a requirement to salute the flag on the grounds that it violated their religious beliefs. He further argues that the main function of the opinion was to overrule *Gobitis*—which rejected an identical religious claim on religious grounds. While conceding that some of the eloquence in Justice Jackson's opinion for the majority "suggests an involvement of freedom of speech," the Attorney General contends we cannot ignore the background of that opinion and the voting pattern of the Court. He points to Justice Frankfurter's dissenting opinion which focused in large part on religious issues and to the separate brief dissent of Justices Roberts and Reed who voted for reversal on the basis of the views expressed in *Gobitis*. He has also referred us to the joint concurring opinion by Justices Black and Douglas in which they state they "are substantially in agreement" with the majority's reasoning but then go on to discuss the free exercise of religion clause. Finally, he notes that Justice Murphy's separate concurring opinion also devoted some discussion to the freedom of worship.

On the basis of this analysis the Attorney General would have us conclude that even if Chief Justice Stone and Justice Rutledge actively favored the purported free speech rationale of the majority opinion by Justice Jackson, the six other members of the Court (three dissenting—three concurring) viewed the decisional issue as freedom of religion. To resolve the questions raised by this suggested interpolation of the Court's vote and the result of its action in *Barnette* we must examine not only the opinion itself but also the constitutional and historical setting in which it was decided.

FROM GOBITIS TO BARNETTE

Instead of settling the flag salute controversy, the decision in Minersville School District v. Gobitis, *supra*, only precipitated a disagreement among the justices on the Supreme Court and exacerbated a growing conflict over the question throughout the country. The eight to one majority ruling that upheld the expulsion of Jehovah's Witnesses school-children for refusing to salute the flag was to become a three to six minority view within three years. During the same period the Witnesses became the butt of an increasing wave of violent persecution as well as discriminatory legal prosecution until their deliverance in *Barnette* and a series of First Amendment cases in which the Supreme Court upheld their right to practice and preach their religion.

The major legal precedent which had blocked the Jehovah's Witnesses was a constitutional doctrine known as the secular regulation rule. Although this rule was to be completely ignored in the *Barnette* majority opinion, the Attorney General is correct in asserting that it received attention in the concurring and dissenting opinions there. The rule also served as the constitutional point of embarkation for Justice Frankfurter's discursive analysis of the flag salute requirement in *Gobitis*. After observing that the First

Amendment, as an historical concept, gave complete protection to religious beliefs, Justice Frankfurter reasoned that religious liberty was not absolute when it collided with the legitimate secular concerns of society.

"The religious liberty which the Constitution protects has never excluded legislation of general scope not directed against doctrinal loyalties of particular sects. Judicial nullification of legislation cannot be justified by attributing to the framers of the Bill of Rights views for which there is no historic warrant. Conscientious scruples have not, in the course of the long struggle for religious toleration, relieved the individual from obedience to a general law not aimed at the promotion or restriction of religious beliefs. The mere possession of religious convictions which contradict the relevant concerns of a political society does not relieve the citizen from the discharge of political responsibilities." 310 U.S. at 594-595, 60 S.Ct. at 1013.

Having established this principle, he concluded that the societal goal of the pledge was the "promotion of national cohesion * * * an interest inferior to none in the hierarchy of legal values." "National unity," he wrote, "is the basis of national security." While "some specific need or interest of secular society," such as health, defenses or taxes might fall before the demands of First Amendment freedoms, national unity was a transcendent overriding interest before which sentiments to the contrary must give away. Pursuing this reasoning, Justice Frankfurter offered a complete justification for the flag salute:

"The ultimate foundation of a free society is the binding tie of cohesive sentiment. Such a sentiment is fostered by all those agencies of the mind and spirit which may serve to gather up the traditions of a people, transmit them from generation to generation, and thereby create that continuity of a treasured common life which constitutes a civilization. 'We live by symbols.' The flag is the symbol of our national unity, transcending all internal differences, however large within the framework of the Constitution." *Id*. 596, 60 S.Ct. 1014.

The only question left unanswered then was whether the state's selection of the flag salute to achieve national unity had some rational basis. To resolve this problem Justice Frankfurter devoted the balance of the opinion to establishing the doctrine of judicial restraint in the field of education law:

"The court-room is not the arena for debating issues of education policy. It is not our province to choose among competing considerations in the subtle process of securing effective loyalty to the traditional ideals of democracy, while respecting at the same time individual idiosyncracies among a people so diversified in racial origins and religious allegiances.

So to hold would in effect make us the school board for the country. That authority has not been given to this Court, nor should we assume it." *Id.* 598, 60 S.Ct. 1014.

He then made the decisive assumption that a flag salute could be required of non-objecting students and reasoned that it would be an unwarranted obstruction of valid legislative judgment for the judiciary to grant exceptional immunity to dissidents:

"Such an exemption might introduce elements of difficulty into the school discipline, might cast doubts in the minds of the other children which would themselves weaken the effect of the exercise." *Id.* 600, 60 S.Ct. 1015.

The opinion terminated with a final analysis of the desirability of judicial restraint and the need to let the representatives of the people take the primary role in defending personal liberties. "To fight out the wise use of legislative authority in the forum of public opinion and before legislative assemblies rather than to transfer such a contest to the judicial arena, serves to vindicate the self-confidence of a free people." *Id.* It would be improper for the Court to interfere with the democratic process by declaring the expulsion of the Gobitis children unconstitutional.

Justice McReynolds merely concurred in this result with only Chief Justice Stone dissenting in a vigorous defense of First Amendment freedoms. The Chief Justice's most telling point was that the freedoms of religion and speech presuppose an even more basic constitutional value: "freedom of the human mind and spirit," which no balancing test could ever diminish and which "must, I think, be deemed to withhold from the state any authority to compel belief or the expression of it * * *." *Id.* 604, 60 S.Ct. 1017. *See* United States v. Carolene Products Co., 304 U.S. 144, 152-153, 58 S.Ct. 778, 82 L.Ed. 1234 n. 4 (1938) (Stone, C.J.).

The reaction to the decision in *Gobitis* has been exhaustively documented and analyzed by David Manwaring in *Render Unto Caesar* (Univ. Chicago Press 1962). A broadstroke sketch based on his five years of research into the entire flag salute controversy should suffice to understand the circumstances leading up to *Barnette.* Following the decision a veritable wave of mob violence, spurred on in large part by the public's apprehension over our impending involvement in World War II, was brought down upon the seemingly unpatriotic Witnesses.[3] Legal prosecutions also followed, in some instances on charges of flag desecration and even sedition, but for the most part hundreds of arrests for violations of local ordinances which prohibited door to door canvassing or which required a license tax for peddling their religious literature.

Scholarly reaction to the opinion also reached a high pitch, mostly critical of the Court. *See, e.g.,* Corwin, The Constitution and What it Means Today, 199 (1941); Rotnem and Folson, Recent Restrictions upon Religious Liberty, 36 Am. Pol.Sci.Rev. 1053, 1063-64 (1942); Note, 26 Cornell L.Q. 127 (1940) and twenty-nine other comments that openly or tacitly questioned the reasoning or the result of the case, collected in Manwaring, *Render Unto Caesar,* 149. Many of the articles appear to contain misconceptions about the complex holding, even those that looked with favor upon it, *see, e.g.,* 14 Temple L.Q. 545 (1940). But in all fairness it should be noted that the rhetorical overtones and effect of the opinion were bound to subject it to bitter criticism for allowing national unity to override religious liberty, especially in the name of judicial self-restraint.

The tide of opinion on the Supreme Court was changing also, but not before reaching its lowest ebb in Jones v. Opelika, 316 U.S. 584, 62 S.Ct. 1231, 86 L.Ed. 1691 (1942), which upheld a statute frequently used against the zealous street preachers: the peddler's license tax. Justice Reed, who wrote the majority opinion, had little difficulty resolving this challenge to a town's right to promulgate non-discriminatory secular regulations over the use of its streets. In spite of the fact that he explicitly disclaimed any reliance on the *Gobitis* opinion, 316 U.S. at 598, 62 S.Ct. 1231, 86 L.Ed. 1691, Justices Black, Murphy and Douglas dissented along with Chief Justice Stone and in a brief separate dissent openly repudiated their adherence to *Gobitis. Id.* 623-624, 62 S.Ct. 1231, 86 L.Ed. 1691. Immediately after Justice Rutledge took his seat on the Court on February 15, 1943, the decision to grant a rehearing in Jones v. Opelika was announced. 318 U.S. 796-797, 63 S.Ct. 658, 87 L.Ed. 1161. *See* Journal of the Supreme Court, October 1942 Term, 153, order at 157. (N.B., 87 L.Ed. 1161 erroneously lists Feb. 14 as the date of the order.)

On May 3, 1943 the Court announced its decision in Murdock v. Pennsylvania, 319 U.S. 105, 63 S.Ct. 870, 87 L.Ed. 1292, Martin v. Struthers, 319 U.S. 141, 63 S.Ct. 862, 87 L.Ed. 1313 and Douglas v. Jeannette, 319 U.S. 157, 63 S.Ct. 877, 87 L.Ed. 1324—all Jehovah's Witnesses cases—which struck down the peddler's license tax, invalidated an anti-doorbell ringing ordinance, and basically ruled as moot a federal injunction against these now unconstitutional statutes. In the same breath (319) U.S. 103, 63 S.Ct. 890, 87 L.Ed. 1290) it reversed the holding in Jones v. Opelika. While relying heavily on a freedom of speech rationale in these decisions, the majority opinions effectively crippled the strict secular regulation rule. Justice Jackson, in a separate opinion appended to these three cases, extensively reviewed and strongly condemned the offensive preaching tactics of the Witnesses, 319 U.S. at 167-174, 63 S.Ct. 877, 87 L.Ed.

1324. In a comment which seemingly favored the continued application of the secular regulation rule, he referred to the new majority's analysis of First Amendment freedoms as "a vague but fervent transcendentalism," *id.* 179, 63 S.Ct. 877, 87 L.Ed. 1324, which *in effect gave a religious sect the privilege of invading the privacy of others. Id.* 181, 63 S.Ct. 877, 87 L.Ed. 1324. Since *Barnette* was argued on the same day as these secular regulation decisions, it strikes us as improbable that Justice Jackson's dissenting views recommended him as the majority opinion writer for yet another secular regulation case. Nevertheless he was the author of the Court's elaborate overruling of *Gobitis*. Admittedly, another member of the new majority in Jones v. Opelika and related cases could have overturned the required flag salute on the basis of the rationale newly articulated there, but without Justice Jackson's support. Their failure to take such a course strongly suggests the Attorney General's analysis of the Court's vote is incorrect.

In writing the opinion for the Court, Justice Jackson addressed a more fundamental issue than that posed by the religiously motivated plaintiffs or framed by the *Gobitis* opinion. He meticulously pointed out that the case did not

"turn on one's possession of particular religious views or the sincerity with which they are held. While religion supplies appellees' motive for enduring the discomforts of making the issue in this case, many citizens who do not share these religious views hold such a compulsory rite to infringe constitutional liberty of the individual. [Footnote with extensive list of scholarly articles opposing the pledge of allegiance omitted.] It is not necessary to inquire whether nonconformist beliefs will exempt from the duty to salute unless we first find power to make the salute a legal duty.

"The *Gobitis* decision, however, *assumed,* as did the argument in that case and in this, that power exists in the State to impose the flag salute discipline upon school children in general." [Emphasis in the original.] West Virginia State Bd. of Edu. v. Barnette, *supra,* 319 U.S. at 634-635, 63 S.Ct. at 1183-1184, 87 L.Ed. 1628.

Having avoided a confrontation with the secular regulation rule, the Court re-examined and rejected the remaining bases of the *Gobitis* decision. The Court first set out to answer Justice Frankfurter's rather strong promotion of national cohesion as an end in itself and indicated that the strength needed for national self-preservation could not be the only standard for resolving challenges against the authority of the state. If this were the case, then governmental interests would always predominate over individual liberties. The whole point of the Bill of Rights, the opinion reasoned, was to limit the inexorable power of

the state, and without it there is doubt if the Constitution would have ever been ratified. 319 U.S. at 636-637, 63 S.Ct. 1178, 87 L.Ed. 1628. Indeed, enforcement of the First Amendment, rather than a source of debilitation, should be viewed as "a means of strength to individual freedom of mind in preference to officially disciplined uniformity * * *." *Id.* 637, 63 S.Ct. 1185, 87 L.Ed. 1628. To carry this reasoning to its logical conclusion the Court elaborated on the need for political neutrality in the public schools.

"Free public education, if faithful to the ideal of secular instruction and political neutrality, will not be partisan or enemy of any class, creed, party, or faction. If it is to impose any ideological discipline, however, each party or denomination must seek to control, or failing that, to weaken the influence of the educational system. Observance of the limitations of the Constitution will not weaken government in the field appropriate for its exercise." *Id.*

Disclaiming any pretense to act as the "school board for the country," the Court was quick to vindicate the extensive discretionary powers of the local boards of education. Nevertheless, as state agencies bound by the Fourteenth Amendment, their functions were circumscribed by the Bill of Rights. *Id.* As for Justice Frankfurter's suggestion that the Court had no "controlling competence" over an issue more appropriately committed to the wisdom of legislative assemblies, the Court interposed this trenchant answer:

"The very purpose of a Bill of Rights was to withdraw certain subjects from the vicissitudes of political controversy, to place them beyond the reach of majorities and officials and to establish them as legal principles to be applied by the courts. One's right to life, liberty, and property, to free speech, a free press, freedom of worship and assembly, and other fundamental rights may not be submitted to vote; they depend on the outcome of no elections." *Id.* 638, 63 S. Ct. 1185, 87 L.Ed. 1628.

Under the Fourteenth Amendment some "rational basis" might well serve to regulate a public utility within the bounds of due process,

"[b]ut freedoms of speech and of press, of assembly, and of worship may not be infringed on such slender grounds. They are susceptible of restriction only to prevent grave and immediate danger to interests which the state may lawfully protect." *Id.* 639, 63 S.Ct. 1186, 87 L.Ed. 1628.

Even heavier constitutional artillery was reserved for the closing pages of the majority opinion—in language which completely refutes the Attorney General's contention that *Barnette* merely "suggests an involvement of free speech." The section begins with a withering attack on the critical assumption made in *Gobitis* that "national unity is the basis of national security" for which the authorities have "the right to select appropriate means for its attainment." *Id.* 640, 63 S.Ct. 1186, 87 L.Ed. 1628. Accepting national unity as a legitimate end to be fostered by persuasion and example, the Court questioned the compulsory flag salute as a constitutionally permissible means to achieve that goal.

"Probably no deeper division of our people could proceed from any provocation than from finding it necessary to choose what doctrine and whose program public educational officials shall compel youth to unite in embracing. * * *

"It seems trite but necessary to say that the First Amendment to our Constitution was designed to avoid these ends by avoiding these beginnings. There is no mysticism in the American concept of the State or of the nature or origin of its authority. We set up government by consent of the governed, and the Bill of Rights denies those in power any legal opportunity to coerce that consent. Authority here is to be controlled by public opinion, not public opinion by authority.

"The case is made difficult not because the principles of its decision are obscure but because the flag involved is our own. Nevertheless, we apply the limitations of the Constitution with no fear that freedom to be intellectually and spiritually diverse or even contrary will disintegrate the social organization. To believe that patriotism will not flourish if patriotic ceremonies are voluntary and spontaneous instead of a compulsory routine is to make an unflattering estimate of the appeal of our institutions to free minds. We can have intellectual individualism and the rich cultural diversities that we owe to exceptional minds only at the price of occasional eccentricity and abnormal attitudes. When they are so harmless to others or to the State as those we deal with here, the price is not too great. But freedom to differ is not limited to things that do not matter much. That would be a mere shadow of freedom. The test of its substance is the right to differ as to things that touch the heart of the existing order.

"If there is any fixed star in our constitutional constellation, it is that no official, high or petty, can prescribe what shall be orthodox in politics, nationalism, religion, or other matters of opinion or force citizens to confess by word or act their faith therein." 319 U.S. at 641-642, 63 S.Ct. at 1186-1187, 87 L.Ed. 1628.

In a joint concurring opinion Justices Black and Douglas stated, "[w]e are substantially in agreement with the opinion just read." While they then proceeded to discuss their "change of view" since *Gobitis* concerning the secular regulation rule, we fail to see how this supplementary religious liberty note to the majority's free speech rationale diminishes their affirmative acceptance of the opinion itself and not merely the result. *Id.* 643-644, 63 S.Ct. 1178, 87 L.Ed. 1628. Justice Murphy's concurring opinion was even more explicit, for he unequivocally stated, "I agree with the opinion of the Court and join in it." *Id.* 643-644, 63 S.Ct. 1188, 87 L.Ed. 1628. He too placed more emphasis on the religious issues than did the majority opinion and he toned down some of its rhetoric. Unlike Justices Black and Douglas and more in the tradition of the *Gobitis* dissent, he linked the freedom of religion with the freedoms of thought and speech, pointing out that these constitutional guaranties include "both the right to speak freely and the right to refrain from speaking at all, except in so far as essential operations of government may require it for the preservation of an orderly society,—as in the case of compulsion to give evidence in court." *Id.* 645, 63 S.Ct. 1189, 87 L.Ed. 1628. The flag salute did not reach this level of required essential conduct. Contrary to the Attorney General's intimations we think that none of these members of the Court rejected the free speech resolution of the flag salute controversy, though they may have added varying pleas for religious freedom to the discussion.

Justice Frankfurter's long dissenting opinion reemphasized and expanded his stringent views on religious liberty and the absolute need for judicial restraint. *Id.* 646-671, 63 S.Ct. 1178, 87 L.Ed. 1628. It would serve no useful purpose to repeat his very personal restatement of the principles set forth in *Gobitis.* Neither Justice Reed nor Roberts adopted this dissent, choosing instead to vote for reversal on the basis of their continued adherence to the *Gobitis* opinion. *Id.* 642-643, 63 S.Ct. 1178, 87 L.Ed. 1628. Whether their cryptically brief dissent was based on stare decisis or a rejection of the views expressed by the Court is a matter of speculation. We do know, however, that on the same day *Barnette* was handed down Justice Roberts announced the Court's unanimous decision in Taylor v. Mississippi, 319 U.S. 583, 63 S.Ct. 1200, 87 L.Ed. 1600 (1943), reversing the convictions of a number of Jehovah's Witnesses for teaching "resistance to governmental compulsion to salute" the flag. Viewing the whole problem as a matter of a fortiori reasoning, completely controlled by *Barnette,* the Court ruled that if the state cannot compel someone to salute the national emblem, "then certainly it cannot punish him for imparting his views on the subject to his fellows and exhorting them to accept those views." 319 U.S. at 589, 63 S.Ct. at 1204, 87 L.Ed. 1600.

Barnette and *Taylor* thus closed a stormy chapter in the history of the Bill of Rights. No doubt a smaller majority of the Supreme Court at the time could have limited the former opinion simply to interpreting the Free Exercise of Religion Clause of the Constitution, but the fact remains they did not do so. In our view

Barnette was unequivocally decided as a question of free speech under the First Amendment; it is binding as such on this Court.

BEYOND BARNETTE

The most significant case since *Barnette* involving the free speech rights of students under the First Amendment is Tinker v. Des Moines Independent Community School Dist., 393 U.S. 503, 89 S.Ct. 733, 21 L.Ed.2d 731 (1969). In that opinion the Supreme Court concluded the silent wearing of black armbands in class to protest the Vietnam war could not be proscribed by school regulations, "at least if it could not be justified by a showing that the students' activities would materially and substantially disrupt the work and discipline of the school." 393 U.S. at 513, 89 S.Ct. at 740, 21 L.Ed.2d 731. Recent flag salute and related cases have turned on this last distinction.

In Banks v. Bd. of Public Instruction, 314 F.Supp. 285 (S.D.Fla.1970) a three judge district court reviewed a Florida flag salute school regulation which provided an exemption for both religious and conscientious objectors but nevertheless required those children to stand while the rest of the class recited the pledge of allegiance. The panel ruled, on the basis of *Barnette* and *Tinker,* that an objecting student could not be expelled or disciplined for his conduct, but it was careful to say, "the unrefuted testimony clearly reflects that the plaintiff's refusal to stand has not caused any disruption in the educational process." 314 F.Supp. at 295.[4] In contrast, the United States District Court for the Eastern District of New York dismissed a bill of complaint for an injunction brought by a school child who refused to stand or leave the room during the recitation of the pledge of allegiance. Richards v. Bd. of Edu. Union Free School Dist. #17, No. 70-C-625, decided July 10, 1970. The court specifically found that the child's conduct had caused some minor disruption and thus ruled that the case fell within the factual exception to the *Tinker* rationale. Hanover v. Northrup, United States Dist.Ct.Conn., 325 F.Supp. 170, decided May 1, 1970 and Frain v. Baron, 307 F.Supp. 27 (E.D.N.Y.1969) declined in accordance with *Barnette* to coerce unwilling school children or teachers into saluting the flag but analyzed the problem before them in terms of the *Tinker* decision. *See also* Sheldon v. Fannin, 221 F.Supp. 766 (D.Ariz. 1963) which allowed children to remain seated during the playing of the national anthem. *But compare* Caldwell v. Craighead, 432 F.2d 213 (6th Cir. 1970), cert. denied, 402 U.S. 953, 91 S.Ct. 1617, 29 L.Ed.2d 123.

The *Tinker* decision is a direct descendant of *Barnette.* It specifically relies on the latter case, using it to demonstrate that neither "students or teachers shed their constitutional rights to freedom of speech or expression at the schoolhouse gate." 393 U.S. at 506, 89 S.Ct. at 736, 21 L.Ed.2d 731. While the Court in *Tinker* affirmed "the comprehensive authority of the States and of school officials, consistent with fundamental constitutional safeguards, to prescribe and control conduct in the schools," *id.* 507, 89 S.Ct. 737, 21 L.Ed.2d 731, the initial safeguard it recognized in this area was that a "student in public school may not be compelled to salute the flag," citing only West Virginia v. Barnette for this proposition. *Id.* Entertaining no doubt that there is ample authority to punish students or teachers who materially disrupt proper school activities, including voluntary patriotic programs, we are far from convinced that the mere refusal to participate in any phase of the pledge of allegiance ritual is punishable. To reach a contrary conclusion would allow the schools to discipline such refusal as "an act of disrespect," even though they may not compel this ceremony in the first place. As the disciplinary provision of Ch. 737 seems to permit this untenable result it too must fall with the general salute requirement.

The posture in which this case comes before us raises no factual issue of potential or actual disruption. We recognize, as did Justice Frankfurter in the *Gobitis* opinion, that one student's failure to join in this group expression "might introduce elements of difficulty into the school discipline, might cast doubts in the minds of the other children which would themselves weaken the effect of the exercise." 310 U.S. at 600, 60 S.Ct. at 1015, 84 L.Ed. 1375. As if in direct response to this assertion, the Court in *Tinker* has answered: "our Constitution says we must take this risk * * *." 393 U.S. at 508, 89 S.Ct. at 737, 21 L.Ed.2d 731. Quite aside from the fact that *Barnette* and *Tinker* are binding constitutional precedents, we also are convinced the First and Fourteenth Amendments of the Constitution require this gamble. The salute requirement and punishment provision of Ch. 737 of the Laws of Maryland 1970 are unconstitutional and void.

Decree affirmed. Appellants to pay the costs.

APPENDIX

STATEMENT OF BELIEF BY AUGUST L. LUNDQUIST

Since the enactment of the statute requiring a flag salute of certain teachers and students I have done much soul searching as to why I feel that I cannot comply with the law. In doing so I must say that I have always been a loyal citizen of this great country, and under any circumstances, will always be one.

In 1944, while still a senior in high school, I enlisted

in the U.S. Navy and served honorably for two years. Shortly after discharge I became a member of the active Naval Reserve program and have continued in the reserves to this time. On my own initiative, during the Korean conflict, I returned to active duty for a period of a year and a half.

As a boy and again as an adult with sons of my own I have been active in the Boy Scout movement, a significant part of which is practicing a serious duty to God and Country. The flag salute and other forms of flag courtesy are an integral part of the scouting program.

As a teacher and more specifically as a social studies teacher, it is my purpose to teach all students about the democratic principles which make this country great. This country is great because it rests on the individual and his faith in his country with its principles of democracy. This country will remain great as long as the individual citizen, by his own conviction, continues to develop his love of country in his own way and to be encouraged to express this love in those ways which seem most appropriate to the individual.

Now I am confronted with an edict that I must not only perform an act daily but I must force others to do the same act or be in fear of the law. This I cannot in good conscience do. To force patriotism down on anyone is extremely repulsive to me; and ultimately an act of futility for patriotism is something you feel, something you believe, something you do as you are a part of your country, but it is something that cannot be forced. I cannot teach democracy one minute and dictate a special form of ceremony the next and be true to myself or my students.

I suppose what I would like to say would be that my conscience will not allow me to be forced or to force others to do acts which must come from the heart.

I love my country, I respect my flag and other symbols of my country, but I am repulsed by the idea that this should be forced on anyone. I cannot in good conscience do it.

NOTES

1. Now codified as Art. 77, § 77, Md.Code (1957, 1969 Repl.Vol. 1970 Cum.Supp.) Ch. 737 provides:

   "It shall be the duty of the board of education of each and every county in the State of Maryland, and of the Board of Education for Baltimore City, in the State of Maryland, to cause to have displayed a flag of the United States of America upon every public school building within their respective jurisdictions while said schools are in session, and to that end shall make all necessary purchase of flags, staffs and appliances therefor and establish rules and regulations for the proper custody, care and display of the flag in said schools; and it shall be the duty of said boards of education to provide each class-room with an American flag; to prepare for each classroom at the beginning of each day of classes in all public schools of the State a program providing for the salute to the flag and other patriotic exercises approved by the United States Government; and to require all students and teachers in charge to stand and face the flag and while so standing render an approved salute, and recite in unison the pledge of allegiance as follows: 'I pledge allegiance to the flag of the United States of America and to the Republic for which it stands; one nation under God, indivisible, with liberty and justice for all'. Any pupil or teacher, for religious reasons, may be excused from actually repeating the words of the pledge of allegiance and from giving any form of hand salute. Any person, however, who may commit an act of disrespect, either by word or action, shall be considered to be in violation of the intent of this act. The said boards of education may provide such other patriotic exercises from time to time as may be deemed by them to be expedient, and under such regulations and instruction as may best meet the various requirements of the different grades in such schools; all to the end that the love of liberty and democracy, signified in the devotion of all true and patriotic Americans to their flag and to their country, shall be instilled in the hearts and minds of the youth of America.

   "Sec. 2. *And be it further enacted,* That this Act is hereby declared to be an emergency measure and necessary for the immediate preservation of the public health and safety and having been passed by a yea and nay vote supported by three-fifths of all the members elected to each of the two houses of the General Assembly, the same shall take effect from the date of its passage."

2. The Supreme Court thus reversed Minersville School Dist. v. Gobitis, 108 F.2d 683 (3d Cir. 1939), aff'g. 24 F.Supp. 271 (E.D.Pa.1938), opinion at 21 F.Supp. 581 (1937). Other flag salute cases were Gabrielli v. Knickerbocker, 306 U.S. 621, 59 S.Ct. 786, 83 L.Ed. 1026 (1939), denying cert. and dismissing appeal from 12 Cal.2d 85, 82 P.2d 391 (1938), rev'g, 74 P.2d 290 (Cal.App.1937); Johnson v. Deerfield, 306 U.S. 621, 59 S.Ct. 791, 83 L.Ed. 1027, aff'g per curiam 25 F.Supp. 918 (D.Mass. 1939) (three judge Dist.Ct.); Hering v. State Board of Education, 303 U.S. 624, 58 S.Ct. 752, 82 L.Ed. 1087 (1938) dismissing appeal from 118 N.J.L. 566, 194 A. 177, aff'g per curiam 117 N.J.L. 455, 189 A. 629 (1937); Leoles v. Landers, 302 U.S. 656, 58 S.Ct. 364, 82 L.Ed. 507 dismissing appeal for want of substantial federal question from 184 Ga. 580, 192 S.E. 218 (1937); State ex rel. Bleich v. Board of Public Instruction, 139 Fla. 43, 190 So. 815 (1939); Nicholls v. Mayor and School Committee of Lynn, 297 Mass. 65, 7 N.E.2d 577 (1937); People ex rel. Fish v. Sandstrom, 279 N.Y. 523, 18 N.E 2d 840 (1939), rev'g, 167 Misc. 436, 3 N.Y.S.2d 1006 (1938); Shinn v. Barrow, 121 S.W.2d 450 (Tex.Civ.App.1938); Reynolds v. Rayborn, 116 S.W.2d 836 (Tex.Civ.App. 1938). In Maryland the flag salute controversy never reached the Court of Appeals, although it erupted with some force at an Oxon Hill school in Prince George's County. In September 1936 the six children of August Ludke, all Jehovah's Witnesses, were expelled for refusing to salute the flag. The Attorney General ruled that the State Board of Education had no authority to decide the constitutional question involved. 21 Op.Atty.Gen. 560 (1936). The Ludkes brought a mandamus action to compel re-admission, but were unsuccessful and did not

appeal. No. 11 at Law, Petitions, October Term 1936, Circuit Court for Prince George's County, Md. Of passing interest, the Board of Education's minutes from the period reveal that Ogle Marbury, later Chief Judge of this Court, served as successful counsel for the Board in the mandamus action. Of equal interest, William L. Henderson, who also became Chief Judge of this Court, was the assistant attorney general who penned the opinion mentioned above.

3. Manwaring has documented such incidents in many states, including Maryland, where a mob broke up a Witness meeting in Rockville on June 19, 1940, only sixteen days after *Gobitis* was announced. *Render Unto Caesar,* 166 and 293, n. 25.

4. On direct appeal to the Supreme Court that judgment was vacated and the case remanded for possible appeal to the 5th Circuit Court of Appeals. 401 U.S. 988, 91 S.Ct. 1223, 28 L.Ed.2d 526 [decided March 29, 1971].

THE United States Court of Appeals, Fifth Circuit, decides against a school district which had prohibited students from wearing black armbands in conjunction with the Vietnam moratorium of October 15, 1969. In deciding for the students, the Court declared: "The use of the ancient symbol of mourning as a propagandistic device is clever precisely for the reason that it should put others differently minded on their best behavior. After all, over 44,000 Americans have died in Vietnam and all of us must mourn them. We differ only in what we think the President and Congress ought to do to end the bloodshed. . . . In the school environment, where no doubt restraints are necessary that the First Amendment would not tolerate on the street, something more is required to establish that they would cause 'disruption' than the *ex cathedra* pronouncement of the superintendent."

Butts v. *Dallas Ind. School District,* 436 F.2d 738 (1971)

NICHOLS, Judge:

Plaintiffs, minors, brought this action by their next friends in the United States District Court for the Northern District of Texas, and appeal from its final judgment dismissing their complaint. We reverse.

The defendants are the Dallas Independent School District, in whose schools plaintiffs were enrolled, and Dr. Nolan Estes, the Superintendent. The action was said to arise under the Fourteenth Amendment and 42 U.S.C. § 1983, which reads as follows:

* * * * * *

Every person who, under color of any statute, ordinance, regulation, custom, or usage, of any State or Territory, subjects, or causes to be subjected, any citizen of the United States or other person within the jurisdiction thereof to the deprivation of any rights, privileges, or immunities secured by the Constitution and laws, shall be liable to the party injured in an action at law, suit in equity, or other proper proceeding for redress. * * *

The alleged wrong was in defendant's refusal to allow plaintiffs to wear black armbands in school on October 15, 1969, and their anticipated continued refusal on later dates. Plaintiffs sought an injunction, a declaratory judgment, and nominal damages of $1.00. The District Judge conducted a hearing and took testimony on a prayer for a temporary injunction, but by stipulation the parties agreed that the hearing and his opinion should be "disposition on merits."

Defendants urge that the School District is immune from suit under § 1983, but this circuit has recently held that such immunity exists only with respect to money damages and not as to equitable relief.

Harkless v. Sweeney Independent School District, 427 F.2d 319 (5th Cir. 1970). *See* also Mayhue v. City of Plantation, Florida, 375 F.2d 447-451 (5th Cir. 1967). We treat the claim for $1.00 damages as waived. No evidence was offered to show pecuniary injury in any amount.

Defendants also say that plaintiffs do not belong to the class protected by § 1983 because the alleged wrong was not inflicted because of race. The absence of a racial question has been ignored in many cases under § 1983, *e.g.,* Tinker v. Des Moines Independent Community School District, 393 U.S. 503, 89 S.Ct. 733, 21 L.Ed.2d 731 (1969); Trister v. University of Mississippi, 420 F.2d 499 (5th Cir. 1969), and is expressly rejected by this circuit in construing the closely related criminal provisions of 18 U.S.C. § 242. Miller v. United States, 404 F.2d 611, 612 (5th Cir. 1968).

Plaintiffs wish to secure a declaratory judgment condemning part of a regulation of the School Board as unconstitutionally vague and overbroad. Identified as Regulation 5133(1) (a) (10), it reads as follows:

(10) Wearing at school any special garb, haircuts, or unusually distracting insignia designed to distinguish members in an excessive way from other students.

The Regulation as a whole is written to implement a Texas statute which undertakes to drive "social clubs," *i.e.*, fraternities, sororities and secret societies from the public schools. It defines certain acts the Board believes to be prohibited, among others those in the paragraph above quoted. The "members" are obviously members of social clubs. The record here reflects that the plaintiffs wished to wear black armbands to show their opposition to United States involvement in the Vietnam hostilities. An organization based in Washington called the National Moratorium Committee had suggested that they do this, and in a loose way they were its supporters, but there is nothing to show it had members in the ordinary sense, as a social club does. In any event, its purposes were political, not social. A separate section of Regulation 5133, not attacked, deals with participation of students in political organizations. Both sides in this litigation, for different purposes of their own, no doubt, seem to agree that paragraph 10 has something to do with this case. Nevertheless, it is an effort to deal with issues wholly distinct from those involved here, and we think it would be improper for us to make any pronouncement upon it. We are not bound by counsels' interpretation of this document. Pitcairn v. American Refrigerator Transit Co., 101 F.2d 929 (8th Cir.), cert. denied, 308 U.S. 566, 60 S.Ct. 78, 84 L.Ed. 475 (1939).

The underbrush cleared away, the main issue of the case emerges. The Supreme Court held in Tinker v. Des Moines Independent Community School District, *supra*, 393 US. at 505, 89 S.Ct. 733, that wearing black armbands in school to protest the Vietnam involvement was "closely akin to pure speech" protected by the First Amendment and could not be prohibited when it did not cause disruption of school discipline or decorum. The Court refers with apparent approval to companion cases in this court: Burnside v. Byars, 363 F.2d 744 (5 Cir., 1966); and Blackwell v. Issaquena County Board of Education, 363 F.2d 749 (5 Cir., 1966). Both involved prohibition against wearing SNCC buttons, by the school authorities. In *Burnside* there was no disruption and the authorities were enjoined. In *Blackwell* there was (in the form of button-wearing students trying to force buttons on the others) and the complaint was dismissed. The duty of the courts in future cases of the same kind therefore seems clear enough, and the trial judge properly proceeded to examine in detail the alleged disruptions and threats of disruption that were considered by the Dallas School Officials on and just before October 15, 1969. To this we now return.

The Vietnam moratorium of October 15, 1969, may end up as a footnote to history but it was tremendous in anticipation. The focal event was to be a mass peaceful demonstration of young people, about the White House in Washington, D.C., but the sponsors issued a manifesto to high school children elsewhere, among others, calling on them to boycott their classes that day, or attend them wearing black armbands as symbols of protest. Someone published a local mimeographed flyer to the same effect. These found their way into the hands of the defendants' school authorities, who concluded that October 15 probably would be a day of disruption in their schools. A former pupil of the District, not directly connected with the Committee or its supporters, threatened to bomb one of the defendants' schools. As the day approached, disruptive sit-ins did occur in the schools of a nearby community, not under defendants' jurisdiction. The organizers of this effort failed, however, to influence defendants' pupils.

The morning of October 15, a Dallas police officer called on school officials to advise that his department expected trouble and to offer what help he could. A group of students massed across the street from one of the schools displaying a large banner reading "Try Peace." A youth of contrary mind snatched this banner and ran away with it. Apparently, however, the schools opened and classes were attended as usual, though perhaps not with full efficiency.

Not all students supported the protest. Besides the one mentioned above, others wore white armbands. None of them testified nor were any manifestos offered, which were attributed to them, and their precise position thus is not in the record, except that they opposed what the black armbands favored. There was also a clique who evidently went further, revering the memory of Adolf Hitler and seeking to establish (or re-establish) white supremacy in this country. One of these soon after October 15, appeared at school wearing a large "swastika" necklace and a like symbol emblazoned on his jacket. He was, of course, speedily removed from the scene.

On learning of the plan to wear black armbands in school, Dr. Estes decided, as he testified, that it was disruptive and contrary to long standing school policy. In support of the long standing of this policy, however, he proffered Regulation 5133, which, as indicated above, fails to show it. The trial court's finding as to the long standing of the policy appears to lack support of substantial evidence. If it makes any difference, it would seem the policy was improvised ad hoc for the occasion. Other "peace symbols" until then had adorned the garments of students without evoking any administration concern. Indication that the policy was new appears also in the fact that the principals of some individual schools were slow in getting the word, with the result that in their schools black armbands were in fact worn for several hours, in one school all day. As the principals and assistant principals learned of the policy, they intercepted wearers of black armbands in the halls and corridors, or called them out of class, requiring them to choose between removing the armbands or going home, being then charged with unexcused absence. The plaintiffs all refused to remove their armbands and left school for the remainder of the day. Many other students took off their armbands. Dr. Estes intended the elimination of the white armbands also, but the record fails to indicate that this was generally achieved, another indication of hasty staff work.

It is undisputed that there occurred in fact no substantial disruption on October 15, 1969, in defendants' schools, either before or after the removal of the black armband wearers. There was also no disruption that day in schools outside defendants' jurisdiction, but in the same general area of Texas, for example in the nearby city of Fort Worth, where the black armbands were tolerated throughout.

None of the school officials who testified expected the wearers of the black armbands to initiate disruption. Rather they believed that the black armbands incensed students not participating in the protest because they gave a false impression of the attitudes general in the schools. The question of public image was important because the media with TV cameras were present at the scene. It was feared that white armband wearers would tear the black armbands off the arms of those who wore them. To dissuade this, school officials urged white armband wearers to restrain themselves, saying that this was an administration matter and administration would take the necessary action. There is no mention of any perceived necessity to urge restraint on black armband wearers.

Nevertheless, counsel for defendants have urged, and still do, that by wearing black armbands plaintiffs and others proclaimed their adherence to the entire program of the Moratorium Committee including its proposals for interruption of school work. Hence, it is said, school officials could use the black armbands to identify the potential disrupters and had a duty to stop them before they could carry out any of their program. This ignores the manifestos referred to above. Exhibit 1 clearly proposes the black armbands as "either—or" alternatives to other measures. Counsel abandons the testimony of defendants' own witnesses as to how the disruption was expected to commence. And he calls on us to subscribe to a kind of "guilt by association" (Elfbrandt v. Russell, 384 U.S. 11, 19, 86 S.Ct. 1238, 16 L.Ed.2d 321 (1966), and cases cited therein), particularly obnoxious in the case of an organization like the Moratorium Committee, having so far as appears, no clearly defined membership. Whatever the black armbands may have communicated, the record is devoid of any evidence that it did in fact communicate to any witness an intention on plaintiffs' part to engage personally in the feared disruptive actions.

We assume that the School Board was not necessarily required by the First Amendment to wait until disruption actually occurred. Likewise, we agree that, antecedently considered, as they had a right and duty to consider the problem, disruption on October 15, 1969, was proved to be a likely contingency. We do not agree that this expectation sufficed *per se* to justify suspending the exercise of what we are taught by *Tinker* is a constitutional right. What more was required at least was a determination, based on fact, not intuition, that the expected disruption would probably result from the exercise of the constitutional right and that foregoing such exercise would tend to make the expected disruption substantially less probable or less severe.

The boy who came to school flaunting his Nazi symbols was also, of course, communicating his ideas in his own fashion. However, the black armbands were more adult, more rational adornments. The use of the ancient symbol of mourning as a propagandistic device is clever precisely for the reason that it should put others differently minded on their best behavior. After all over 44,000 Americans have died in Vietnam and all of us must mourn them. We differ only in what we think the President and Congress ought to do to end the bloodshed. The difference between merely unwise or unpopular language and "fighting words" is well recognized in First Amendment cases. *Compare,* Terminiello v. Chicago, 337 U.S. 1, 4, 69 S.Ct. 894, 93 L.Ed. 1131 (1949), and Edwards v. South Carolina, 372 U.S. 229, 236, 83 S.Ct. 680, 9 L.Ed.2d 697 (1963), with Feiner v. New York, 340 U.S. 315, 71 S.Ct. 303, 95 L.Ed. 267 (1951). What seems clear is that black armbands are not *per se* akin to "fighting words," just because armbands of other colors, or shirts, or hats, have sometimes been so. Therefore, even in the school environment, where no doubt restraints are necessary that the First Amendment would not tolerate on the street, something more is required to establish that they would cause "disruption" than the *ex cathedra* pronouncement of the superintendent.

There is nothing in the instant record to show, *e.g.* conferences with leaders of the student factions, which might have developed solid information as to their attitudes and intentions. The school system had programs in which students were encouraged to speak out about current issues including Vietnam, in order to develop them as national leaders of the future, but no use apparently was made of this machinery to bring leaders of the white armband faction together with the black armbands to agree on mutual respect for each other's constitutional rights. If this had been tried and failed, the failure would have tended to establish that armbands of all colors should be banned. In short, it appears to us that the school system was confronted with a rapidly developing crisis, for which it had no policy predetermined, and instead of obtaining an answer through democratic processes, it responded with a hasty ukase.

Our difference with the trial court therefore is that we do not agree that the precedential value of the *Tinker* decision is nullified whenever a school system is confronted with disruptive activities or the possibility of them. Rather we believe that the Supreme Court has declared a constitutional right which school authorities must nurture and protect, not extinguish, unless they find the circumstances allow them no practical alternative. As to the existence of such circumstances, they are the judges, and if within the range where reasonable minds may differ, their decisions will govern. But there must be some inquiry, and establishment of substantial fact, to buttress the determination.

So far as the record shows, the plaintiffs would still like to wear black armbands to school and defendants would prevent their doing so. If these conflicting resolves have in any way moderated, the record does not so disclose, and mootness is not suggested. Therefore, plaintiffs are entitled to the injunction they request.

The complaint alleged that their exclusion from classes caused them to miss instruction they would otherwise have received. Except for one young man who was excluded from IBM work for the remainder of the term, the amount of teaching that was missed was slight and no doubt was soon made up. The IBM work was not a credit course. If, however, any makeup work is required to put any plaintiff where he would have been as to school advancement if not excluded because of his black armband, the District Judge can provide for the situation in framing the injunction.

The order entered by the District Court denying the injunction sought is hereby vacated, the judgment is reversed and the cause is remanded with direction to the District Court to grant an injunction enjoining defendants from interfering with plaintiffs in the exercise of their First Amendment right by wearing black armbands to school to protest the Vietnam war.

Reversed and remanded.

A United States District Court in Pennsylvania decides that the First Amendment rights of students who had participated in a sit-in at their high school were not violated when the school authorities terminated the sit-in by suspending the students involved. The Court declared: "Although we recognize that the students attempted to conduct their sit-in with respect for the orderly operation of the school, we find that the conduct of the sit-in participants did substantially interfere with appropriate school discipline. 'Appropriate discipline in the operation of the school' certainly requires students to attend their scheduled classes and to refrain from preventing other students from attending classes in their scheduled location. School officials may act to prevent demonstrating students from disrupting classes by moving noisily through the halls. . . . We find that the actions of the students disrupted the educational program of the school and therefore that the action of the school officials in terminating the sit-in by suspending the students did not violate the First Amendment rights of the students."

Gerbert v. *Hoffman*, 336 F.Supp. 694 (1972)

JOSEPH S. LORD, III, Chief Judge.

Plaintiffs filed this class action suit on December 17, 1970. In that complaint it was alleged, generally, that on December 14 and 15 various students who attend Abington High School engaged in sit-in demonstrations during and after school hours. It was further alleged that the defendant members of the Board of School Directors responded to these sit-ins by (1) obtaining a preliminary injunction, issued ex parte on December 14 in the Court of Common Pleas of Montgomery County, restraining such behavior, (2) suspending approximately thirty-six students from school, and (3) enforcing the suspensions. Plaintiffs contended that all the above activity violated rights granted by the First, Fifth and Fourteenth Amendments of the United States Constitution and by 42 U.S.C. § 1983. Jurisdiction is founded upon 28 U.S.C. § 1343(3).

On December 18, 1970, we entered a temporary restraining order which enjoined the defendants from continuing to prosecute the state court action and from continuing the suspensions in force. An evidentiary hearing was held in this matter on February 1-3, 1971. On June 7, 1971, we vacated the restraining order insofar as it prohibited further prosecution of the state court action. At the same time we retained jurisdiction over the claims relating to student suspensions. Gebert et al. v. Hoffman et al., 328 F.Supp. 574 (E.D. Pa., 1971).

On December 15, 1970, the plaintiffs were cleared from Abington High School pursuant to a state court preliminary injunction. At this time they were also informed that they were suspended from school. Later that day, letters sent to the parents of the suspended students stated that the students had been suspended "for participating in a sit-in at South Campus, an activity disruptive to the normal operation of the school." The school principal testified that the basis for the suspensions was rule 14 of the 1970-71 Abington Handbook which provides that "[a]ny other serious breach of proper conduct" is a ground for suspension. N.T. 298-301.

In the afternoon of December 15th, Gay Jewell and Robin Mack, students at Abington High School, were arrested by a Deputy Sheriff of Abington Township while they were on school property. Testimony indicated that the sheriff made the arrest after consulting a list of students who were not allowed in school. The girls were taken to the police station, questioned, and then released. No charges were lodged against either girl.

Plaintiffs contend that their sit-in activity was protected by the First Amendment or, alternatively, if that activity was not constitutionally protected, that they were not put on notice by the school disciplinary rules that it was impermissible. It is prayed that we therefore enjoin defendants from "continuing to effectuate the school suspensions" and from "engaging in any other conduct, including state court proceedings, by which the constitutional rights of plaintiffs are abridged."

We read the complaint as asking for the following

relief. Plaintiffs' request to enjoin defendants from "continuing to effectuate the school suspensions" of December 15, 1970 seeks to prevent the reinstatement of the temporary suspensions and the use of the records of the suspension. Plaintiffs' request to enjoin the defendants from engaging in any other conduct which abridges the constitutional rights of the students seeks to enjoin future temporary suspensions for sit-ins and the use of the police or resort to state court proceedings against students for engaging in constitutionally protected activities.

At the outset we can dispose of three of the plaintiffs' requests for relief. First, we find that there is no threat that the temporary suspensions of December 15 will be reinstated to bar the students from school in the future. N.T. 114-116. Therefore, insofar as plaintiffs' complaint seeks relief from such reinstatement, we consider the issue as moot. Second, we find that the evidence is insufficient to indicate that the police arrested Gay Jewell and Robin Mack at the behest of the defendants. We find that there is no threat that the defendants will use the police in the future to enforce their will in violation of the constitutional rights of the plaintiffs, and we therefore deny the request or injunctive relief on this ground. Third, we find no threat of future state court proceedings by defendants against plaintiffs which would justify an injunction. There is no evidence that the defendants would fail to abide by any decision of this court defining plaintiffs' constitutional rights.

We are therefore left with the request to enjoin future temporary suspensions and the use of records. In order to determine whether to grant plaintiffs' request for relief, we must determine whether defendants' actions in suspending the students on December 15 was in violation of their constitutional rights.

Plaintiffs contend that the sit-in was protected activity under the First and Fourteenth Amendments, and therefore the action of the school administrators in suspending the students for such activity constituted a legally cognizable wrong under 42 U.S.C. § 1983 for which injunctive relief is appropriate. The Supreme Court has stated that:

"First Amendment rights, applied in light of the special characteristics of the school environment, are available to teachers and students. It can hardly be argued that either students or teachers shed their constitutional rights to freedom of speech or expression at the schoolhouse gate." Tinker v. Des Moines Community School District, 393 U.S. 503, 506, 89 S.Ct. 733, 736, 21 L.Ed.2d 731 (1969).

However, even outside the school environment, the Court has held that where speech is mixed with conduct, as in the case of a sit-in, the state may reasonably regulate the time, place and manner of such activity in order to prevent serious interference

with the normal usage of the facility or area in which the demonstration is to take place. Cox v. Louisiana, 379 U.S. 536, 554-557, 85 S.Ct. 453, 13 L.Ed.2d 471 (1965); Cox v. Louisiana, 379 U.S. 559, 563, 85 S.Ct. 476, 13 L.Ed.2d 486 (1965); Shuttlesworth v. Birmingham, 394 U.S. 147, 152-155, 89 S.Ct. 935, 22 L.Ed.2d 162 (1969); Kunz v. New York, 340 U.S. 290, 293-295, 71 S.Ct. 312, 95 L.Ed. 280 (1951).

In a school case involving conduct "akin to pure speech," the Supreme Court has defined the limits of permissible regulation of First Amendment activities of students as follows:

"* * * [A student] may express his opinions, even on controversial subjects * * *, if he does so without 'materially and substantially interfer[ing] with the requirements of appropriate discipline in the operation of the school' and without colliding with the rights of others. * * * [Burnside v. Byars, 363 F.2d 744, 749 (5 Cir. 1966).] But conduct by the student, in class or out of it, which for any reason—whether it stems from time, place, or type of behavior—materially disrupts classwork or involves substantial disorder or invasion of the rights of others is, of course, not immunized by the constitutional guarantee of freedom of speech." Tinker, supra, 393 U.S. at 513, 89 S.Ct. at 740, 21 L.Ed.2d 731.

In the present case, there is evidence that the sit-in disrupted the normal operation of the school: the students involved in the sit-in did not attend classes; the sit-in forced the removal of a few classes from their scheduled locations; students engaging in the demonstration moved noisily through the halls possibly disturbing classes in session in the area; non-participating students were attracted to and congregated in the halls near the sit-in area; and school administrators could not attend to their regular duties. The issue before the court is whether these disruptions materially and substantially interfered with the requirements of appropriate discipline in the operation of the school so as to permit regulation of the conduct.

In deciding this issue, we believe that the courts can only consider the conduct of the demonstrators and not the reaction of the audience.

"In order for the State in the person of school officials to justify prohibition of a particular expression of opinion, it must be able to show that its action was caused by something more than a mere desire to avoid the discomfort and unpleasantness that always accompany an unpopular viewpoint." Tinker, supra, 393 U.S. at 509, 89 S.Ct. at 738, 21 L.Ed.2d 731. See also Terminiello v. Chicago, 337 U.S. 1, 69 S.Ct. 894, 93 L.Ed. 1131 (1949).

Therefore the fact that the demonstrations attracted a crowd which congregated in the hallways cannot be a basis for punishing the demonstrators' exercise of their First Amendment rights.

Similarly, the fact that the school administrators could not attend to their normal duties cannot be a basis for suspending the students' First Amendment rights. A sit-in is a form of demonstration in which the participants cease to engage in their normal activities and gather together to express their views on a particular issue. In the context of a high school particularly, it is likely that the school administration will want to keep close watch on such activity to insure that it does not substantially disrupt the school program. The fact that these administrators cannot therefore attend to their scheduled duties is not a basis for determining that the sit-in itself has materially disrupted the school program. If the test of material interference depends alone on what others do in response to the demonstrators' activity then all forms of constitutionally protected expression could be barred from the schools by a showing that administrators could not attend to their scheduled duties on any grounds related to the conduct engaged in by the students. We must therefore distinguish evidence that administrators left scheduled duties in order to keep an eye on potentially disruptive conditions in the school from evidence that disruptive activity by demonstrators actually occurred.

Although we recognize that the students attempted to conduct their sit-in with respect for the orderly operation of the school, we find that the conduct of the sit-in participants did substantially interfere with appropriate school discipline. "Appropriate discipline in the operation of the school" certainly requires students to attend their scheduled classes and to refrain from preventing other students from attending classes in their scheduled location. School officials may act to prevent demonstrating students from disrupting classes by moving noisily through the halls. One of the "special characteristics of the school environment" is the need to maintain order and discipline to promote the educational program. We find that the actions of the students disrupted the educational program of the school and therefore that the action of the school officials in terminating the sit-in by suspending the students did not violate the First Amendment rights of the students.

We need not reach the issues raised by the plaintiffs' further argument concerning the school rules which were the basis of the student suspensions. The plaintiffs have failed to establish any reasonable probability of injury to them as a result of the continued existence and use of those rules which would justify their request for injunctive relief against future temporary suspensions or the use of the records of the December 15 suspensions. If in the future the plaintiffs can establish actual or threatened harm as a result of the application of the school disciplinary rules, we have no reason to doubt that the state courts will fairly and adequately consider the merits of the plaintiffs' claims and protect their constitutional rights.

$\mathbb{T}$HE United States Court of Appeals, Second Circuit, gives First Amendment protection to an eleventh grade English teacher who had worn a black armband in class as symbolic protest against the war in Vietnam. In deciding for the teacher, the Court declared: "Several factors present here compel the conclusion that the Board of Education arbitrarily and unjustifiably discharged James [the teacher] for wearing the black armband. Clearly, there was no attempt by James to proselytize his students. It does not appear from the record that any student believed the armband to be anything more than a benign symbolic expression of the teacher's personal views. Moreover, we cannot ignore the fact that James was teaching 11th grade (high school) English. His students were approximately 16 and 17 years of age, thus more mature than those junior high school students in *Tinker*. Recently, this country enfranchised 18 year-olds. It would be foolhardy to shield our children from political debate and issues until the eve of their first venture into the voting booth. . . . Under the circumstances present here, there was a greater danger that the school, by power of example, would appear to the students to be sanctioning the very 'pall of orthodoxy,' condemned in *Keyishian,* which chokes freedom of dissent."

James v. *Board of Education,* 461 F.2d 566 (1972)

IRVING R. KAUFMAN, Circuit Judge:

The first amendment proscription against any law abridging freedom of expression, perhaps more than any other constitutional guarantee, frequently brings into sharp focus the inexorable tension between enduring concerns for individual freedom and the authority required to preserve the democracy so crucial to realizing that freedom. For several decades, the courts have struggled with principles and concepts necessary to strike a functional balance between protected speech and the government's legitimate interest in protecting our democracy.[1]

The Supreme Court has more than once instructed that "[t]he vigilant protection of constitutional freedoms is nowhere more vital than in the community of American schools." Shelton v. Tucker, 364 U.S. 479, 487, 81 S.Ct. 247, 251, 5 L.Ed.2d 231 (1960), *quoted in* Keyishian v. Board of Regents, 385 U.S. 589, 603, 87 S.Ct. 675, 17 L.Ed.2d 629 (1967); Tinker v. Des Moines Independent Community School District, 393 U.S. 503, 512, 89 S.Ct. 733, 21 L.Ed.2d 731 (1969). Rightly called the "cradle of our democracy," our schools bear the awesome responsibility of instilling and fostering early in our nation's youth the basic values which will guide them throughout their lives. Appellant is quick to agree that we cannot tolerate undisciplined, coercive, intimidating or disruptive activities on the part of teachers or students which threaten the essential functions of our schools, and that such conduct requires a disciplinary response. But, the issue in this case is whether, in assuming the role of judge and disciplinarian, a Board of Education may forbid a teacher to express a political opinion, however benign or noncoercive the manner of expression. We are asked to decide whether a Board of Education, without transgressing the first amendment, may discharge an 11th grade English teacher who did no more than wear a black armband in class in symbolic protest against the Vietnam War, although it is agreed that the armband did not disrupt classroom activities, and as far as we know did not have any influence on any students and did not engender protest from any student, teacher or parent. We hold that the Board may not take such action.

The facts essential to a resolution of the conflicting interests are undisputed. On June 7, 1969, Charles James was employed as an 11th grade English teacher at Addison High School, located near Elmira, New York. He previously had taught in the New York City public schools. After moving to the Elmira area, James, a practicing Quaker, joined the Elmira Meeting of the Religious Society of Friends.

When November 14 and December 12, 1969, were designated as "moratorium" days by the opponents of the Vietnam War, the Elmira Meeting determined to observe the two days by wearing black armbands.[2] On

November 14 James affixed one of the armbands, which had been prepared by the Meeting, to the sleeve of his jacket. He since has stated that he "resolved to wear one of the black armbands as an expression of [his] religious aversion to war in any form and as a sign of [his] regret over the loss of life in Vietnam."

Shortly after school began that day, Carl Pillard, the Principal, entered James's homeroom, noticed the armband, but made no comment. Pillard waited until midway through the second period when James was teaching poetry, apparently without any incident or discussion whatsoever relating to Vietnam or the armband, to summon James to his office and to request him to remove the armband. When James refused to remove it, Pillard sent him to the District Principal, Edward J. Brown. Brown ordered James to remove the armband or risk suspension or dismissal because the armband constituted a symbolic expression of his political views.[3] In addition, Brown feared that "wearing the armband would tend to be disruptive and would possibly encourage pupils to engage in disruptive demonstrations." When James again refused to remove the armband, Brown summarily suspended him and ordered James to leave the school at once.

The following day James received a letter from the Board of Education of Central District No. 1, reinstating him on "the understanding that [he] engage in no political activities while in the school."[4] James resumed his teaching duties, but, steadfastly abiding by his principles, whether religious (Quakers are doctrinally opposed to war) or political in nature, he came to school wearing an armband on December 12, the second moratorium day. He was summarily suspended as soon as Brown learned that James again had worn an armband. Here, too, the record is barren of a scintilla of evidence indicating that there were any incidents or threats to school discipline, that any students or teachers had complained of or were offended by James's first or second symbolic protest, or that the armband constituted more than a silent expression of James's own feelings. On January 13, however, without affording James a hearing, the Board of Education of Central District No. 1 discharged him from his teaching position in accordance with § 3013(1) of the Education Law of New York, McKinney's Consol.Laws, c. 16.[5]

James appealed his dismissal to the New York State Commissioner of Education, Ewald B. Nyquist, asserting that his dismissal infringed upon his first amendment rights and deprived him of due process of law.[6] The "hearing" before the Commissioner, as we were informed at the argument of this appeal, was no more than an informal roundtable discussion between the Commissioner, the parties and their attorneys. No transcript of the proceedings was made. On September 23, 1970, Commissioner Nyquist filed his decision.

Although he recognized that a board of education does not have unfettered discretion to dismiss a probationary teacher,[7] he concluded that James had violated "sound educational principles" and that his actions "were not constitutionally protected." In addition, he reaffirmed the Board of Education's absolute right to dismiss a probationary teacher without affording the teacher a hearing or explaining the basis of the discharge.

Thereupon, James instituted this action in the Western District of New York against the Board of Education of Central District No. 1, Edward Brown, Carl Pillard and Robert Andrews, President of the School District Board of Trustees, alleging that his dismissal violated 42 U.S.C. § 1983.[8] Judge Burke, in a brief memorandum, denied James's motion for summary judgment and granted the defendants' motion for a judgment, summarily dismissing the complaint on the merits, seemingly on two grounds: first, that the issues raised by the complaint were *res judicata,* and second, that none of James's federally protected rights was violated.[9]

I.

At the outset we are presented with the contention that the claims asserted below are *res judicata.* We consider this to be wholly without merit. Appellees argue that James, at his own choosing, was given the full opportunity to litigate his claims before the Commissioner of Education, a "judicial officer" of the State, and therefore that James should be bound by the Commissioner's decision. Judge Burke buttressed their position with a pointed reference to James's failure to appeal the Commissioner's decision to the New York courts.[10]

It is no longer open to dispute that a plaintiff with a claim for relief under the Civil Rights Act, 42 U.S.C. § 1983, is not required to exhaust state judicial remedies. *See, e.g.,* Monroe v. Pape, 365 U.S. 167, 81 S.Ct. 473, 5 L.Ed.2d 492 (1961); Rodriguez v. McGinnis, 456 F.2d.79 (2d Cir. 1972) (*in banc*); Sostre v. McGinnis, 442 F.2d 178, 182 (2d Cir. 1971) (*in banc*), cert. denied, 404 U.S. 1049, 92 S.Ct. 719, 30 L.Ed.2d 740 (1972). It is still the law in this Circuit, however, that a Civil Rights plaintiff must exhaust state administrative remedies. Eisen v. Eastman, 421 F.2d 560 (2d Cir. 1969), cert. denied, 400 U.S. 841, 91 S.Ct. 82, 27 L.Ed.2d 75 (1970). It hardly can be suggested that a plaintiff having followed the course laid out by *Eisen,* was to be barred henceforth from pressing his claim to final judicial review or to be deprived of his opportunity to litigate his constitutional claims in the judicial forum of his choice. To adopt the full implication of appellees' argument would be to effect a judicial repeal of 42 U.S.C. § 1983 and strike down the Supreme Court's decision in Monroe v. Pape, *supra*. James would be placed in the paradoxical position of being barred from the federal courts if he had not exhausted administrative remedies and barred if he had.[11]

II.

We come now to the crucial issue we must decide—did the Board of Education infringe James's first amendment right to freedom of speech?[12]

Any meaningful discussion of a teacher's first amendment right to wear a black armband in a classroom as a symbolic protest against this nation's involvement in the Vietnam War must begin with a close examination of the case which dealt with this question as it applied to a student. Tinker v. Des Moines Independent Community School District, *supra*. Mary Beth Tinker, a junior high school student, her older brother and his friend, both high school students, were suspended from school for wearing black armbands in school to publicize their opposition to the war in Vietnam. Noting that neither students nor teachers "shed their constitutional rights to freedom of speech or expression at the schoolhouse gate," 393 U.S. at 506, 89 S.Ct. at 736, the Supreme Court held that a school cannot bar or penalize students' exercise of primary first amendment rights akin to "pure speech" without "a showing that the students' activities would materially and substantially disrupt the work and discipline of the school." *Id.* at 513, 89 S.Ct. at 740.

With respect to both teacher and student, the responsibility of school authorities to maintain order and discipline in the schools remains the same. The ultimate goal of school officials is to insure that the discipline necessary to the proper functioning of the school is maintained among both teachers and students. Any limitation on the exercise of constitutional rights can be justified only by a conclusion, based upon reasonable inferences flowing from concrete facts and not abstractions, that the interests of discipline or sound education are materially and substantially jeopardized, whether the danger stems initially from the conduct of students or teachers. Although it is not unreasonable to assume that the views of a teacher occupying a position of authority may carry more influence with a student than would those of students *inter sese*, that assumption merely weighs upon the inferences which may be drawn. It does not relieve the school of the necessity to show a reasonable basis for its regulatory policies. As the Court has instructed in discussing the state's power to dismiss a teacher for engaging in conduct ordinarily protected by the first amendment: "The problem in any case is to arrive at a balance between the interests of the teacher, as a citizen, in commenting upon matters of public concern

and the interest of the State, as an employer, in promoting the efficiency of the public services it performs through its employees." Pickering v. Board of Education, 391 U.S. 563, 568, 88 S.Ct. 1731, 1734, 20 L.Ed.2d 811 (1968).[13]

It is to be noted that in this case, the Board of Education has made no showing whatsoever at any stage of the proceedings that Charles James, by wearing a black armband, threatened to disrupt classroom activities or created any disruption in the school. Nor does the record demonstrate any facts "which might reasonably have led school authorities to forecast substantial disruption of or material interference with school activities. . . ." Tinker v. Des Moines Independent Community School District, 393 U.S. at 514, 89 S.Ct. at 740. All we can learn from the record is that in the opinion of Edward Brown, the District Principal, "wearing the armband would tend to be disruptive and would possibly encourage pupils to engage in disruptive demonstrations." "But," the Supreme Court warned in *Tinker*, "in our system, undifferentiated fear or apprehension of disturbance is not enough to overcome the right to freedom of expression."[14] *Id.* at 508, 89 S.Ct. at 737.

Appellees urge us not to conclude that schools must wait until disruption is on the doorstep before they may take protective action. We do not suggest this course, but if anything is clear from the tortuous development of the first amendment right, freedom of expression demands breathing room. To preserve the "marketplace of ideas" so essential to our system of democracy, we must be willing to assume the risk of argument and lawful disagreement. *Id.* at 508-509; Terminiello v. Chicago, 337 U.S. 1, 69 S.Ct. 894, 93 L.Ed. 1131 (1949). This is entirely different, however, from saying that the school must await open rebellion, violence or extensive disruption before it acts. *Compare* Burnside v. Byars, 363 F.2d 744 (5th Cir. 1966), *with* Blackwell v. Issaquena County Board of Education, 363 F.2d 749 (5th Cir. 1966).[15]

III.

That does not end our inquiry, however. The interest of the state in promoting the efficient operation of its schools extends beyond merely securing an orderly classroom. Although the pros and cons of progressive education are debated heatedly, a principal function of all elementary and secondary education is indoctrinative—whether it be to teach the ABC's or multiplication tables or to transmit the basic values of the community. "[S]ome measure of public regulation is inherent in the very provision of public education." Note, Developments in the Law-Academic Freedom, 81 Harv.L.Rev. 1045, 1053 (1968). Accordingly, courts consistently have affirmed that curriculum controls belong to the political process and local school authorities. "Courts do not and cannot intervene in the resolution of conflicts which arise in the daily operation of school systems and which do not directly and sharply implicate constitutional values." Epperson v. Arkansas, 393 U.S. 97, 104, 89 S.Ct. 266, 270, 21 L.Ed.2d 228 (1968).[16]

Appellees argue that this broad power extends to controlling a teacher's speech in public schools, that "assumptions of the 'free marketplace of ideas' on which freedom of speech rests do not apply to school-aged children, especially in the classroom where the word of the teacher may carry great authority." Note, Developments in the Law-Academic Freedom, 81 Harv.L.Rev. at 1053. Certainly there must be some restraints because the students are a "captive" group. But to state the proposition without qualification is to uncover its fallacy. More than a decade of Supreme Court precedent leaves no doubt that we cannot countenance school authorities arbitrarily censoring a teacher's speech merely because they do not agree with the teacher's political philosophies or leanings. This is particularly so when that speech does not interfere in any way with the teacher's obligations to teach, is not coercive and does not arbitrarily inculcate doctrinaire views in the minds of the students. *Cf.* Keyishian v. Board of Regents, *supra.*

As we have indicated, there is merit to appellees' argument that *Tinker* does not control this case, because a teacher may have a far more pervasive influence over a student than would one student over another. Although sound discussions of ideas are the beams and buttresses of the first amendment, teachers cannot be allowed to patrol the precincts of radical thought with the unrelenting goal of indoctrination, a goal compatible with totalitarianism and not democracy. When a teacher is only content if he persuades his students that his values and only his values ought to be their values, then it is not unreasonable to expect the state to protect impressionable children from such dogmatism. But, just as clearly, those charged with overseeing the day-to-day interchange between teacher and student must exercise that degree of restraint necessary to protect first amendment rights. The question we must ask in every first amendment case is whether the regulatory policy is drawn as narrowly as possible to achieve the social interests that justify it, or whether it exceeds permissible bounds by unduly restricting protected speech to an extent "greater than is essential to the furtherance of" those interests. *See* United States v. O'Brien, 391 U.S. 367, 377, 88 S.Ct. 1673, 1679, 20 L.Ed.2d 672 (1968). Thus, when a teacher presents a colorable claim that school authorities have infringed on his first amendment rights and arbitrarily transgressed on these transcendent values, school authorities must demonstrate a reasonable basis for concluding that the teacher's conduct threatens to impair their legitimate interests in regulating the school curriculum. What we require, then, is only that rules formulated by school officials be reasonably related to the needs of the educational process and that any disciplinary action taken pursuant to those rules have a basis in fact.

Several factors present here compel the conclusion that the Board of Education arbitrarily and unjustifiably discharged James for wearing the black armband.[17] Clearly, there was no attempt by James to proselytize his students.[18] It does not appear from the record that any student believed the armband to be anything more than a benign symbolic expression of the teacher's personal views. Moreover, we cannot ignore the fact that James was teaching 11th grade (high school) English. His students were approximately 16 or 17 years of age, thus more mature than those junior high school students in *Tinker.*

Recently, this country enfranchised 18-year-olds.[19] It would be foolhardy to shield our children from political debate and issues until the eve of their first venture into the voting booth. Schools must play a central role in preparing their students to think and analyze and to recognize the demagogue. Under the circumstances present here, there was a greater danger that the school, by power of example, would appear to the students to be sanctioning the very "pall of orthodoxy," condemned in *Keyishian*, which chokes freedom of dissent.[20]

Finally, James was first removed from class while he was teaching poetry. There is no suggestion whatsoever that his armband interfered with his teaching functions, or, for that matter, that his teaching ever had been deficient in any respect.[21]

IV.

We emphasize that we do not question the broad discretion of local school authorities in setting classroom standards, nor do we question their expertise in evaluating the effects of classroom conduct in light of the special characteristics of the school environment. The federal courts, however, cannot allow unfettered discretion to violate fundamental constitutional rights.[22] Professor Jaffe put it aptly in an analogous area of the federal courts' review power: " . . . expertness is not a magic wand which can be indiscriminately waved over the corpus of an agency's findings to preserve them from review." L. Jaffe, Judicial Control of Administrative Action 613 (1965). We cannot abdicate our responsibility to form our own conclusions when, having thoroughly searched the record, we find no sound constitutional basis for the Board's or the Commissioner's conclusions.

The dangers of unrestrained discretion are readily

apparent. Under the guise of beneficent concern for the welfare of school children, school authorities, albeit unwittingly, might permit prejudices of the community to prevail. It is in such a situation that the will of the transient majority can prove devastating to freedom of expression. Indeed, James has alleged in his complaint that another teacher, "without incurring any disciplinary sanction, prominently displayed the slogan 'Peace with Honor' on a bulletin board in his classroom." This slogan has been associated with our foreign policy. If the allegation is true, and we must assume that it is in light of the summary dismissal of the complaint, it exemplifies the concern we have expressed. The Board's actions under such circumstances would indicate that its regulation against political activity in the classroom may be no more than the fulcrum to censor only that expression with which it disagrees. *See* Tinker v. Des Moines Independent Community School District, 393 U.S. at 510-511, 89 S.Ct. 733, 21 L.Ed.2d 731 (petitioners were barred from wearing black armbands, but other students were allowed to wear political campaign buttons and the Iron Cross, a traditional symbol of Nazism). By requiring the Board of Education to justify its actions when there is a colorable claim of deprivation of first amendment rights, we establish a prophylactic procedure that automatically tempers abuse of properly vested discretion.

It is characteristic of resolutions of first amendment cases, where the price of freedom of expression is so high and the horizons of conflict between countervailing interests seemingly infinite, that they do not yield simplistic formulas or handy scales for weighing competing values. "The best one can hope for is to discern lines of analysis and advance formulations sufficient to bridge past decisions with new facts. One must be satisfied with such present solutions and cannot expect a clear view of the terrain beyond the periphery of the immediate case." Eisner v. Stamford Board of Education, 440 F.2d 803, 804 n. 1 (2d Cir. 1971).

It is appropriate, however, lest our decision today (which is based on the total absence of any facts justifying the Board of Education's actions) be misunderstood, that we disclaim any intent to condone partisan political activities in the public schools which reasonably may be expected to interfere with the educational process.

Accordingly, we conclude that the district court erred. The judgment of the district court is reversed and the case remanded for proceedings not inconsistent with this opinion.

NOTES

1. *See generally,* Kaufman, The Medium, the Message and the First Amendment, 45 N.Y.U.L.Rev. 761 (1970) (The James Madison Lecture).

2. In a statement signed after James had been dismissed, the members of the Elmira Meeting explained their motivation:

    It is from this religious context [Quaker belief in the futility and immorality of war] that Charles James drew his moral imperative to act as he did, in wearing a black armband—symbol of sympathy and mourning for the dead—on those days accepted nationally as the time to demonstrate for peace and for an end to the killing in Vietnam. His action was as one member of this meeting, along with other members, who chose out of the same deep convictions, to wear a black armband all and every day of the moratoriums.

3. Brown apparently assured James that there was no question as to his right to hold political views or to participate in political activities outside of school. Controversial issues, he said, should not be discussed in school unless they are relevant to the subject matter being taught and all points of view are objectively presented. He relied in part on a letter of November 3, 1969, from Herbert F. Johnson, Deputy Commissioner of the Department of Education of New York, which set forth the Department's policies with respect to the upcoming moratorium days: "The school posture should be neutral and objective. Administrators and staff members should avoid taking positions on controversial matters which may reflect on the objectivity of the school." In addition, Brown suggested that it was a breach of professional ethics to use the classroom to promote partisan politics. See New York State Teachers Ass'n, Joint Code of Ethics.

4. The letter in full read:

    The Board of Education of Addison Central School District has conferred with counsel and very thoroughly discussed the facts of your situation. The Board has, unanimously, confirmed the action of District Principal Edward J. Brown regarding your suspension on Friday, November 14, 1969.

    The Board deems your action to be a political act. As such, it is prohibited in the School. It is, also, deemed unethical action on the part of a teacher to engage in such activity.

    You may return to class on Monday, November 17, 1969, with the understanding that you engage in no political activities while in the School.

    Of course, the Board recognizes fully your absolute right to express outside of the School any beliefs that you may have.

5. James, in his first year of teaching at Addison, was appointed as a "probationary" teacher. Under the provisions of § 3013(1) of the Education Law of New York, the services of a probationary teacher "may be discontinued at any time during such probationary period, upon the recommendation of the district superintendent, by a majority vote of the board of education or trustees."

6. *See* Education Law of New York § 310.

7. Commissioner Nyquist relied on his earlier decision in Matter of Collins, Decision No. 8051, August 26, 1969:

    While I fully agree that a board of education has broad powers over a probationary teacher and may dismiss a probationer without giving a reason, the exercise of these powers by a board must be made "within the ambit of the purpose for which they were granted and in a manner consistent with our basic Constitutional framework."

See also Puentes v. Board of Education, 24 N.Y.2d 996, 302 N.Y.S.2d 824, 250 N.E.2d 232 (1969), rev'g 24 A.D.2d 628 (1966).

8. 42 U.S.C. § 1983 provides:

Every person who, under color of any statute, ordinance, regulation, custom, or usage, of any State or Territory, subjects, or causes to be subjected, any citizen of the United States or other person within the jurisdiction thereof to the deprivation of any rights, privileges, or immunities secured by the Constitution and laws, shall be liable to the party injured in an action at law, suit in equity, or other proper proceeding for redress.

James's complaint asserts violations of his rights to free speech, free exercise of religion, procedural due process and equal protection of the laws.

9. In this posture of the proceedings, we must accept all factual allegations in the complaint as true.

10. Although § 310 of the Education Law of New York provides that any decision of the Commissioner "shall be final and conclusive, and not subject to question or review in any place or court whatever," New York courts have reviewed decisions where there is a claim that the decision was arbitrary or an abuse of discretion. *See e.g.,* Board of Education v. Allen, 6 N.Y.2d 127, 188 N.Y.S.2d 515, 160 N.E.2d 60 (1959).

11. Appellees' reliance on Judge Weinstein's opinion in Taylor v. New York City Transit Authority, 309 F.Supp. 785 (E.D.N.Y.), aff'd. 433 F.2d 665 (2d Cir. 1970), is misplaced. Judge Weinstein's determination that Taylor could not raise his procedural due process claim in the federal courts, after he had appealed his discharge as a Transit Authority employee to the New York City Civil Service Commission and then the New York courts, was based on Taylor's failure to raise that claim before the administrative agency. The decision was nothing more than a logical extension of Eisen v. Eastman, *supra,* through the application of traditional notions of merger and bar. Since no transcript of the proceedings before Commissioner Nyquist was made, James cannot be charged with the failure to raise any of his claims. Suffice it to say that appellees conceded at oral argument that the broad range of James's grievances were discussed informally before the Commissioner.

12. In view of our decision, it is unnecessary to reach the claims that the discharge violated his rights to free exercise of religion and equal protection of the laws.

13. *Pickering* dealt with the power of the Board of Education to discharge a high school teacher for sending a letter to the local newspaper criticizing the Board and the district superintendent of schools for their fiscal policies. The Board insisted that the letter was disruptive of faculty discipline and would tend to foment "controversy, conflict and dissension" among teachers, administrators, and residents of the district. The Court held that the Board had violated the teacher's first amendment rights. Appellees would distinguish *Pickering* by having us draw an arbitrary line between first amendment rights exercised in school and out of school. The distinction is deceptively simple and cannot withstand scrutiny. *See* Goldwasser v. Brown, 417 F.2d 1169 (D.C.Cir.), cert. denied, 397 U.S. 922, 90 S.Ct. 918, 25 L.Ed.2d 103 (1969) (*Pickering* test applies to teacher's classroom speech at Air Force language

school). Appellees concede, as they must, that James has a constitutional right to wear a black armband off school premises—every day if he so pleases. But, it is not unreasonable to assume that James, as a teacher, might gain notoriety for such out-of-school conduct and become a vanguard of the local opposition to the Vietnam War. In that event, one could not divorce his person from the idea, and he would become an embodiment of his symbolic protest no matter where or how he appeared—even if temporarily without his armband. Although we can imagine situations in which a teacher would be so controversial because of his tenets or beliefs that he would be a disruptive force in the school, no one would suggest that he could be dismissed merely because he was *identified* with a particular cause if he did not preach that cause in class.

14. The facts here call more clearly for the protection of James's rights than did those in *Tinker.* In his dissenting opinion in *Tinker,* Justice Black emphasized that "[e]ven a casual reading of the record shows that the armband did divert students' minds from their regular lessons, and that talk, comments, etc., made John Tinker 'self-conscious' in attending school with his armband." 393 U.S. at 518, 89 S.Ct. at 742. The record in this case does not support similar inferences.

15. In Burnside v. Byars, the Fifth Circuit ordered that school authorities be enjoined from enforcing a regulation against wearing freedom buttons when there was no evidence of disruption. The same panel of the Fifth Circuit on the same day in *Issaquena* upheld a similar regulation in another school because students wearing the buttons had attempted to force unwilling students to wear the buttons. When the offending students were ordered to remove their buttons and cease distributing them in school, they engaged in disruptive activities.

16. Even in this area there are constitutional limitations. In *Epperson,* for example, the Court held that a state could not prevent a high school biology teacher from teaching students about Darwin's theory of evolution because the regulation would be an establishment of religion in violation of the first amendment. Nor can a state prevent the teaching of modern foreign languages under the guise of promoting "civic development." Meyer v. Nebraska, 262 U.S. 390, 43 S.Ct. 625, 67 L.Ed. 1042 (1923).

17. In light of our holding, we find it unnecessary to decide whether the Board of Education violated James's due process rights by not affording him an evidentiary hearing before he was dismissed. *Compare* Roth v. Board of Regents, 446 F.2d 806 (7th Cir.), cert. granted, 404 U.S. 909, 92 S.Ct. 227, 30 L.Ed.2d 181 (1971), and Sindermann v. Perry, 430 F.2d 939 (5th Cir. 1970), cert. granted, 403 U.S. 917, 91 S.Ct. 2226, 29 L.Ed.2d 694 (1971) (a probationary teacher has a right to a hearing when he has a colorable claim that his dismissal violates the first amendment), *with* Parker v. Board of Education, 348 F.2d 464 (4th Cir. 1965) (a probationary teacher has no constitutional right to a hearing when his contract is not renewed). *See also* Drown v. Portsmouth School District, 435 F.2d 1182, 1188 (1st Cir. 1970), cert. denied, 402 U.S. 972, 91 S.Ct. 1659, 29 L.Ed.2d 137 (1971); Orr v. Trinter, 444 F.2d 128, 135 (6th Cir. 1971), petition for cert. filed, 40 U.S.L.W. 3126 (Aug. 18, 1971); Shirck v. Thomas, 447 F.2d 1025, 1026 (7th Cir. 1971), petition for cert. filed, 40 U.S.L.W. 3321 (Dec. 3, 1971), 40 U.S.L.W 3375 (Jan. 21, 1972); Note, 85 Harv. L.Rev. 1327 (1972). The Supreme Court has heard

argument in both *Roth* and *Sindermann,* and its decision may well be dispositive of this issue.

18. Appellees argue that James's political activity was unacceptable in the classroom because the armband was "the projection of an idea . . . it asks no comments in return and it invites no discussion." This fact alone cannot condemn a protected medium of expression.

19. Eighteen-year-olds, in addition, are now eligible to serve on federal juries. Pub. L. No. 92-269 (Apr. 6, 1972).

20. *See* Hanover v. Northrup, 325 F.Supp. 170 (D.Conn. 1970) (violation of first amendment rights to dismiss a junior high school teacher who refused to lead her class in the Salute to the Flag because she believed the phrase "with liberty and justice for all" was an untrue statement).

21. Appellees rely extensively on Goldwasser v. Brown, *supra,* which is clearly inapposite. Goldwasser, a civilian, was employed as a language instructor in the Air Force Language School to teach English to foreign military officers. After repeated warnings against discussing controversial subjects during class hours, he was discharged for antiwar statements and comments about anti-Semitism in America. In upholding the dismissal in the face of a first amendment challenge, the court relied on findings that his conduct interfered with the proper performance of his duties because he unduly sacrificed classroom teaching hours. 417 F.2d at 1176-1177.

22. The Supreme Court decision in *Tinker* instructs that the federal courts must not accept unquestioningly the school authorities' judgment as to the effects of classroom conduct or speech. *See,* Note, The Supreme Court, 1968 Term, 83 Harv.L.Rev. 7, 158 (1969) : "By not deferring to the administrative expertise of school officials, *Tinker* imposes new limitations on the power of the state to restrain students from speech or conduct which would clearly be protected by the first amendment if engaged in by adults."

THE United States Court of Appeals, Sixth Circuit, in deciding that a high school student's suspension for his refusal to stop wearing a Confederate flag patch on the sleeve of his jacket was not violative of his First and Fourteenth Amendment rights, supported the District Court's distinction between this case and *Tinker*, District Court Judge Wilson having said: "Unlike the *Tinker* case, where the Court found no evidence of either actual or potential disruptive conduct, but only an 'undifferentiated fear or apprehension of disturbance,' the record in the present case reflects quite clearly that there was substantial disorder at Brainerd High School throughout the 1969-1970 school year, that this disorder most materially disrupted the functioning of the school, so much so that the school was in fact closed upon two occasions, that much of the controversy the previous year had centered around the use of the Confederate flag as a school symbol and that the school officials had every right to anticipate that a tense racial situation continued to exist as of the opening of school in September of 1970."

In his dissenting opinion, Judge Miller argued that "the evidence in this case clearly brings it within the ambit of *Tinker*. . . . The fact is that despite the racial strife of the year before the circumstances were altogether different in the school year beginning in the fall of 1970, and there is no substantial basis to support the principal's apprehension and fear that a small emblem worn by a single student on the sleeve of his jacket, which was merely symbolic of one of the historic facts of American life, would activate anew the kind of turmoil which had previously existed and which had been caused by entirely different circumstances."

Melton v. Young, 465 F.2d 1332 (1972)

KEITH, District Judge.

This is an appeal from a judgment of the District Court for the Eastern District of Tennessee, 328 F.Supp. 88, determining that the suspension of appellant Rod Melton from Brainerd High School at Chattanooga, Tennessee was not violative of his constitutional rights.

Appellant[1] instituted this action in the District Court under 42 U.S.C. § 1983 for declaratory and injunctive relief alleging appellant's various constitutional rights were violated because the principal of his high school suspended him for wearing an emblem depicting a Confederate flag on the sleeve of his jacket.

The background of this case is recited in the extensive opinion entered by the District Judge and we will merely capsulize the factual circumstances leading to appellant's suspension.

Brainerd is a public high school in the city of Chattanooga, Tennessee. Until 1966 Brainerd was operated as an all white school which had adopted as its nickname the word "Rebel" and used the Confederate flag as the school flag along with the song Dixie as its pep song. The school has been attended by both white and black students since 1966; by 1969 the student body consisted of 170 black and 1224 white students.

The record indicates that with the advent of the 1969 school year the student body became racially polarized as a result of continuing controversy over the use of the Confederate flag and the song Dixie at various school functions. It also appears that on October 8, 1969 demonstrations took place at the school which disrupted classes and that on the evening of the same day a motorcade drove through various parts of the city waving Confederate flags. Thereafter various disturbances took place in the city finally culminating in the imposition of a city-wide curfew for four nights from October 13 through October 17, 1969. The District Court also found that throughout the remainder of the fall semester considerable racial tension existed within the student body which continued on into the following spring. During this period it was necessary to call for police assistance amid several confrontations and also to close the school for the purpose of restoring order and calming tensions.

In May, 1970, the Brainerd school administration and P.T.A. appointed a committee of citizens to study the difficulties of the past year and recommend remedial action for the ensuing year. Among the conclusions of the committee were the nickname "Rebel," the song Dixie, and the Confederate flag were precipitating causes of tension and disorder within the school. As a corrective measure the committee recommended that the use of the Confederate flag as a school symbol and the use of the song Dixie as the school pep song be discontinued but that the nickname "Rebel" be retained. These recommendations were adopted as official policy by the School Board at its meeting on July 8, 1970 along with the directive to school administrators that each principal develop and disseminate within the student body a "code of conduct"[2] consistent with the recommendations by the opening of the school in September, 1970. It is this code and the consequences of its enforcement that gave rise to this lawsuit.

Appellant, after both he and his parents were informed of the new rules, wore a jacket to school with an emblem depicting a Confederate flag on one sleeve. He was asked to remove the emblem or cease wearing the jacket while in school by the principal but declined to do so. After he was allowed to return to class several complaints from both faculty and students caused the principal to call appellant to his office and request him to remove the jacket, which request was again refused. The principal then indicated that it was his judgment that the emblem was "provocative" and in violation of the school code and thereupon he directed that appellant either remove the jacket or leave the school. Appellant chose to absent himself from the campus.

The following day appellant presented himself at the school with the same jacket and emblem and upon being sent to the principal's office and being requested to remove the jacket stated that he was merely demonstrating pride in his Confederate heritage by the wearing of the flag and that he had no other motive. Appellant was then told to leave school and not return until he was willing to stop displaying the Confederate emblem while in school. The above two suspensions occurred on September 8 and September 9, 1970 respectively and letters were sent to appellant's parents on both occasions stating the reasons for the suspension.

The District Court issued an opinion finding, inter alia, that the portion of the school regulation forbidding students from wearing "provocative symbols" upon their clothing was unconstitutionally "vague, broad, and imprecise" in derogation of the precepts of both the First and Fourteenth Amendments to the United States Constitution. Appellee does not argue this determination on appeal hence we will not discuss it.

Although the plaintiff-appellant was suspended pursuant to a regulation that was subsequently determined to be unconstitutional, the District Court apparently felt that the suspension was nevertheless valid for the reason that the suspension would have been a legitimate exercise of the school officials' inherent authority to curtail disruption of the educational process even in the absence of a regulation. This Court agrees with the District Court's finding.

Turning now to the substance of this appeal we note that counsel for appellant has engaged in a proselytizing diatribe bordering on the edge of uncivility at the most, and poor professional taste at the least, in an effort to expand the issues facing this Court. In our view the only question for determination is whether a public high school student's suspension for his unwillingness to stop wearing a Confederate flag patch was violative of the First and Fourteenth Amendments under the circumstances in existence at the time of the suspension?

This is a troubling case; on the one hand we are faced with the exercise of the fundamental constitutional right to freedom of speech, and on the other with the oft conflicting, but equally important, need to maintain decorum in our public schools so that the learning process may be carried out in an orderly manner. It is abundantly clear that this Court will not uphold arbitrary or capricious restrictions on the exercise of such jealously guarded and vitally important constitutional tenets. However, it is contended here that the circumstances at the time of appellant's suspension were such that the District Court could properly find that

> "[t]he Principal had every right to anticipate that a tense, racial situation continued to exist at Brainerd High School as of the school [sic] in September of 1970 and that repetition of the previous year's disorders might reoccur if student use of the Confederate symbol was permitted to resume."

It is our view after an independent examination[3] of the record that the conclusions of the District Court are fully supported by the evidence.

In the leading case of Tinker v. Des Moines Independent Community School District, 393 U.S. 503, 89 S.Ct. 733, 21 L.Ed.2d 731, the Supreme Court stated, inter alia, that student conduct which "materially disrupts class work or involves substantial disorder or invasion of the rights of others" is not afforded the cloak of protection provided by the First Amendment. Recognizing the problems discussed in Tinker, this Court, in the case of Guzick v. Drebus, 431 F.2d 594 (6 Cir. 1970) indicated its belief that

"... the potentiality and imminence of the admitted rebelliousness in the Shaw students support the wisdom of the no-symbol rule. Surely those charged with providing a place and atmosphere for educating young Americans should not have to fashion their disciplinary rules only after good order has been at least once demolished."

In this regard it should be noted that District Judge Frank Wilson's opinion reflects a careful and studied consideration of the precepts of *Tinker* and its application to the case before the Court. In the language of the trial court

"Unlike the *Tinker* case, where the Court found no evidence of either actual or potential disruptive conduct, but only an 'undifferentiated fear or apprehension of disturbance,' the record in the present case reflects quite clearly that there was substantial disorder at Brainerd High School throughout the 1969-70 school year, that this disorder most materially disrupted the functioning of the school, so much so that the school was in fact closed upon two occasions, that much of the controversy the previous year had centered around the use of the Confederate flag as a school symbol and that the school officials had every right to anticipate that a tense racial situation continued to exist as of the opening of school in September of 1970."

We conclude that this determination is fully supported by the evidence presented to the Court. We also think that Judge Wilson was correct in his determination that *Guzick, supra,* permitted the school authorities to stave off any potential danger resulting from appellant's conduct.[4]

It is therefore our conclusion that under all of the circumstances herein presented that appellant's suspension was not violative of his First and Fourteenth Amendment rights and that the judgment below was proper.

Affirmed.

WILLIAM E. MILLER, Circuit Judge (dissenting).

The plaintiff in this case, Rod Melton, a student at Brainerd High School in Chattanooga, was suspended from school by the Principal because of his refusal to cease wearing a small shoulder patch sewn on one sleeve of his jacket and depicting the Confederate Flag. The sole reason for such suspension, as found by the district court and established by the evidence, was that the student, in the judgment of the Principal, had violated that portion of a school code of conduct which provided as follows: "*Also, provocative symbols on clothing will not be allowed.*" The district court held, and I think correctly so, that this regulation was invalid and unenforceable because of its vagueness and lack of specificity. If the rule under the sole authority of which the student was suspended is invalid because it infringed upon the rights of the student to freedom of speech and expression, as the district court clearly held, it follows, in my opinion, that the student was entitled to have the suspension itself declared illegal and to have the benefit of the injunctive relief which he sought by his complaint.

It is interesting to note that the district court, in invalidating this provision of the code, stated:

Although elsewhere in the regulations Confederate symbols were barred from use as school symbols and although there is evidence that the words 'provocative symbols' were construed by the school principal to mean 'that which would cause a substantial disruption of the student body,' such an interpretation is subjective to the principal, for nowhere in the regulatory scheme are the words 'provocative symbols' defined.

Yet the district court proceeded in its opinion to find that the Principal had every reason to believe, because of the disturbances which occurred in the prior school year, that the wearing of the shoulder patch was provocative and might lead to a disruption of the proper functions of the school. If his judgment in construing the regulation was subjective to him when he undertook to apply the code of conduct and assigned such code as the sole reason for suspension, it is difficult for me to fathom why his judgment should not be regarded equally as subjective in attempting to assess the validity of the suspension upon the hypothetical assumption of the district court that the Principal could have acted, although he did not, on the basis of his inherent authority over the operation of the school.

Since the Principal acted pursuant to the regulation alone and that regulation is void, it necessarily follows that the student's constitutional rights were infringed and that he is entitled to appropriate relief. One cannot escape the conclusion that if the regulation itself is void on its face it cannot be validly applied in fact as the Principal in this case sought to do.

But even accepting the district court's premise that the Principal's action in suspending the student because of his refusal to remove the emblem is not dependent upon the validity of the regulation, I still hold the view that the district court's conclusion that the student's constitutional rights were not infringed is wrong.

I do not in any way quarrel with the finding of the district court with respect to the tense racial situation and disturbances which disrupted the school in the 1969-70 school year. As the district court, as well as the special Citizens Committee, found, the disturbances which occurred during that year were provoked primarily because of the use of a number of official or semi-official school symbols which appeared to be offensive to a minority group of the students in the school, including (a) the name "The Rebels" to designate the school's athletic teams; (b) the song "Dixie"; and (c) the "Confederate Flag." No finding was made with regard to the individual wearing of shoulder patches or insignia. It was recommended by the Committee, followed by later approval by the Board of Education, that the name "Rebel" or "Rebels" be retained, but that the Confederate Flag as a school symbol and the use of the song "Dixie" as a school pep song should be discontinued. These recommendations were implemented as codes of conduct at each of the schools, including the provision with respect to "provocative symbols" which the district court has held to be invalid.

The evidence in this case clearly brings it within the ambit of Tinker v. Des Moines Independent Community School District, 393 U.S. 503, 89 S.Ct. 733, 21 L.Ed.2d 731 (1969). It is my firm conviction that the Principal in suspending the student simply over-reacted and was motivated by the kind of "undifferentiated fear or apprehension of disturbance" which the court in Tinker held to be insufficient to overcome the right to freedom of expression. True enough, in this case the Principal was aware of the disturbances which had occurred during the prior school year, but he failed to take into account, in acting so hastily and precipitately, the following differentiating factors which appear to me to be of controlling significance:

1. The protests of the previous year were against a group of school symbols which by long usage and custom, if not by express official sanction, carried the impact of official sanction, whereas the wearing of the small sleeve insignia in this case by a single student could in no way represent an official ruling or have the appearance of doing so.

2. In the early part of the 1970-71 school year (in September) a football game was played by the school team when some students imprudently and in violation of the school's code of conduct waved Confederate flags, with no resulting protests or outbreaks of violence, indicating a lessening of racial tension at the school.

3. In the interim between school years, the Board of Education, acting upon the recommendation of a citizens committee which had made an intensive study of the events of 1969-70, mandated the discontinuance at Brainerd of the song "Dixie" and the Confederate Flag as *school symbols,* but retained the designation of "Rebels" for the school's athletic teams. If such continued use officially of a term equally as suggestive of the Confederacy as the flag caused no disruption, it is difficult to conceive how the wearing of a confederate flag insignia could be seriously taken as disruptive.

4. There was no finding by the Committee that the wearing of confederate symbols on clothing by in-

dividual students as matters of personal choice had contributed to the previous trouble or that it should be prohibited for the future.

5. The complaints received by the Principal concerning this student's display of the Confederate Flag on his sleeve were, at best, minimal if not trivial.

6. As of the time this student was suspended there had been no acts of violence at the school and no significant threats of disruption, despite the continued "official" use of the team name "Rebels" and the events at the opening football game. There was every reason to believe that the official steps taken by the School Board in abolishing the school song and flag had satisfied the demands of those who protested the year before.

7. The nature of the "symbolism" in this case (entitled under *Tinker* to the same reverence as "pure speech") is of significance: It was small; it was worn as a part of an article of clothing; and it had no inherent qualities for causing disruption or disturbance.

8. The emblem was worn by the student in a quiet, peaceful and dignified manner with no untoward gestures or remarks.[1]

9. The Principal conducted no substantial inquiry to ascertain the true facts as to whether the wearing of the insignia would lead to further trouble.

The fact is that despite the racial strife of the year before the circumstances were altogether different in the school year beginning in the fall of 1970, and there is no substantial basis to support the Principal's apprehension and fear that a small emblem worn by a single student on the sleeve of his jacket, which was merely symbolic of one of the historic facts of American life, would activate anew the kind of turmoil which had previously existed and which had been caused by entirely different circumstances. After all, it should be emphasized, the school symbols which were discontinued, such as the song "Dixie" and the Confederate Flag, at least bore the appearance of officialdom and could hardly be compared with the personal choice of a single student to decorate his jacket with a harmless emblem of the Confederate Flag.

The language of the Fifth Circuit in Burnside v. Byars, 363 F.2d 744, 748 (1966), appears to me to be pertinent in the present context:

. . . . Thus it appears that the presence of "freedom buttons" did not hamper the school in carrying on its regular schedule of activities; nor would it seem likely that the simple wearing of buttons unaccompanied by improper conduct would ever do so. Wearing buttons on collars or shirt fronts is certainly not in the class of those activities which inherently distract students and break down the regimentation of the classroom such as carrying banners, scattering leaflets, and speechmaking, all of which are protected methods of expressions, but all of which have no place in an orderly classroom. If the decorum had been so disturbed by the presence of the "freedom buttons," the principal would have been acting within his authority and the regulation forbidding the presence of buttons on school grounds would have been reasonable.

Since no question is made on appeal as to the validity of the district court's ruling in striking down the "provocative symbol" regulation, I would reverse the remainder of the judgment and remand the case with directions to modify the judgment below so as to grant the injunctive relief sought and for further proceedings on the issue of damages.

NOTES

1. When used through this opinion "appellant" refers to the minor, Rod Melton.
2. Relevant portions of the code provided as follows:
   a) "Also, provocative symbols on clothing will not be allowed."
   b) Re: Brainerd High School. . . . year 1970-71
   SYMBOLS:
   According to the Board of Education, July 8th, 1970, meeting the status of symbols for Brainerd High School is as follows:

The Confederate Flag and Confederate Soldier cannot be used as symbols for any public school in Chattanooga, therefore, all displays of the Flag and Soldier are removed from the school premises and cannot be used in any display where Brainerd is involved.
SONG DIXIE:
The song "Dixie" can no longer be used as a fight or pep song at Pep Meetings, Athletic contests or other school functions. It may be played in concert when other music of similar kind composes the program.

3. Edwards v. South Carolina, 372 U.S. 229, 235, 83 S.Ct. 680, 9 L.Ed.2d 697 (1963); Jacobellis v. Ohio, 378 U.S. 184, 189, 84 S.Ct. 1676, 12 L.Ed.2d 793 (1964).
4. See also Norton v. Discipline Committee of East Tennessee State University, 419 F.2d 195 (6th Cir. 1969).

DISSENTING JUDGE'S NOTE

1. There was evidence pro and con as to the student's conduct in connection with prior racial situations, but the district court made no finding, and the record justifies none, that he was a troublemaker or that he wore the insignia other than for the purposes stated by him. His stated purpose was to indicate his pride in his Confederate heritage.

THE United States Court of Appeals, Second Circuit, decides for a high school art teacher who had refused to comply with a school regulation requiring her to participate with her class in the pledge of allegiance. In deciding to give First Amendment protection to the teacher, the Court stated: "We emphasize, too, that despite our holding that Mrs. Russo may not be dismissed for refusing to pledge allegiance to the flag, we do not share her views. But because the First Amendment ranks among the most important of our constitutional rights we must recognize that the precious right of free speech requires protection even when the speech is personally obnoxious. . . . It is our conclusion that the right to remain silent in the face of an illegitimate demand for speech is as much a part of First Amendment protections as the right to speak out in the face of illegitimate demand for silence."

Russo v. *Central School Dist. No. 1,* 469 F.2d 623 (1972)

IRVING R. KAUFMAN, Circuit Judge:

Events that occur in small towns sometimes have a way of raising large constitutional questions. Henrietta, New York, a town of approximately 6,500 residents, is the geographic setting of this important case, in which we are asked to decide whether the dismissal of Mrs. Susan Russo, a high school art teacher, for what in the end amounts to a silent refusal to participate in her school's daily flag salute ceremonies, violated her constitutional rights under the First Amendment. As in James v. Board of Education, 461 F.2d 566 (2d Cir. 1972), decided by the Court just a few months ago, we must ascertain, and ultimately assess, the sometimes conflicting interests of the state on the one hand, in maintaining and promoting the discipline necessary to the proper functioning of schools, and the interest of a teacher, on the other, freely to exercise fundamental rights of expression and belief guaranteed by the Bill of Rights. There is, however, more to this case than even that difficult balancing test requires, for we are mindful of the fact that the problems associated with the short-hand phrase, "flag salute," bare a complex of deep emotions, calling into question the meaning of patriotism and loyalty, and the different significance those words have for different people. This case, therefore, is made more difficult for us, "not because the principles of decision are obscure but because the flag involved is our own." West Virginia State Board of Education v. Barnettte, 319 U.S. 624, 641, 63 S.Ct. 1178, 1187, 87 L.Ed. 1628 (1943).

I.

The facts, which we glean from the trial record below, are as follows. Susan Russo was appointed by the Board of Education for the Rush-Henrietta School District, as a probationary art teacher, and assigned, as of September 1, 1969, to the James E. Sperry High School in Henrietta. As a condition of her employment, Mrs. Russo was required by New York Education Law, McKinney's Consol.Laws, c. 16, § 3002 to sign a loyalty oath affirming her support of the Constitution of the United States and of New York State. She signed that oath, without reservation, on August 27, 1969.

In September, 1969, shortly after the school year began, a notice appeared on the school's bulletin board announcing that the "pledge of allegiance" would be recited each day and that "all students and staff members [were] expected to salute the flag." The practice at the Sperry School was to have the pledge read into the school's intercommunication system by a faculty member or a student. Students and teachers would then stand in their homeroom classes, and recite the pledge along with the voice over the public address system.

Mrs. Russo, in addition to her duties as an art instructor, was assigned to homeroom duty and charged with supervision of between twenty and twenty-five children, ranging from fourteen to sixteen years of age. Mrs. Catherine Adams, a teacher with seven years experience in the Rush-Henrietta school district, was also assigned to supervise the same homeroom, and to exercise senior authority in the classroom.

Although Mrs. Adams saluted the flag and recited the pledge each morning with her class, Mrs. Russo did not. From her first day in school, when it came time to recite the pledge, Mrs. Russo rose and faced the flag, but neither recited the pledge nor saluted the flag. She simply stood at respectful attention, with her hands at her sides. Significantly, there is no evidence in the record indicating that Mrs. Russo ever tried to influence her students to follow her example, and no evidence disclosing even a trace of disruption in the classroom as a result of her action. The students all knew the pledge and, under Mrs. Adams's guidance, recited it each day, without incident. Mrs. Russo's belief, the sincerity of which is unchallenged in these proceedings, was that the phrase "liberty and justice for all" appearing in the pledge, which to most of us represents the spirit and abiding genius of our institutions, in her mind simply did not reflect the quality of life in America today. For this reason, she felt it to be an act of hypocrisy on her part to mouth the words of the pledge when she lacked a belief in either their accuracy or efficacy.

Although Mrs. Russo had not recited the pledge from the start of the school year in September, her action did not come to the attention of school officials until some time in April, 1970. In fact, as late as April 17, 1970, a teacher's report based on actual observation was prepared by James Bennett, an assistant principal at the Sperry school. He evaluated Mrs. Russo's classroom performance as favorable in all respects.[1]

About that time, in April 1970, certain students and parents reported to the principal, Donald Loughlin, that Mrs. Russo was not saluting the flag. On the morning of April 19, Loughlin entered Mrs. Russo's homeroom class and observed her standing in silence as the pledge was being recited. The following day Mrs. Russo was summoned to Loughlin's office and asked to explain her behavior. Mrs. Russo did so, as we have indicated, adding that her unwillingness to recite the pledge and salute the flag was a matter of personal conscience.

It was hardly coincidence that school officials were informed of Mrs. Russo's behavior in the spring of 1970. During the preceding months the school's flag salute regulations had become a matter of some controversy in Henrietta, and its surrounding towns. A directive of the school Board issued on February 2 reminded school principals that all students were to stand during the pledge. On April 14, the Board reversed itself and announced that students who were unable to participate in the pledge ceremonies because of sincere conscientious belief, would be permitted to remain seated during the pledge if they chose to do so. This Board regulation was the subject of bitter dispute at an open meeting of the school Board. A few days later, on May 1, Principal Loughlin visited Mrs. Russo's class for a second time and observed her activity during the pledge. At a subsequent meeting in his office, Loughlin told Mrs. Russo that he intended to recommend that her probationary appointment not be renewed unless she resigned. Mrs. Russo asked

Loughlin for the reasons underlying his decision, but he refused to supply any, stating that he was not compelled to explain his action with respect to a probationary teacher.[2] Mrs. Russo refused to resign.

On May 12, Loughlin wrote Superintendent of Schools Richard E. TenHaken, recommending that Mrs. Russo not be reappointed for the coming academic year, and that her employment status be terminated, effective June 30. On the evening of May 12, however, the school board announced new regulations governing student conduct during the pledge. The new regulations modified the policy adopted on April 14 by requiring all students who refused to salute the flag to stand in respectful silence. Finally, at a meeting of the school board, held on June 23, Mrs. Russo was dismissed from service at the Sperry school. No reasons for her dismissal were set forth by the Board. A notice of termination sent to Mrs. Russo by the District Clerk similarly did not provide any statement of the grounds for her dismissal.

II.

This action was brought by Mrs. Russo pursuant to provisions of the Civil Rights Act, 42 U.S.C. § 1983,[3] and 28 U.S.C. § 1343,[4] alleging that her dismissal for refusing to pledge allegiance to the flag violated her First Amendment rights, and that the Board's failure to state reasons for her dismissal denied her the procedural protections safeguarded by the Due Process Clause of the Fourteenth Amendment. Mrs. Russo seeks reinstatement with back pay, and damages. In view of our decision on the merits of the First Amendment challenge,[5] we do not reach Mrs. Russo's Due Process claim.[6]

As a preliminary matter we are constrained to comment on the cryptic findings filed by the court below. After trial, Judge Burke dismissed Mrs. Russo's complaint on the merits, holding, in a brief series of findings and conclusions unaccompanied by any opinion, that neither First nor Fourteenth Amendment rights were violated in the dismissal of June 30, 1970. Judge Burke recited without explanation that Mrs. Russo's probationary appointment was terminated because of: (1) "her failure to follow school regulations," (2) "her refusal to teach a course in the art department," (3) "her lack of cooperation," (4) "her refusal to participate in the pledge of allegiance," (5) "her failure to perform all her duties," and (6) "her involvement of the student body in her conflict with the school."

Ordinarily, of course, Rule 52, F.R.Civ.P., binds us to accept findings of fact made by the district court unless they are "clearly erroneous." But equally compelling is the demand in Rule 52(a) that "in all actions tried upon the facts without a jury . . . the court shall find the facts specially. . . . " The degree of specificity and particularity with which the facts must be found may vary, depending upon the circumstances of each case, see Kelley v. Everglades Drainage District, 319 U.S. 415, 63 S.Ct. 1141, 87 L.Ed. 1485 (1943). But we must remember that an important function of findings of facts is to aid an appellate court on review, see Advisory Committee Note to Rule 52(a) (1946); 5A Moore, Federal Practice ¶ 52.01 [5]. Findings that are nothing but cold rhetoric, couched in extraordinarily broad and general terms, and stripped of underlying analysis or justification or an accompanying memorandum or opinion shedding some light on the reasoning employed, invite closer scrutiny, especially when the case concerns fundamental constitutional freedoms. See, Schneiderman v. United States, 320 U.S. 118, 129-131, 63 S.Ct. 1333, 87 L.Ed. 1796 (1943). The need for precision and clarity in fact-finding and the use of cold conclusory statements as a shield to prevent penetrating the absence of facts is made more significant because of the "clearly erroneous" standard, for while errors of law are always correctable by an appellate court, errors of fact rarely are, unless an appellant can scale the high wall which that standard places before him.[7] It stands to reason that unless due care is given to the process of fact finding, the reliability of the district court's conclusions will be subject to question, thus compelling a reviewing court to scrutinize the findings with a sharper eye than is ordinarily appropriate.

"A finding is 'clearly erroneous' when although there is evidence to support it, the reviewing court on the entire evidence is left with the definite and firm conviction that a mistake has been committed." United States v. United States Gypsum Co., 333 U.S. 364, 395, 68 S.Ct. 525, 542, 92 L.Ed. 746 (1948). We are of the view that except with regard to the finding concerning Mrs. Russo's refusal to recite the pledge, the "findings of facts" by the district court with respect to her dismissal are clearly erroneous.

Although Judge Burke lists six grounds for Mrs. Russo's dismissal, his findings discuss only the refusal to salute the flag and the "ceramics incident," a matter about which we shall have more to say in a moment. We are at a loss to understand what Judge Burke meant by his comments upon Mrs. Russo's "failure to follow school regulations," "her lack of cooperation," and her "failure to perform all her duties," unless these "findings" in some way refer to her failure to recite the pledge.[8] Although there was mention in the record of one occasion on which Mrs. Russo, because of some confusion, did not report for hall duty as assigned, we hardly imagine that Judge Burke gave such weight to this trivial occurrence as to attach to it three separate violations. Finally, the court found that Mrs. Russo had involved the student body in her dispute with the principal. We find no

evidence in the record to support such a finding.[9]

The ceramics incident remains an obscure contretemps characterizing the personal relationships at Sperry High School. It is obscure inasmuch as principal Loughlin's account of the occurrence was constantly interrupted by the court, making cogent narration of the event a virtual impossibility. It appears that Loughlin and three members of the school's art department, including Mrs. Russo, met on April 15, 1970 to discuss the qualifications of a teacher who had already been hired to teach ceramics the following year. At that time, Mrs. Russo made the statement that she would not teach ceramics. Loughlin testified quite clearly, however, that he had never asked Mrs. Russo to teach ceramics. Mrs. Russo's version, as she explained to the court, was that she intended her statement as advice to Mr. Loughlin, which she offered in her capacity as one of the three art department teachers present at the meeting. She did not intend to indicate a refusal to teach ceramics, for that issue was not in question. She meant only to say that if she were possessed of the minimal qualifications and training of the replacement ceramics teacher she would not undertake to teach that course. In view of Loughlin's testimony that Mrs. Russo was never asked to teach ceramics, and the fact that a new teacher had already been hired to serve that function, it simply is not believable that Mrs. Russo's statement was meant in any way as a challenge to Loughlin's authority, or that it could have been construed as such.

We are left, then, with the ultimate conclusion that Mrs. Russo's dismissal resulted directly from her refusal to engage in the school's daily flag ceremonies and that all the remaining findings were trimmings to cloak the conduct of the Board and to justify the court's conclusions. We do, however, accept the lower court's findings that school policy required teachers to lead their classes in the pledge exercise and that Mrs. Russo was aware of her responsibility in this respect.

The question, then, is whether dismissal of a high school teacher may be sustained when the sole ground for that dismissal is the teacher's refusal to comply with a school regulation which required her to participate with her class in the pledge of allegiance. To this question we now turn.

III.

If the central character in this drama were one of Mrs. Russo's students, rather than the teacher herself, we might dispose of this case with a simple reference to the Supreme Court's decision in West Virginia State Board of Education v. Barnette, supra. There the Court was of the view that "in connection with the pledge, the flag salute is a form of utterance." 319 U.S. at 632, 63 S.Ct. at 1182. "To sustain the compulsory flag salute," the Court said, "we are required to say that a Bill of Rights which guards the individual's right to speak his own mind, left it open to public authorities to compel him to utter what is not in his mind." 319 U.S. at 634, 63 S.Ct. at 1183. The Court declined to do so, and invalidated a West Virginia statute and a Board of Education resolution promulgated under its authority, that required all students to recite the pledge, or suffer expulsion from school.

Thus, there is no question but that the refusal to recite the pledge and salute the flag is a form of expression, and it matters not that the expression takes the form of silence, *see* Brown v. Louisiana, 383 U.S. 131, 86 S.Ct. 719, 15 L.Ed.2d 637 (1966). But here we are concerned with a teacher, and we are asked to determine whether the responsibilities which that teacher has voluntarily assumed, to shape and to direct the supple and still impressionable minds of her students in accordance with policies of the school board, somehow lessen the constitutional rights she would otherwise enjoy. In a related context the Supreme Court has said: "To the extent that the [lower] Court's opinion may be read to suggest that teachers may constitutionally be compelled to relinquish the First Amendment rights they would otherwise enjoy as citizens to comment on matters of public interest in connection with the operation of the public schools in which they work, it proceeds on a premise that has been unequivocally rejected in numerous prior decisions of this Court [citations omitted]. 'The theory that public employment which may be denied altogether may be subjected to any conditions, regardless of how unreasonable, has been uniformly rejected.' Keyishian v. Board of Regents [385 U.S. 589 (1970)] at 605-606, 87 S.Ct. [675] at 685, 17 L.Ed. 629." Pickering v. Board of Education, 391 U.S. 563, 568, 88 S.Ct. 1731, 1734, 20 L.Ed.2d 811 (1968); *see also* Van Alstyne, The Demise of the Right-Privilege Distinction in Constitutional Law, 81 Harv.L.Rev. 1439 (1968). Nevertheless, it is also true that society will not "tolerate undisciplined, coercive, intimidating or disruptive activities on the part of teachers or students which threaten the essential functions of our schools. . . ." James v. Board of Education, *supra,* 461 F.2d, at 568, and that Boards of Education retain substantial discretion in controlling the educational process in their schools, *see generally,* Note, Developments in the Law—Academic Freedom, 81 Harv.L.Rev. 1045, 1098 (1968). Reasonable regulations designed to effect legitimate purposes, are well within the Board's power, and will be upheld against challenge, by the courts. *See, e. g.,* Presidents Council, Dist. 25 v. Community School Board, 457 F.2d 289, (2d Cir.) cert. denied, 309 U.S. 998, 93 S.Ct. 308, 34 L.Ed.2d 260 (1972).

It has been stated that children, in many instances, have more limited First Amendment rights than do adults. *See, e. g.,* Ginsberg v. New York, 390 U.S. 629, 88 S.Ct. 1274, 20 L.Ed.2d 195 (1968) (obscenity) ; Emerson, Toward A General Theory of the First Amendment, 72 Yale L.J. 877, 938, 939 (1963); *see also,* Tinker v. Des Moines Independent School Dist., 393 U.S. 503, 512, 89 S.Ct. 733, 21 L.Ed.2d 731 (1969), (Stewart concurrence). But here, the school board, as it did in James v. Board of Education, *supra,* would have us decide that the rights enjoyed by school children are broader than the First Amendment rights of their teachers. In *James,* we declined that invitation. The *James* case, which called into question the right of a teacher to silently protest America's involvement in the Vietnam war by wearing a black armband in school, was decided after the Supreme Court's decision in *Tinker* which expressly granted that right to children, where no substantial disruption resulted from the protest. We held that Mr. James could not be dismissed from his employment as a teacher for engaging in protected expression. Similarly, in this instance, the Supreme Court's *Barnette* decision teaches that school children may not be compelled to utter the pledge of allegiance when it offends their conscientiously held beliefs to do so. There is little room in what Mr. Justice Jackson once called the "majestic generalities of the Bill of Rights," West Virginia State Board of Education v. Barnette, *supra,* 319 U.S., at 639, 63 S.Ct., at 1186, for an interpretation of the First Amendment that would be more restrictive with respect to teachers than it is with respect to their students, where there has been no interference with the requirements of appropriate discipline in the operation of the school, Tinker v. Des Moines Independent School Dist., *supra,* 393 U.S., at 509, 89 S.Ct. 733. We add, however, as we did in *James,* that nothing in the First Amendment requires a school administration to wait until disruption has actually occurred before it may take protective action. Conduct which leads, or is likely to lead, to violence in the schools is not to be tolerated. James v. Board of Education, *supra,* 461 F.2d, at 572. But such conduct is not involved in this case. We take guidance, instead, from the Supreme Court's instruction in *Tinker,* whose lesson is that neither students nor teachers "shed their constitutional rights to freedom of speech or expression at the schoolhouse gate." 393 U.S. at 506, 89 S.Ct. at 736; *see also* Hanover v. Northrup, 325 F.Supp. 170 (D. Conn.1971).[10]

Schools, of course, have a substantial interest in maintaining flag salute programs. New York's Education Law, § 802, imposes a duty upon the Commissioner of Education to prepare a program of flag salute for the public schools, and this duty has been given effect in Regulations of the New York Commissioner of Education, 8 CRRNY §§ 108.5, 108.7.[11] It is a proper, and appropriate function of our educational system to instill in young minds a healthy respect for the symbols of our national government. School officials, therefore, may enforce regulations whose purpose is to give effect to this legitimate state aim. But such regu?altions must be narrowly drawn for "[p]recision of regulation must be the touchstone in an area so closely touching our most precious freedoms." NAACP v. Button, 371 U.S. 415, 438, 83 S.Ct. 328, 340, 9 L.Ed.2d 405 (1963), quoted in the United States v. Robel, 389 U.S. 258, 265, 88 S.Ct. 419, 19 L.Ed.2d 508 (1967). Traditional First Amendment teaching requires that when "legitimate [state] concerns are expressed in a [provision] which imposes a substantial burden on protected First Amendment activities, [the state] must achieve its goal by means which have a 'less drastic' impact on the continued vitality of First Amendment freedoms." (citations omitted). United States v. Robel, supra, at 268, 88 S.Ct., at 426; see Note, Less Drastic Means and the First Amendment, 78 Yale L.J. 464 (1969). This kind of precision and less restrictive effect are noticeably lacking in the Board of Education regulations involved in this case and therefore do not meet the test of constitutional exactness required by the First Amendment.

Mrs. Russo neither disrupted her classes nor attempted to prevent her students from reciting the pledge. The record indicates that the class participated in the flag salute program each day under the capable supervision of the senior instructor, Mrs. Catherine Adams. During the pledge, Mrs. Russo acted in a way that can only be described as respectful: she stood in silence with her hands at her sides. We recall, at this point, that the April 14 action of the Board permitted protesting students to remain seated. We note, moreover, that although the federal statute which treats the pledge of allegiance, 36 U.S.C. § 172, suggests that the pledge be rendered by placing the hand over the heart, it also provides that "civilians will always show full respect to the flag when the pledge is given merely by standing at attention. . . . "

In view of all the circumstances in this case, it is clear that the state's interest in maintaining a flag salute program was well-served in Mrs. Russo's classroom, even without her participation in the pledge ceremonies. We do well to note that her pupils were not fresh out of their cradles: she had charge of a tenth grade homeroom class consisting of students ranging in ages between fourteen and sixteen years. Young men and women at this stage of development are approaching an age when they form their own judgments. They readily perceive the existence of conflicts in the world around them; indeed, unless we are to screen them from all newspapers and television, it will be only a rather isolated teenager who does not have some understanding of the political divisions that exist and have existed in this country. Nor is this knowledge something to be dreaded. As we said in James, "schools must play a central role in preparing their students to think and analyze and to recognize the demagogue." Mrs. Russo made no attempt to proselytize her students. Instead, she provided her high school students with a second, but quiet, side of the not altogether new flag-salute debate: one teacher led the class in recitation of the pledge, the other remained standing in respectful silence. There is nothing to indicate that this demonstration had any effect—certainly no evidence of a destructive effect—on Mrs. Russo's students. Indeed, had it not been for the Board's precipitous action in dismissing her, the very fact that Mrs. Russo was permitted to refrain from saluting the flag would clearly have been evidence to her students that the injustice and intolerance against which she was quietly protesting was not merely not well-founded but a demonstrable falsehood at least within the confines of one school's homeroom class.

VI.

By our holding today we do not mean to limit the traditionally broad discretion that has always rested with local school authorities to prescribe curriculum, set classroom standards, and evalute conduct of teachers and students "in light of the special characteristics of the school environment." James v. Board of Education, supra. Nor do we imply that school officials are limited in their power to dismiss inept or obstreperous instructors, except, of course, to the extent they choose to so limit themselves. Public employment is not a sinecure to be retained regardless of merit simply by shouting loudly that any threat of dismissal is motivated by an anti-First Amendment animus. But where in fact, as in this case, a dismissal is directed because a teacher has engaged in constitutionally protected activity, that dismissal may not stand.

We emphasize, too, that despite our holding that Mrs. Russo may not be dismissed for refusing to pledge allegiance to the flag, we do not share her views. But because the First Amendment ranks among the most important of our constitutional rights we must recognize that the precious right of free speech requires protection even when the speech is personally obnoxious. Freedom of expression, as we said in James, requires "breathing room." Patriotism, particularly at a time when that virtuous quality appears much maligned, should not be the object of derision. But patriotism that is forced is a false patriotism just as loyalty that is coerced is the very antithesis of loyalty. We ought not impugn the loyalty of a citizen—especially one whose convictions appear to be as genuine and conscientious as Mrs. Russo's—merely for refusing to pledge allegiance, any more than we ought necessarily to praise the loyalty of a citizen who without conviction or meaning, and with mental reservation, recites the pledge by rote each morning. Surely patriotism and loyalty go deeper than that.

It is our conclusion that the right to remain silent in the face of an illegitimate demand for speech is as much a part of First Amendment protections as the right to speak out in the face of an illegitimate demand for silence, *see* Sweezy v. New Hampshire, 354 U.S. 234, 77 S.Ct. 1203, 1 L.Ed.2d 1311 (1957); West Virginia State Board of Education v. Barnette, *supra.* Beliefs, particularly when they touch on sensitive questions of faith, when they involve not easily articulated intuitions concerning religion, nation, flag, liberty and justice, are most at home in a realm of privacy, and are happiest in that safe and secluded harbour of the mind that protects our innermost thoughts. To compel a person to speak what is not in his mind offends the very principles of tolerance and understanding which for so long have been the foundation of our great land. "If there is any fixed star in our constitutional constellation," Mr. Justice Jackson said in *Barnette*, "it is that no official, high or petty, can prescribe what shall be orthodox in politics, nationalism, religion, or other matters of opinion or force citizens to confess by word or act their faith therein. If there are any circumstances which permit an exception, they do not now occur to us." West Virginia State Board of Education v. Barnette, *supra*, 319 U.S., at 642, 63 S.Ct., at 1187. We believe that to be an accurate and thoughtful statement of the underlying spirit of the First Amendment and we abide by it here.

Accordingly, the judgment is reversed, and the case is remanded to the district court for proceedings not inconsistent with this opinion.

NOTES

1. The portion of Bennett's report, listed as "Summary and Recommendations" appears below:

    I have taken the opportunity to "pass through" several of Mrs. Russo's classes throughout the year and observe her students at work and I have observed her Studio in Art class for an entire period. The current project in that class is a work, preferably in 3-D or a stylistic interpretation, involving social commentary.

    Comments—

    Mrs. Russo has a congenial, relaxed personality and meets students at their level. The pupil-teacher relationship has always appeared quite good.

    Teaching methods and techniques appear to be resourceful and appropriate to individualized instruction in a creative atmosphere. The teacher adopts the role of resource person and helper—guiding individual initiative.

    The teacher plans basic time periods for each project but is flexible in regard to completion time so as to allow for individual differences. Those that finish a project early are encouraged to practice drawing and painting skills.

    Student participation has generally appeared to be at a high school level—most seem busy at work generally.

    "....."

    By this account, Mrs. Russo appears to have been an exemplary teacher.

2. New York Education Law sec. 3012, Tenure, provides:

    1. Teachers, principals, supervisors and all other members of the teaching and supervising staff shall be appointed by the board of education ... upon the recommendation of [the] superintendent of schools, for a probationary period of three years. The service of a person appointed to any of such positions may be discontinued at any time during such probationary period, on the recommendation of the superintendent of schools, by a majority vote of the board of education.

    2. At the expiration of the probationary term of a person appointed for such term, subject to the conditions of this section, the superintendent of schools shall make a written report to the board of education recommending for appointment on tenure those persons who have been found competent, efficient and satisfactory....

3. 42 U.S.C. sec. 1983, Civil Action for Deprivation of Rights provides:

    Every person who, under color of any statute, ordinance, regulation, custom, or usage, of any State or Territory, subjects, or causes to be subjected, any citizen of the United States or other person within the jurisdiction thereof to the deprivation of any rights, privileges, or immunities secured by the Constitution and laws, shall be liable to the party injured in an action at law, suit in equity, or other proceeding for redress.

4. 28 U.S.C. sec. 1343. Civil Rights and Elective Franchise, provides:

    The district courts shall have original jurisdiction of any civil action authorized by law to be commenced by any person:

    *   *   *

    (3) To redress the deprivation, under color of any State law, statute, ordinance, regulation, custom or usage, of any right, privilege or immunity secured by the Constitution of the United States or by any Act of Congress providing for equal rights of citizens or of all persons within the jurisdiction of the United States;

    (4) To recover damages or to secure equitable or other relief under any Act of Congress providing for the protection of civil rights, including the right to vote.

5. We reach the merits here because Mrs. Russo did not have any state administrative remedies to exhaust before filing this action under 42 U.S.C. sec. 1983, *see* Eisen v. Eastman, 421 F.2d. 560 (2d Cir. 1969), cert. denied, 400 U.S. 841, 91 S.Ct. 82, 27 L.Ed.2d 75 (1970). Mrs. Russo did file a grievance notice pursuant to the contractual grievance procedure in the district. The

Superintendent of Schools informed Mrs. Russo that non-renewal determinations of probationary teachers were not subject to grievance procedures. Of course, exhaustion of state judicial remedies is not a predicate to a federal court's jurisdiction in a sec. 1983 claim, Monroe v. Pape, 365 U.S. 167, 81 S.Ct. 473, 5 L.Ed.2d 492 (1961); Sostre v. McGinnis, 442 F.2d 178 (2d Cir. 1971) (en banc), cert. denied, 404 U.S. 1049, 92 S.Ct. 719, 30 L.Ed.2d 740 (1972).

6. Because we hold that Mrs. Russo was dismissed solely because of the exercise of her First Amendment rights we need not decide what effect the Supreme Court's recent decisions in Board of Regents v. Roth, 408 U.S. 564, 92 S.Ct. 2701, 33 L.Ed.2d 548 (1972) and Perry v. Sindermann, 408 U.S. 593, 92 S.Ct. 2694, 33 L.Ed.2d 570 (1972), might have on future dismissals of probationary teachers in New York. We note only that by statute, probationary teachers in New York are hired for a period of three years. Whether this is a sufficient period to establish the kind of "claim of entitlement" which the Court spoke of in *Sindermann* as being in the nature of a property right in employment that triggers the application of procedural safeguards before such a claim may be taken away is a question we leave for another day. In this context, however, we note the admirable efforts of the New York legislature to afford protection to probationers. A recent 1972 amendment to New York's Education Law specifically requires that teachers who are not recommended for tenure or who are recommended for dismissal henceforth will be entitled to a written statement giving the reasons for such recommendation. New York Education Law § 3031, McKinney's Sessions Laws, c. 866, 1972.

7. *See,* United States v. Forness, 125 F.2d 928 (2d Cir.) cert. denied, City of Salamanca v. United States, 316 U.S. 694, 62 S.Ct. 1293, 86 L.Ed. 1764 (1942). Judge Frank, for the court wrote:

> Chief Justice Hughes once remarked, "An unscrupulous administrator might be tempted to say 'Let me find the facts for the people of my country, and I care little who lays down the general principles.'" That comment should be extended to include facts found without due care as well as unscrupulous fact-finding: for such lack of due care is less likely to reveal itself than lack of scruples, which, we trust, seldom exists. And Chief Justice Hughes' comment is just as applicable to the careless fact-finding of a judge as to that of an administrative officer. The judiciary properly holds administrative officers to high standards in the discharge of the fact-finding function. The judiciary should at least measure up to the same standards.

> 125 F.2d at 942.

8. Loughlin's testimony at trial would appear to indicate that this is indeed the case. He said: "I also told the school board that she [Russo] had failed to comply with school regulations. It happened to be saluting the flag, but it was a school regulation. . . ." Loughlin also offered testimony that indicated that the failure to salute and the ceramics incident were the only significant factors involved in the decision to dismiss Mrs. Russo. He said: "I stated to the Board, as I had to the Superintendent, that I would not recommend Mrs. Russo because she had been insubordinate in refusing to follow a school regulation. And this coupled with her attitude on the statement she made concerning not teaching ceramics generally was the basis (for non-renewal)."

The extent to which Loughlin was influenced by Mrs. Russo's silent refusal to salute the flag is well-illustrated by a teacher "observation" report he filed concerning Mrs. Russo's classroom performance. The report rates Mrs. Russo's "professional characteristics" as "below average" or "poor" in five of six categories, and concludes with the comment: "Mrs. Russo, a first year teacher, has not met her responsibilities to my satisfaction." The report is dated June, 1970, and appears to refer to the entire 1969-1970 school year. Curiously, Loughlin did not see fit to submit a report about Mrs. Russo's classroom performance until he decided to dismiss her, and he did not decide to dismiss her until he learned of her refusal to participate in the pledge exercise. When Loughlin's report is contrasted with Bennett's glowing evaluation, submitted two months earlier, Loughlin's "observation" clearly appears to have been an after-thought and a mere contrivance to establish non-first amendment grounds to justify Mrs. Russo's dismissal.

9. There is some evidence in the record that the school's student body president discussed Mrs. Russo's situation in the school lunchroom, but there is not the slightest hint that Mrs. Russo encouraged him to do so. Indeed, there is evidence indicating that when Mrs. Russo learned of the situation she asked the boy to stop speaking. A petition was circulated by certain students in Mrs. Russo's behalf. Again there is no evidence even tending to show that she encouraged that activity.

10. In Hanover v. Northrup, *supra,* a district court, per Blumenfeld, J., applied the test of *Tinker* and held that the refusal of a teacher to lead or recite the pledge was expression which could not be forbidden at the risk of loss of employment.

11. New York Education Law § 802. Instruction Relating to Flag: Holidays

> 1. It shall be the duty of the commissioner of education to prepare, for the use of the public schools of the state, a program providing for a salute to the flag and a daily pledge of allegiance to the flag, for instruction in its correct use and display and such other patriotic exercises as may be deemed by him to be expedient, under such regulations and instructions as may best meet the varied requirements of the different grades in such schools.

> Regulations of the Commissioner of Education.

> 108.5 Pledge to the Flag. (a) It is recommended that schools use the following pledge to the flag:

> "I pledge allegiance to the flag of the United States of America and to the Republic for which it stands, one Nation, under God, indivisible, with liberty and justice for all."

> (b) In giving the pledge to the flag, the procedure is to render the pledge by standing with the right hand over the heart.

> 108.7 Other Instructions. Instruction concerning the flag as a symbol of American life should not be limited to the observance of Flag Day. Before leaving the elementary school each child should come to think of himself as a "maker of the flag" and each pupil who passes through the secondary school should be guided in sober thought as to the meaning of "liberty and justice for all."

THE United States Court of Appeals, Ninth Circuit, decides for a student who had been suspended for bringing onto the high school campus signs protesting the school's refusal to renew the teaching contract of an English instructor; part of the protest involved a planned "walkout" at an athletic awards ceremony and students staging a "walkout" from classes. In deciding for the student, the Court declared: "That the primary reason for suspension was the sign activity is . . . demonstrated by the fact that the school officials would have shortened the suspension to three days if he had agreed to refrain from bringing similar signs onto the campus. The sign activity in this case constituted the exercise of pure speech rather than conduct. . . . As such, it comes within the protective umbrella of the First Amendment."

Karp v. *Becken,* 477 F.2d 171 (1973)

WALLACE, Circuit Judge:

Appellant brought this action in the District Court pursuant to the Civil Rights Act (42 U.S.C. § 1983) for alleged violation of his First Amendment rights. The action was brought against school officials (appellees) who suspended appellant for five days from Canyon del Oro High School in Pima County, Arizona. Appellant sought to enjoin the school officials permanently from enforcing the suspension order. After a trial, the District Court entered findings of fact and conclusions of law in favor of the school officials.

Several students, including appellant, planned a chant and "walkout" at an athletic awards ceremony which was to be held at the high school in order to protest the refusal of the school to renew the teaching contract of an English instructor. Appellant gave notice of the plans to the news media the day before it was to occur, apparently resulting in an article about the planned walkout in the morning paper on the day of the assembly.

Before the ceremony began, the school officials were told by student body officers that if a "walkout" did take place, certain members of the Lettermen Club (the school athletes) would likely attempt to prevent it. Fearing a possibly violent confrontation, the school officials cancelled the assembly. Notwithstanding the cancellation, some students did stage a "walkout" from classes.

As part of his efforts to publicize a demonstration to be held later in the morning, appellant again notified the news media. During the lunch hour, students and newsmen gathered in the area of the school's multi-purpose room. At one point, appellant, who had been at this gathering, went out to his car in the parking lot and brought back signs supporting the English instructor and distributed them to other students.

The Vice-Principal ordered the students to surrender their signs, claiming they were not permitted to have them. There was no specific rule prohibiting the bringing of signs on campus.[1] All signs were surrendered immediately except those held by appellant. He asserted a Constitutional right to have and distribute the signs. When asked a second time, appellant gave up the signs and then accompanied the Vice-Principal into the administrative office, upon the latter's request. While appellant was in the administrative office, students began chanting, and pushing and shoving developed between the demonstrators and some Lettermen. Shortly after intervention by school officials, the demonstration broke up.

A couple of days later, after consultation with appellant's parents (who were out of town at the time of the activities noted), school officials advised appellant he was to be suspended for five days. School officials then offered to reduce the suspension to three days if appellant would agree to refrain from bringing similar signs on the campus. Appellant and his father refused to make such an agreement.

The difficulties inherent in federal court supervision of disciplinary problems in the 23,390 public school systems of this country were anticipated by Justice Black in his dissent in Tinker v. Des Moines School District, 393 U.S. 503, 515, 89 S.Ct. 733, 21 L.Ed.2d 731 (1962).[2] The reason for his concern is amply demonstrated in this case, which presents a conflict between asserted Constitutional rights and good-faith actions by school officials.

Tinker, of course, provides the standards. It is clear that public high school students have a right to freedom of speech which is not shed at the schoolhouse gates. 393 U.S. at 506, 511, 89 S.Ct. 733. However, it is equally clear that the daily administration of public education is committed to school officials. Epperson v. Arkansas, 393 U.S. 97, 104, 89 S.Ct. 266, 21 L.Ed.2d 228 (1968). That responsibility carries with it the inherent authority to prescribe and control conduct in the schools. When conflict does arise, *Tinker* then provides that the students' rights to free speech may not be abridged in the absence of "facts which might reasonably have led school authorities to forecast substantial disruption of or material interference with school activities . . . ." 393 U.S. at 514, 89 S.Ct. at 740. Thus, the courts have recognized that the interest of a state in the maintenance of its educational system is a compelling one, provoking a balancing of First Amendment rights with a state's efforts to preserve and protect its educational process. Bayless v. Martine, 430 F.2d 873, 877 (5th Cir. 1970); Burnside v. Byars, 363 F.2d 744, 748 (5th Cir. 1966).

The *Tinker* rule is simply stated; application, however, is more difficult. Years ago, in a free speech case, Chief Justice Vinson noted "that neither Justice Holmes nor Justice Brandeis ever envisioned that a shorthand phrase should be crystallized into a rigid rule to be applied inflexibly without regard to the circumstances of each case." Dennis v. United States, 341 U.S. 494, 508, 71 S.Ct. 857, 866, 95 L.Ed. 1137 (1951). The shorthand phrase referred to in *Dennis* was "clear and present danger," but the remarks are equally appropriate to "substantial disruption or material interference"; federal courts should treat the *Tinker* rule as a flexible one dependent upon the totality of relevant facts in each case. See Grayned v. City of Rockford, 408 U.S. 104, 119, 92 S.Ct. 2294, 33 L.Ed.2d 222 (1972).

The difficulty of application is even more pronounced because disruptive conduct was absent in *Tinker;* there were "no disturbances or disorders on the school premises. . . ." 393 U.S. at 514, 89 S.Ct. at 740. The *Tinker* court borrowed the phraseology of the rule from the Fifth Circuit decision in Burnside v. Byars, *supra;* but there too, disruption or interference was absent, there being only a "mild curiosity." 363 F.2d at 748. Consequently, the two cases which provided the rule give little assistance in its application to specific facts. However, the Fifth Circuit panel which decided *Burnside* also decided Blackwell v. Issaquena County Board of Education, 363 F.2d 749 (5th Cir. 1966). In *Blackwell*, they found more than a "mild curiosity"; in fact, "there was an unusual degree of commotion, boisterous conduct, a collision with the rights of others, an undermining of authority, and a lack of order, discipline and decorum." 363 F.2d at 754. Evidently, such conduct resulted in substantial

disruption, for the court upheld a regulation banning the wearing of buttons though the regulation was similar to the one struck down in *Burnside.*

Thus, mild curiosity alone will not justify abridgement though Blackwellian disorder and disruption will. The question presented by the present case is whether incidents falling between the two extremes might also permit the imposition of restraints. For three reasons, we believe so. First, the First Amendment does not require school officials to wait until disruption actually occurs before they may act.[3] In fact, they have a duty to prevent the occurrence of disturbances. Second, *Tinker* does not demand a certainty that disruption will occur, but rather the existence of facts which might reasonably lead school officials to forecast substantial disruption. 393 U.S. at 514, 89 S.Ct. 733. And finally, because of the state's interest in education, the level of disturbance required to justify official intervention is relatively lower in a public school than it might be on a street corner.

It should also be obvious that the actions of one claiming free speech abridgement on a school campus cannot be dissected from reality and observed in a vacuum. The same false cry of "fire" may be permissible in an empty theater, but certainly not when there is a capacity crowd. Schenk v. United States, 249 U.S. 47, 52, 39 S.Ct. 247, 63 L.Ed. 470 (1919) (Holmes, J.). The striking of a match may have no effect in an open field, but be lethal in a closed room filled with gases. Similarly, in making a determination in this case, in addition to consideration of the acts of appellant, all other circumstances confronting the school administrators which might reasonably portend disruption must be evaluated.

The court in *Tinker* emphasized that there was no evidence documenting the school officials' forecast of disruption of the educational processes. 393 U.S. at 508-509, 514, 89 S.Ct. 733.[4] In contrast, the record here reflects the following facts, justifying a reasonable forecast of material interference with the school's work:

1. On the morning involved, there was a newspaper article relating to the planned assembly walkout. The article indicated that the newspaper's source of information was a reporter's conversation with appellant.

2. The highschool Principal and other school officials testified that the school athletes had threatened to stop the proposed demonstration.

3. The assembly was cancelled because school officials feared a walkout might provoke violence.

4. Later in the morning, newsmen appeared on the campus and set up their equipment. During this time, appellant and other students, during a free period, were milling around outside the building talking with these newsmen.

5. The Vice-Principal testified to his impression that there was a general atmosphere of excitement and expectation pervading the campus and classrooms. There was an intense feeling something was about to happen.

6. Some students actually walked out from class, notwithstanding the cancellation of the assembly.

7. About the time when the assembly walkout would have occurred, someone pulled the school fire alarm, which, had it not been previously disconnected by the Vice-Principal, would have emptied every room in the entire school.

8. Approximately fifty students gathered in the area of the multi-purpose room who talked among themselves and with news media personnel.

9. Excited by the situation, twenty to thirty of the junior high students who share facilities with the highschool and who were eating at the highschool cafeteria during their lunch period, interrupted their lunch and ran into the area of the multi-purpose room to watch the group of students and news people gathered there. The junior high students ran about the group excitedly and, as a result, their supervisors determined their lunch period should be shortened and they were returned to their classrooms earlier than usual.

10. Appellant went to the school parking lot and took the signs from his car to the area where the students had congregated near the multi-purpose room and proceeded to distribute them.

In view of these facts, the sole question is whether this evidence is substantial enough to support the school officials' forecast of a reasonable likelihood of substantial disruption. The temptation to be a "Monday morning quarterback" should be resisted—focus should be upon whether the apprehension of the school officials was unreasonable under the circumstances. The officials in *Tinker* anticipated a level of disruption which did not justify curtailment of free speech. The officials in this case testified, and the trier of fact apparently believed, that they feared the provocation of an incident, including possible violence, and that they took the signs from the appellant in an effort to prevent such an incident. Considering all the facts, we do not find that such an anticipation, or forecast, was unreasonable.

However, a determination that the school officials were justified in taking the signs from appellant (and thus curtailing his exercise of claimed First Amendment rights) does not terminate our inquiry. The second question is whether the school officials properly suspended him from school for five days. The district court found that the suspension resulted from "his activities in connection with the planned 'walkout', the demonstration, and, principally, because of his con-

duct in bringing the signs on campus and attempting to distribute them." That the primary reason for suspension was the sign activity is further demonstrated by the fact that the school officials would have shortened the suspension to three days if he had agreed to refrain from bringing similar signs onto the campus.

The sign activity in this case constituted the exercise of pure speech rather than conduct. Cohen v. California, 403 U.S. 15, 18-19, 91 S.Ct. 1780, 29 L. Ed.2d 284 (1971); *Tinker, supra,* 393 U.S. at 508, 89 S.Ct. 733. As such, it comes within the protective umbrella of the First Amendment. We have already held that school officials may curtail the exercise of First Amendment rights when they can reasonably forecast material interference or substantial disruption. However, for discipline resulting from the use of pure speech to pass muster under the First Amendment, the school officials have the burden to show justification for their action. Here they failed to do so. Absent justification, such as a violation of a statute or school rule, they cannot discipline a student for exercising those rights. The balancing necessary to enable school officials to maintain discipline and order allows curtailment but not necessarily punishment. Consequently, appellant could not be suspended for his activities with the signs. We need not reach the question of whether the remaining two of the three reasons for the suspension were constitutionally permissible. There is no way to determine, based upon this record, what part of the five days was solely for the sign activities. Therefore, we are left with no choice but to invalidate the entire suspension.

What we have said does not mean that the school officials could not have suspended appellant for violating an existing reasonable rule. In fact, in securing the signs, he broke a regulation by going to the parking lot during school hours. However, this was not a basis of the suspension. See Eisner v. Stamford Board of Education, 440 F.2d 803 (2d Cir. 1971). We have only held that, under the circumstances of this case, appellant could not be suspended on the sole basis of his exercising pure free speech when no justification was demonstrated.

Reversed and remanded for further proceedings consistent with this opinion.

NOTES

1. The absence of a specific regulation prohibiting signs is not a constitutional flaw. *See* Richards v. Thurston, 424 F.2d 1281, 1282 (1st Cir. 1970).
2. *See also* Karr v. Schmidt, 401 U.S. 1201, 91 S.Ct. 592, 27 L.Ed.2d 797 (Black, Circuit Justice, 1971). As of the decision in Karr v. Schmidt, 460 F.2d 609 (5th Cir.) (en banc), cert. denied, 409 U.S. 989, 93 S.Ct. 307, 34 L.Ed.2d 256 (1972), the federal circuit courts had in-

vested the time necessary to decide at least twenty-two cases involving the length of student hair.

3. *See* Butts v. Dallas Independent School Dist., 436 F.2d 728, 731 (5th Cir. 1971); Norton v. Discipline Comm. of E. Tenn. State Univ., 419 F.2d 195, 199 (6th Cir. 1969),

cert. denied, 399 U.S. 906, 90 S.Ct. 2191, 26 L.Ed.2d 562 (1970).

4. *See also* Butts v. Dallas Independent School Dist., 436 F.2d 728, 731 (5th Cir. 1971); Burnside v. Byars, 363 F.2d 744, 748 (5th Cir. 1966).

THE United States Court of Appeals, Second Circuit, decides for a senior at Shaker High School in Latham, New York, who had refused to participate in the Pledge of Allegiance because he believed "that there [isn't] liberty and justice for all in the United States." In deciding for the student, who refused to leave the classroom during the pledge and refused to stand during the salute ceremony, the Court stated: "If the state cannot compel participation in the pledge, it cannot punish non-participation. And being required to leave the classroom during the pledge may reasonably be viewed by some as having that effect, however benign defendants' motives may be. . . . while we do not share plaintiff's resistance to pledging allegiance to this nation, his reservations of belief must be protected. In time, perhaps, he will recognize that such protection is sound ground for a firmer trust in his country."

Goetz v. *Ansell,* 477 F.2d 636 (1973)

FEINBERG, Circuit Judge:

Plaintiff Theodore Goetz, a senior at Shaker High School in Latham, New York, an honor student and the president of his class, refuses to participate in the Pledge of Allegiance because he believes "that there [isn't] liberty and justice for all in the United States." Defendants George S. Ansell, President of the Board of Education of North Colonie Central School District, Charles Szuberla, Superintendent of Schools in that district, the Board of Education of the district, and Arthur E. Walker, principal of Shaker High School, have offered plaintiff the option of either leaving the room or standing silently during the pledge ceremony. But plaintiff maintains that he has a first amendment right to remain quietly seated, even though if he adheres to that position, he faces suspension from school. This is the basis of his action brought by his next friend Jane Sanford in the United States District Court for the Northern District of New York under 42 U.S.C § 1983. After a hearing before Chief Judge James T. Foley on plaintiff's application for a preliminary injunction, the judge dismissed the complaint for failure to exhaust administrative remedies and, alternatively, ruled against plaintiff on the merits. We conclude that both rulings were erroneous.

I

Judge Foley clearly had in mind that "[a]ny person conceiving himself aggrieved" by the act of a school official may, under N.Y.Educ.Law § 310, McKinney's Consol.Laws, c. 16, appeal to the New York State Commissioner of Education. The judge also referred in his opinion to a possible appeal to defendant Board of Education. Putting to one side the question whether the doctrine of exhaustion of administrative remedies still applies in a section 1983 suit,[1] invoking it on these facts was clearly unwarranted. The Board of Education had ruled on the precise point only a year earlier in a case involving plaintiff's older brother; indeed, plaintiff had testified before the Board as a witness in that case. Thus, this remedy was "certainly or probably futile." Eisen v. Eastman, supra note 1, 421 F.2d at 569. Similarly, the State Commissioner of Education had ruled on the issue in 1970, holding that requiring a student "either to stand silently or to leave the classroom" did not infringe his rights.[2] The Commissioner cited that decision with implicit approval the following year,[3] and thereafter issued guidelines that indicated no subsequent change of heart.[4] Under these circumstances, there was no real remedy to exhaust.[5]

II

This brings us to the merits of plaintiff's case. In West Virginia State Board of Education v. Barnette, 319 U.S. 624, 63 S.Ct. 1178, 87 L.Ed. 1628 (1943), the Court made clear, in Mr. Justice Jackson's memorable words, that

no official, high or petty, can prescribe what shall be orthodox in politics, nationalism, religion, or other matters of opinion or force citizens to confess by word or act their faith therein.

Id. at 642, 63 S.Ct. at 1187. It is true that the Court dealt in that case with the compulsion of saluting the flag and reciting the pledge, whereas here plaintiff is given the option of standing silently. But the Court in *Barnette* was aware that the state might demand other "gestures of acceptance or respect: . . . a bowed or bared head, a bended knee," id. at 632, 63 S.Ct. at 1182, and reiterated that the state may not compel students to affirm their loyalty "by word or act." Id. at 642, 63 S.Ct. 1178. In this case, the act of standing is itself part of the pledge. New York State Regulations so provide;[6] and standing "is no less a gesture of acceptance and respect than is the salute or the utterance of the words of allegiance." Banks v. Board of Public Instruction, 314 F.Supp. 285, 296 (S.D. Fla.1970) (three-judge court), aff'd mem., 450 F.2d 1103 (5th Cir. 1971).[7] Therefore, the alternative offered plaintiff of standing in silence is an act that cannot be compelled over his deeply held convictions. It can no more be required than the pledge itself.

Defendants point out, however, that plaintiff has the option of leaving the classroom; he is not, as in *Barnette*, excluded from the school. While we agree that the effect upon plaintiff of adhering to his convictions is far less drastic than in *Barnette*, we do not believe that this disposes of the case. If the state cannot compel participation in the pledge, it cannot punish non-participation. And being required to leave the classroom during the pledge may reasonably be viewed by some as having that effect, however benign defendants' motives may be. See Abington School District v. Schempp, 374 U.S. 203, 292, 83 S.Ct. 1560, 1608, 10 L.Ed.2d 844 (1963) (Brennan, J., concurring) ("[T]he excluded pupil loses caste with his fellows, and is liable to be regarded with aversion, and subjected to reproach and insult.").

Recognizing the force of *Barnette* and of Tinker v. Des Moines Independent Community School District, 393 U.S. 503, 89 S.Ct. 733, 21 L.Ed.2d 731 (1969) (upholding right of students to wear black arm band), defendants concede that plaintiff has a protected first amendment right not to participate in the pledge. They argue, however, that the other students also have rights and that *Tinker* does not protect conduct that

> materially disrupts classwork or involves substantial disorder or invasion of the rights of others. . . .

Id. at 513, 89 S.Ct. at 740. The argument is sound, but the facts of this case do not justify applying it. There is no evidence here of disruption of classwork or disorder or invasion of the rights of others. The record is just to the contrary: Plaintiff took a poll of his approximately 30 classmates; 25 said that it did not disturb them that plaintiff had remained seated during the pledge earlier in the year and the other five he "could not contact or else they did not see" him. Defendants ask where, if plaintiff prevails, the line is to be drawn. May plaintiff "kneel, lie down, stand on his hands? May he make derisive motions?"[8] Those situations are not before us,

and we doubt that they will occur in the North Colonie Central School District, any more than they have occurred in the New York City school system after Judge Judd's decision in Frain v. Baron, supra note 4, which wholly accepted plaintiff's position. Of course, if such disruptive acts should occur, we would have no hesitancy in holding them unprotected. But we do not believe that a silent, non-disruptive expression of belief by sitting down may similarly be prohibited.[9] While we do not share plaintiff's resistance to pledging allegiance to this nation, his reservations of belief must be protected. In time, perhaps, he will recognize that such protection is sound ground for a firmer trust in his country.

Judgment reversed.

NOTES

1. See H. Friendly, Federal Jurisdiction: A General View 100 & n. 111 (1973) (discussing Eisen v. Eastman, 421 F.2d 560, 569 (2d Cir. 1969), cert. denied, 400 U.S. 841, 91 S.Ct. 82, 27 L.Ed.2d 75 (1970)); Russo v. Central School District No. 1, 469 F.2d 623, 628 n. 5 (2d Cir. 1972), cert. denied, 411 U.S. 932, 93 S.Ct. 1899, 36 L.Ed.2d 391 (1973); James v. Board of Education, 461 F.2d 566, 570-571 (2d Cir. 1972), cert. denied, 409 U.S. 1042, 93 S.Ct. 529, 34 L.Ed.2d 491 (1972). But see Carter v. Stanton, 405 U.S. 669, 670-671, 92 S.Ct. 1232, 31 L.Ed.2d 569 (1972) (per curiam); Wilwording v. Swenson, 404 U.S. 249, 251-252, 92 S.Ct. 407, 30 L.Ed.2d 418 (1971) (per curiam).
2. In re Bielenberg, 9 Ed.Dept.Rep. 196 (1970).
3. In re Bustin, 10 Ed.Dept.Rep. 168, 169 (1971).
4. New York State Education Dep't, Guidelines for Students Rights and Responsibilities 16 (undated pamphlet), which, while citing a recent district court decision upholding the Commissioner's position, Richards v. Board of Education, 70-C-625 (E.D.N.Y. July 10, 1970), unaccountably makes no reference to a decision of the same court enjoining enforcement of this very rule in New York City schools. Frain v. Baron, 307 F.Supp. 27 (E.D.N.Y.1969).
5. This probably explains why defendants do not press the exhaustion argument on appeal.
6. "In giving the pledge to the flag, the procedure is to render the pledge by *standing* with the right hand over the heart." 8 CRRNY § 108.5(b). (Emphasis added.)
7. The decision of the three-judge court in *Banks* was appealed to the Supreme Court, which vacated and remanded "so that a fresh decree may be entered from which a timely appeal may be taken to the United States Court of Appeals. . . ." 401 U.S. 988, 91 S.Ct. 1223, 28 L.Ed.2d 526 (1971). The single judge then entered an order adopting the findings of fact and conclusions of law of the three-judge court concerning the first amendment issue. This order was then affirmed by the circuit court, as indicated in the text.
8. Appellees' Brief, at 8.
9. Contrary to defendants' suggestion, this court's decision in Russo v. Central School District No. 1, supra note 1, does not represent a rejection of the holding in Frain v. Baron, supra note 4, and is in no sense contrary to the result that we reach here.

THE United States Court of Appeals, Third Circuit, declares unconstitutional that part of the New Jersey statutory provision which required students to stand at attention during the Pledge of Allegiance. In deciding for Deborah Lipp, a sixteen year old pupil who had objected to the requirement that she stand during the pledge, the Court stated: "*Banks* and *Goetz* are precisely on point. They interdict the State from requiring a student to engage in what amounts to implicit expression by standing at respectful attention while the flag salute is being administered and being participated in by other students."

Lipp v. *Morris,* 579 F.2d 834 (1978)

PER CURIAM:

This case involves the constitutionality of a New Jersey statute requiring school students to stand at attention during the salute to the flag. The appeal brings before the court two questions: (1) Did the District Judge abuse his discretion in declining to abstain because the New Jersey statute involved here is clear and unambiguous, and (2) Is the statute unconstitutional because it compels an affirmation of belief or punishes protected activity in violation of the First and Fourteenth Amendments of the Constitution of the United States.

District Judge H. Curtis Meanor held for the plaintiff, severed the following language of a New Jersey statute (N.J.Stat.Ann. § 18A:36-3(c), and declared this segment to be unconstitutional;[1] . . . but shall be required to show full respect to the flag while the pledge is being given merely by standing at attention . . .[2] We affirm.

Plaintiff, Deborah Lipp, a 16-year-old, alleged that because the statute directed that she stand during the recitation of the pledge of allegiance to the flag, compelling her to make what she termed a "symbolic gesture," it violated her rights under the First and Fourteenth Amendments. The action was brought under 42 U.S.C. § 1983 (1970). Plaintiff was a student at Mountain Lakes High School, New Jersey. Defendants were Harry Morris, principal of the high school; Robert Lautenstack, president of the board of education; and William F. Hyland, attorney general of New Jersey. Plaintiff emphasized that in her belief, the words of the pledge were not true and she stood only because she had been threatened if she did not do so.

Defendant argues first that the district court should have abstained from ruling on the constitutionality of the New Jersey statute to permit a New Jersey court to construe the law and thereby avoid a decision on federal constitutional grounds. The clearest answer to this argument is the statement of the District Judge which we adopt: "I can only do that [abstain] where the statute is open to an alternative construction which would avoid the Constitutional issue. This statute permits no such construction. It's plain, simple, blunt English." As the U.S. Supreme Court said in *Zwickler* v. *Koota*, 389 U.S. 241, 251 n.14, 88 S.Ct. 391, 397, 19 L.Ed.2d 444 (1967):

We have frequently emphasized that abstention is not to be ordered unless the state statute is of an uncertain nature, and is obviously susceptible of a limiting construction.

Here we hold that the statute is not of an uncertain nature and, therefore, the case does not qualify for application of the abstention doctrine.

Secondly, defendant asserts that being required to stand while others engage in the flag salute ceremony is in no way a violation of the First and Fourteenth Amendments. The attorney general of New Jersey argues that mere standing does not rise to the level of "symbolic speech." Defendant suggests that standing silently is the same as just remaining seated, and that by the simple act of standing, the plaintiff in no way engages in protected activity.

Citing *Board of Education* v. *Barnette*, 319 U.S. 624, 63 S.Ct. 1178, 87 L.Ed. 1628 (1943); *Goetz* v. *Ansell*, 477 F.2d 636 (2nd Cir. 1973), and *Banks* v. *Board of Public Instruction*, 314 F.Supp. 285 (S.D.Fla. 1970),[3] Deborah Lipp urges that her right to remain silent and not to be forced to stand springs directly from the precise First Amendment right against compelled participation in the flag ceremony recognized in *Barnette*.

Banks and *Goetz* are precisely on point. They interdict the state from requiring a student to engage in what amounts to implicit expression by standing at respectful attention while the flag salute is being administered and being participated in by other students. *Cf. Wooley* v. *Maynard*, 430 U.S. 705, 97 S.Ct. 1428, 51 L.Ed.2d 752 (1977).

In the words of Judge Meanor: "I find this statute to be severable, that is, the portion thereof attacked as unconstitutional may rationally be severed from the remainder of the statute. * * * This mandatory condition upon the student's right not to participate in the flag salute ceremony is an unconstitutional requirement that the student engage in a form of speech and may not be enforced. The unconstitutionality of this severable portion of the statute is declared at this time." We concur.

Accordingly, after consideration of all submissions of the parties and the amicus curiae, and after argument, the judgment of the district court will be affirmed.

NOTES

1. Judge Meanor also dismissed Robert Lautenstack as a defendant. The question of dismissal was not raised on appeal.
2. N.J.Stat.Ann § 18A:36-3 provides in part: "Every board of education shall:

"(c) Require the pupils in each school in the district on every school day to salute the United States flag and repeat the following pledge of allegiance to the flag: 'I pledge allegiance to the flag of the United States of America and to the republic for which it stands, one nation, under God, indivisible, with liberty and justice for all,' which salute and pledge of allegiance shall be rendered with the right hand over the heart, except that pupils who have conscientious scruples against such pledge or salute, or are children of accredited representatives of foreign governments to whom the United States Government extends diplomatic immunity, shall not be required to render such salute and pledge but shall be required to show full respect to the flag while the pledge is being given merely by standing at attention, the boys removing the headdress."

3. *Banks* originated as a three-judge case. It was reversed and remanded for a fresh decree by the Supreme Court. 401 U.S. 988, 91 S.Ct. 1223, 28 L.Ed.2d 526 (1971). Upon remand, the district judge entered an order adopting the findings of fact and conclusions of law of the three-judge court pertaining to the unconstitutionality of requiring a student to stand during the pledge of allegiance. The Fifth Circuit affirmed. 450 F.2d 1103 (5th Cir. 1971).

T HE United States Supreme Court decides, 7-2, against Matthew Fraser, a high school student who had been disciplined for delivering at a school assembly a one-minute student campaign speech containing metaphorical sexual double entendres, a speech described by Chief Justice Burger as "offensively lewd and indecent." Delivering the opinion of the Court, the Chief Justice wrote: "The First Amendment does not prevent the school officials from determining that to permit a vulgar and lewd speech such as respondent's would undermine the school's basic educational mission. A high school assembly or classroom is no place for a sexually explicit monologue directed towards an unsuspecting audience of teenage students." The disciplinary rule which Fraser had violated read: "conduct which materially and substantially interferes with the educational process is prohibited, including the use of obscene, profane language or gestures." Fraser's argument that he had no way of knowing that the delivery of his speech would subject him to disciplinary sanctions was rejected by Chief Justice Burger.

Bethel School Dist. No. 403 v. *Fraser,* 106 S.Ct. 3159 (1986)

Chief Justice BURGER delivered the opinion of the Court.

We granted certiorari to decide whether the First Amendment prevents a school district from disciplining a high school student for giving a lewd speech at a school assembly.

I

A

On April 26, 1983, respondent Matthew N. Fraser, a student at Bethel High School in Bethel, Washington, delivered a speech nominating a fellow student for student elective office. Approximately 600 high school students, many of whom were 14-years-olds, attended the assembly. Students were required to attend the assembly or to report to the study hall. The assembly was part of a school-sponsored educational program in self-government. Students who elected not to attend the assembly were required to report to study hall. During the entire speech, Fraser referred to his candidate in terms of an elaborate, graphic, and explicit sexual metaphor.

Two of Fraser's teachers, with whom he discussed the contents of his speech in advance, informed him that the speech was "inappropriate and that he probably should not deliver it," App. 30, and that his delivery of the speech might have "severe consequences." *Id.,* at 61.

During Fraser's delivery of the speech, a school counselor observed the reaction of students to the speech. Some students hooted and yelled; some by gestures graphically simulated the sexual activities pointedly alluded to in respondent's speech. Other students appeared to be bewildered and embarrassed by the speech. One teacher reported that on the day following the speech, she found it necessary to forgo a portion of the scheduled class lesson in order to discuss the speech with the class. *Id.,* at 41-44.

A Bethel High School disciplinary rule prohibiting the use of obscene language in the school provides:

"Conduct which materially and substantially interferes with the educational process is prohibited, including the use of obscene, profane language or gestures."

The morning after the assembly, the Assistant Principal called Fraser into her office and notified him that the school considered his speech to have been a violation of this rule. Fraser was presented with copies of five letters submitted by teachers, describing his conduct at the assembly; he was given a chance to explain his conduct, and he admitted to having given the speech described and that he deliberately used sexual innuendo in the speech. Fraser was then informed that he would be suspended for three days, and that his name would removed from the list of candidates for graduation speaker at the school's commencement exercises.

Fraser sought review of this disciplinary action through the School District's grievance procedures. The hearing officer determined that the speech given by respondent was "indecent, lewd, and offensive to the modesty and decency of many of the students and faculty in attendance at the assembly." The examiner determined that the speech fell within the ordinary meaning of "obscene," as used in the disruptive-conduct rule, and affirmed the discipline in its entirety. Fraser served two days of his suspension, and was allowed to return to school on the third day.

B

Respondent, by his father as guardian *ad litem*, then brought this action in the United States District Court for the Western District of Washington. Respondent alleged a violation of his First Amendment right to freedom of speech and sought both injunctive relief and monetary damages under 42 U.S.C. § 1983. The District Court held that the school's sanctions violated respondent's right to freedom of speech under the First Amendment to the United States Constitution, that the school's disruptive-conduct rule is unconstitutionally vague and overboard, and that the removal of respondent's name from the graduation speaker's list violated the Due Process Clause of the Fourteenth Amendment because the disciplinary rule makes no mention of such removal as a possible sanction. The District Court awarded respondent $278 in damages, $12,750 in litigation costs and attorney's fees, and enjoined the School District from preventing respondent from speaking at the commencement ceremonies. Respondent, who had been elected graduation speaker by a write-in vote of his classmates, delivered a speech at the commencement ceremonies on June 8, 1983.

The Court of Appeals for the Ninth Circuit affirmed the judgment of the District Court, 755 F.2d 1356 (1985), holding that respondent's speech was indistinguishable from the protest armband in *Tinker* v. *Des Moines Independent Community School Dist.*, 393 U.S. 503, 89 S.Ct. 733, 21 L.Ed.2d 731 (1969). The court explicitly rejected the School District's argument that the speech, unlike the passive conduct of wearing a black armband, had a disruptive effect on the educational process. The Court of Appeals also rejected the School District's argument that it had an interest in protecting an essentially captive audience of minors from lewd and indecent language in a setting sponsored by the school, reasoning that the school board's "unbridled discretion" to determine what discourse is "decent" would "increase the risk of cementing white, middle-class standards for determining what is acceptable and proper speech and behavior in our public schools." 755 F.2d, at 1363. Finally, the Court of Appeals rejected the School District's argument that, incident to its responsibility for the school curriculum, it had the power to control the language used to express ideas during a school-sponsored activity.

We granted certiorari, 474 U.S.—, 106 S.Ct. 56, 88 L.Ed.2d 45 (1985). We reverse.

II

This Court acknowledged in *Tinker v. Des Moines Independent Community School Dist.*, *supra*, that students do not "shed their constitutional rights to freedom of speech or expression at the schoolhouse gate." *Id.*, 393 U.S., at 506, 89 S.Ct., at 736. The Court of Appeals read that case as precluding any discipline of Fraser for indecent speech and lewd conduct in the school assembly. That court appears to have proceeded on the theory that the use of lewd and obscene speech in order to make what the speaker considered to be a point in a nominating speech for a fellow student was essentially the same as the wearing of an armband in *Tinker* as a form of protest or the expression of a political position.

The marked distinction between the political "message" of the armbands in *Tinker* and the sexual content of respondent's speech in this case seems to have been given little weight by the Court of Appeals. In upholding the students' right to engage in a nondisruptive, passive expression of a political viewpoint in *Tinker*, this Court was careful to note that the case did "not concern speech or action that intrudes upon the work of the schools or the rights of other students." *Id.*, at 508, 89 S.Ct., at 737.

It is against this background that we turn to consider the level of First Amendment protection accorded to Fraser's utterances and actions before an official high school assembly attended by 600 students.

III

The role and purpose of the American public school system was well described by two historians, saying "public education must prepare pupils for citizenship in the Republic. . . . It must inculcate the habits and manners of civility as values in themselves conducive to happiness and as indispensable to the practice of self-government in the community and the nation." C. Beard & M. Beard, New Basic History of the United States 228 (1968). In *Ambach v. Norwick*, 441 U.S. 68, 76-77, 99 S.Ct. 1589, 1594, 60 L.Ed.2d 49 (1979), we echoed the essence of this statement of the objectives of public education as the "inculcat[ion of] fundamental values necessary to the maintenance of a democratic political system."

These fundamental values of "habits and manners of civility" essential to a democratic society must, of course, include tolerance of divergent political and religious views, even when the views expressed may be unpopular. But these "fundamental values" must also take into account consideration of the sensibilities of others, and, in the case of a school, the sensibilities of fellow students. The undoubted freedom to advocate unpopular and controversial views in schools and classrooms must be balanced against the society's countervailing interest in teaching students the boundaries of socially appropriate behaviour. Even the most heated political discourse in a democratic society requires consideration for the personal sensibilities of other participants and audiences.

In our Nation's legislative halls, where some of the most vigorous political debates in our society are carried on, there are rules prohibiting the use of expressions offensive to other participants in the debate. The Manual of Parliamentary Practice, drafted by Thomas Jefferson and adopted by the House of Representatives to govern the proceedings in that body, prohibits the use of "impertinent" speech during debate and likewise provides that "[n]o person is to use indecent language against the proceedings of the House." Jefferson's Manual of Parliamentary Practice, §§ 359, 360, reprinted in Manual and Rules of House of Representatives, H.R. Doc. No. 97-271, pp. 158-159 (1982); see *id.*, at 111, n. *a* (Jefferson's Manual governs the House in all cases to which it applies). The Rules of Debate applicable in the Senate likewise provide that a Senator may be called to order for imputing improper motives to another Senator or for referring offensively to any State. See Senate Procedure, S.Doc. No. 97-2, Rule XIX, pp. 568-569, 588-591 (1981). Senators have been censured for abusive language directed at other Senators. See Senate Election, Expulsion and Censure Cases from 1793 to 1972, S.Doc. No. 92-7, pp. 95-98 (1972) (Sens. McLaurin and Tillman); *id.*, at 152-153 (Sen. McCarthy). Can it be that what is proscribed in the halls of Congress is beyond the reach of school officials to regulate?

The First Amendment guarantees wide freedom in matters of adult public discourse. A sharply divided Court upheld the right to express an antidraft viewpoint in a public place, albeit in terms highly offensive to most citizens. See *Cohen* v. *California*, 403 U.S. 15, 91 S.Ct. 1780, 29 L.Ed.2d 284 (1971). It does not follow, however, that simply because the use of an offensive form of expression may not be prohibited to adults making what the speaker considers a political point, that the same latitude must be permitted to children in a public school. In *New Jersey* v. *T.L.O.*, 469 U.S. 325, __, 105 S.Ct. 733, __, 83 L.Ed.2d 720 (1985), we reaffirmed that the constitutional rights of students in public school are not automatically coextensive with the rights of adults in other settings. As cogently expressed by Judge Newman, "the First Amendment gives a high school student the classroom right to wear Tinker's armband, but not Cohen's jacket." *Thomas* v. *Board of Education, Granville Central School Dist.*, 607 F.2d 1043, 1057 (CA2 1979) (opinion, concurring in result).

Surely it is a highly appropriate function of public school education to prohibit the use of vulgar and offensive terms in public discourse. Indeed, the "fundamental values necessary to the maintenance of a democratic political system" disfavor the use of terms of debate highly offensive or highly threatening to others. Nothing in the Constitution prohibits the states from insisting that certain modes of expression are inappropriate and subject to sanctions. The inculcation of these values is truly the "work of the schools." *Tinker*, 393 U.S., at 508, 89 S.Ct., at 737; see *Ambach* v. *Norwick, supra*. The determination of what manner of speech in the classroom or in school assembly is inappropriate properly rests with the school board.

The process of educating our youth for citizenship in public schools is not confined to books, the curriculum, and the civics class; schools must teach by example the shared values of a civilized social order. Consciously or otherwise, teachers—and indeed the older students—demonstrate the appropriate form of civil discourse and political expression by their conduct and deportment in and out of class. Inescapably, like parents, they are role models. The schools, as instruments of the state, may determine that the essential lessons of civil, mature conduct cannot be conveyed in a school that tolerates lewd, indecent, or offensive speech and conduct such as that indulged in by this confused boy.

The pervasive sexual innuendo in Fraser's speech was plainly offensive to both teachers and students—indeed to any mature person. By glorifying male sexuality, and in its verbal content, the speech was acutely insulting to teenage girl students. See App.77-81. The speech could well be seriously damaging to its less mature audience, many of whom were only 14 years old and on the threshold of awareness of human sexuality. Some students were reported as bewildered by the speech and the reaction of mimicry it provoked.

This Court's First Amendment jurisprudence has acknowledged limitations on the otherwise absolute interest of the speaker in reaching an unlimited audience where the speech is sexually explicit and the audience may include children. In *Ginsberg* v. *New York*, 390 U.S. 629, 88 S.Ct. 1274, 20 L.Ed.2d 195 (1968), this Court upheld a New York statute banning the sale of sexually oriented material to minors, even though the material in question was entitled to First Amendment protection with respect to adults. And in addressing the question whether the First Amendment places any limit on the authority of public schools to remove books from a public school library, all Members of the Court, otherwise sharply divided, acknowledged that the school board has the authority to remove books that are vulgar. *Board of Education v. Pico,* 457 U.S. 853, 871-872, 102 S.Ct. 2799, 2814-15, 73 L.Ed.2d 435 (1982) (plurality opinion); *id.,* at 879-881, 102 S.Ct., at 2814-15 (BLACKMUN, J., concurring); *id.,* at 918-920, 102 S.Ct., at 2834-35 (REHNQUIST, J., dissenting). These cases recognize the obvious concern on the part of parents, and school authorities acting *in loco parentis* to protect children—especially in a captive audience—from exposure to sexually explicit, indecent, or lewd speech.

We have also recognized an interest in protecting minors from exposure to vulgar and offensive spoken language. In *FCC v. Pacifica Foundation,* 438 U.S. 726, 98 S.Ct. 3026, 57 L.Ed.2d 1073 (1978), we dealt with the power of the Federal Communications Commission to regulate a radio broadcast described as "indecent but not obscene." There the Court reviewed an administrative condemnation of the radio broadcast of a self-styled "humorist" who described his own performance as being in "the words you couldn't say on the public, ah, airwaves, um, the ones you definitely wouldn't say ever." *Id.,* at 729, 98 S.Ct., at 3030; see also *id.,* at 751-755, 98 S.Ct., at 3041-43 (appendix). The Commission concluded that "certain words depicted sexual and excretory activities in a patently offensive manner, [and] noted that they 'were broadcast at a time when children were undoubtedly in the audience.' " The Commission issued an order declaring that the radio station was guilty of broadcasting indecent language in violation of 18 U.S.C. § 1464. 438 U.S., at 732, 98 S.Ct., at 3031. The Court of Appeals set aside the Commission's determination, and we reversed, reinstating the Commission's citation of the station. We concluded that the broadcast was properly considered "obscene, indecent, or profane" within the meaning of the statute. The plurality opinion went on to reject the radio station's assertion of a First Amendment right to broadcast vulgarity:

"These words offend for the same reasons that obscenity offends. Their place in the hierarchy of First Amendment values was aptly sketched by Mr. Justice Murphy when he said: '[S]uch utterances are no essential part of any exposition of ideas, and are of such slight social value as a step to truth that any benefit that may be derived from them is clearly outweighed by the social interest in order and morality.' *Chaplinsky v. New Hampshire,* 315 U.S. [568], at 572 [62 S.Ct. 766, at 769, 86 L.Ed. 1031 (1942)]." *Id.,* at 746, 98 S.Ct., at 3039.

We hold that petitioner School District acted entirely within its permissible authority in imposing sanctions upon Fraser in response to his offensively lewd and indecent speech. Unlike the sanctions imposed on the students wearing armbands in *Tinker,* the penalties imposed in this case were unrelated to any political viewpoint. The First Amendment does not prevent the school officials from determining that to permit a vulgar and lewd speech such as respondent's would undermine the school's basic educational mission. A high school assembly or classroom is no place for a sexually explicit monologue directed towards an unsuspecting audience of teenage students. Accordingly, it was perfectly appropriate for the school to disassociate itself to make the point to the pupils that vulgar speech and lewd conduct is wholly inconsistent with the "fundamental values" of public school education. Justice Black, dissenting in *Tinker,* made a point that is especially relevant in this case:

"I wish therefore,... to disclaim any purpose ... to hold that the federal Constitution compels the teachers, parents and elected school officials to surrender control of the American public school system to public school students." 393 U.S., at 522, 526, 89 S.Ct., at 744, 746.

IV

Respondent contends that the circumstances of his suspension violated due process because he had no way of knowing that the delivery of the speech in question would subject him to disciplinary sanctions. This argument is wholly without merit. We have recognized that "maintaining security and order in the schools requires a certain degree of flexibility in school disciplinary procedures, and we have respected the value of preserving the informality of the student-teacher relationship." *New Jersey v. T.L.O.,* 469 U.S., at —, 105 S.Ct., at 743. Given the school's need to be able to impose disciplinary sanctions for a wide range of unanticipated conduct disruptive of the educational process, the school disciplinary rules need not be as detailed as a criminal code which imposes criminal sanctions. Cf. *Arnett v. Kennedy,* 416 U.S. 134, 161, 94 S.Ct. 1633, 1647-48, 40 L.Ed.2d 15 (1974) (REHNQUIST, J., concurring). Two days' suspension from school does not rise to the level of a penal sanction calling for the full panoply of procedural due process protections applicable to a criminal prosecution. Cf. *Goss v. Lopez,* 419 U.S. 565, 95 S.Ct. 729, 42 L.Ed.2d 725 (1975). The school disciplinary rule proscribing "obscene" language and the prespeech admonitions of teachers gave adequate warning to Fraser that his lewd speech could subject him to sanctions.*

The judgment of the Court of Appeals for the Ninth Circuit is

Reversed.

Justice BLACKMUN concurs in the result.
Justice BRENNAN, concurring in the judgment.
Respondent gave the following speech at a high

school assembly in support of a candidate for student government office:

"'I know a man who is firm—he's firm in his pants, he's firm in his shirt, his character is firm—but most . . . of all, his belief in you, the students of Bethel, is firm.

"'Jeff Kuhlman is a man who takes his point and pounds it in. If necessary, he'll take an issue and nail it to the wall. He doesn't attack things in spurts—he drives hard, pushing and pushing until finally—he succeeds.

"'Jeff is a man who will go to the very end—even the climax, for each and every one of you.

"'So vote for Jeff for A.S.B. vice-president—he'll never come between you and the best our high school can be.'" App. 47.

The Court, referring to these remarks as "obscene" "vulgar," "lewd," and "offensively lewd," concludes that school officials properly punished respondent for uttering the speech. Having read the full text of respondent's remarks, I find it difficult to believe that it is the same speech the Court describes. To my mind, the most that can be said about respondent's speech— and all that need be said—is that in light of the discretion school officials have to teach high school students how to conduct civil and effective public discourse, and to prevent disruption of school educational activities, it was not unconstitutional for school officials to conclude, under the circumstances of this case, that respondent's remarks exceeded permissible limits. Thus, while I concur in the Court's judgment, I write separately to express my understanding of the breadth of the Court's holding.

The Court today reaffirms the unimpeachable proposition that students do not "'shed their constitutional rights to freedom of speech or expression at the schoolhouse gate.'" *Ante,* at 3163 (quoting *Tinker v. Des Moines School District,* 393 U.S. 503, 506, 89 S.Ct. 733, 736, 21 L.Ed.2d 731 (1969)). If respondent had given the same speech outside of the school environment, he could not have been penalized simply because government officials considered his language to be inappropriate, see *Cohen v. California,* 403 U.S. 15, 91 S.Ct. 1780, 29 L.Ed.2d 284 (1971); the Court's opinion does not suggest otherwise.[1] Moreover, despite the Court's characterizations, the language respondent used is far removed from the very narrow class of "obscene" speech which the Court has held is not protected by the First Amendment. *Ginsberg v. New York,* 390 U.S. 629, 635, 88 S.Ct. 1274, 1278, 20 L.Ed.2d 195 (1968); *Roth v. United States,* 354 U.S. 476, 485, 77 S.Ct. 1304, 1309, 1 L.Ed.2d 1498 (1957). It is true, however, that the State has interests in teaching high school students how to conduct civil and effective public discourse and in avoiding disruption of

educational school activities. Thus, the Court holds that under certain circumstances, high school students may properly be reprimanded for giving a speech at a high school assembly which school officials conclude disrupted the school's educational mission.[2] Respondent's speech may well have been protected had he given it in school but under different circumstances, where the school's legitimate interests in teaching and maintaining civil public discourse were less weighty.

In the present case, school officials sought only to ensure that a high school assembly proceed in an orderly manner. There is no suggestion that school officials attempted to regulate respondent's speech because they disagreed with the views he sought to express. Cf. *Tinker, supra.* Nor does this case involve an attempt by school officials to ban written materials they consider "inappropriate" for high school students, cf. *Board of Education v. Pico,* 457 U.S. 853, 102 S.Ct. 2799, 73 L.Ed.2d 435 (1982), or to limit what students should hear, read, or learn about. Thus, the Court's holding concerns only the authority that school officials have to restrict a high school student's use of disruptive language in a speech given to a high school assembly.

The authority school officials have to regulate such speech by high school students is not limitless. See *Thomas v. Board of Education, Granville Central School Dist.,* 607 F.2d 1043, 1057 (CA2 1979) (Newman, J., concurring in result) ("[S]chool officials . . . do [not] have limitlesss discretion to apply their own notions of indecency. Courts have a First Amendment responsibility to insure that robust rhetoric. . . . is not suppressed by prudish failures to distinguish the vigorous from the vulgar"). Under the circumstances of this case, however, I believe that school officials did not violate the First Amendment in determining that respondent should be disciplined for the disruptive language he used while addressing a high school assembly.[3] Thus, I concur in the judgment reversing the decision of the Court of Appeals.

Justice MARSHALL, dissenting.

I agree with the principles that Justice BRENNAN sets out in his opinion concurring in the judgment. I dissent from the Court's decision, however, because in my view the school district failed to demonstrate that respondent's remarks were indeed disruptive. The District Court and Court of Appeals conscientiously applied *Tinker v. Des Moines School District,* 393 U.S. 503, 89 S.Ct. 733, 21 L.Ed.2d 731 (1968), and concluded that the board had not demonstrated any disruption of the educational process. I recognize that the school administration must be given wide latitude to determine what forms of conduct are inconsistent with the school's educational mission; nevertheless, where speech is involved, we may not unquestioningly accept a teacher's or administrator's assertion that certain pure speech interfered with education. Here the board, despite a clear opportunity to do so, failed to bring in evidence sufficient to convince either of the two lower courts that education at Bethel School was disrupted by respondent's speech. I therefore see no reason to disturb the Court of Appeals' judgment.

Justice STEVENS, dissenting.

"Frankly, my dear, I don't give a damn."

When I was a high school student, the use of those words in a public forum shocked the Nation. Today Clark Gable's four-letter expletive is less offensive than it was then. Nevertheless, I assume that high school administrators may prohibit the use of that word in classroom discussion and even in extracurricular activities that are sponsored by the school and held on school premises. For I believe a school faculty must regulate the content as well as the style of student speech in carrying out its educational mission.[1] It does seem to me, however, that if a student is to be punished for using offensive speech, he is entitled to fair notice of the scope of the prohibition and the consequences of its violation. The interest in free speech protected by the First Amendment and the interest in fair procedure protected by the Due Process Clause of the Fourteenth Amendment combine to require this conclusion.

This respondent was an outstanding young man with a fine academic record. The fact that he was chosen by the student body to speak at the school's commencement exercises demonstrates that he was respected by his peers. This fact is relevant for two reasons. It confirms the conclusion that the discipline imposed on him—a three-day suspension and ineligibility to speak at the school's graduation exercises—was sufficiently serious to justify invocation of the School District's grievance procedures. See *Goss v. Lopez*, 419 U.S. 565, 574-575, 95 S.Ct. 729, 736, 42 L.Ed.2d 725 (1975). More importantly, it indicates that he was probably in a better position to determine whether an audience composed of 600 of his contemporaries would be offended by the use of a four-letter word—or a sexual metaphor—than is a group of judges who are at least two generations and 3,000 miles away from the scene of the crime.[2]

The fact that the speech may not have been offensive to his audience—or that he honestly believed that it would be inoffensive—does not mean that he had a constitutional right to deliver it. For the school—not the student—must prescribe the rules of conduct in an educational institution.[3] But it does mean that he should not be disciplined for speaking frankly in a school assembly if he had no reason to anticipate punitive consequences.

One might conclude that respondent should have known that he would be punished for giving this speech on three quite different theories: (1) It violated the "Disruptive Conduct" rule published in the student handbook; (2) he was specifically warned by his teachers; or (3) the impropriety is so obvious that no specific notice was required. I discuss each theory in turn.

The Disciplinary Rule

At the time the discipline was imposed, as well as in its defense of this lawsuit, the school took the position that respondent violated the following published rule:

"'In addition to the criminal acts defined above, the commission of, or participation in certain non-criminal activities or acts may lead to disciplinary action. Generally, these are acts which disrupt and interfere with the educational process.

.   .   .   .   .

"'*Disruptive Conduct.* Conduct which materially and substantially interferes with the educational process is prohibited, including the use of obscene, profane language or gestures.'" 755 F.2d 1356, 1357, n. 1 (CA9 1985).

Based on the findings of fact made by the District Court, the Court of Appeals concluded that the evidence did not show "that the speech had a materially disruptive effect on the educational process." *Id.,* at 1361. The Court of Appeals explained the basis for this conclusion:

"[T]he record now before us yields no evidence that Fraser's use of a sexual innuendo in his speech materially interfered with activities at Bethel High School. While the students' reaction to Fraser's speech may fairly be characterized as boisterous, it was hardly disruptive of the educational process. In the words of Mr. McCutcheon, the school counselor whose testimony the District relies upon, the reaction of the student body 'was not atypical to a high school auditorium assembly.' In our view, a noisy response to the speech and sexually suggestive movements by three students in a crowd of 600 fail to rise to the level of a material interference with the educational process that justifies impinging upon Fraser's First Amendment right to express himself freely.

"We find it significant that although four teachers delivered written statements to an assistant principal commenting on Fraser's speech, none of them suggested that the speech disrupted the assembly or otherwise interfered with school activities. *See,* Finding of Fact No. 8. Nor can a finding of material disruption be based upon the evidence that the speech proved to be a lively topic of conversation among students the following day." *Id.*, at 1360-1361.

Thus, the evidence in the record, as interpreted by the District Court and the Court of Appeals, makes it perfectly clear that respondent's speech was not "conduct" prohibited by the disciplinary rule.[4] Indeed, even if the language of the rule could be stretched to encompass the nondisruptive use of obscene or profane language, there is no such language in respondent's speech. What the speech does contain is a sexual metaphor that may unquestionably be offensive to some listeners in some settings. But if an impartial judge puts his or her own views about the metaphor to one side, I simply cannot understand how he or she could conclude that it is embraced by the above-quoted rule. At best, the rule is sufficiently ambiguous that without a further explanation or construction it could not advise the reader of the student handbook that the speech would be forbidden.[5]

The Specific Warning by the Teachers

Respondent read his speech to three different teachers before he gave it. Mrs. Irene Hicks told him that she thought the speech "was inappropriate and that he probably should not deliver it." App. 30. Steven DeHart told respondent "that this would indeed cause problems in that it would raise eyebrows." *Id.*, at 61. The third teacher, Shawn Madden, did not testify. None of the three suggested that the speech might violate a school rule. *Id.*, at 49-50.

The fact that respondent reviewed the text of his speech with three different teachers before he gave it does indicate that he must have been aware of the possibility that it would provoke an adverse reaction, but the teachers' responses certainly did not give him any better notice of the likelihood of discipline than did the student handbook itself. In my opinion, therefore, the most difficult question is whether the speech was so obviously offensive that an intelligent high school student must be presumed to have realized that he would be punished for giving it.

Obvious Impropriety

Justice Sutherland taught us that a "nuisance may be merely a right thing in the wrong place,—like a pig in the parlor instead of the barnyard." *Euclid v. Ambler Realty Co.*, 272 U.S. 365, 388, 47 S.Ct. 114, 118, 71 L.Ed. 303 (1926). Vulgar language, like vulgar animals, may be acceptable in some contexts and intolerable in others. See *FCC v. Pacifica Foundation*, 438 U.S. 726, 750, 98 S.Ct. 3026, 3041, 57 L.Ed.2d 1073 (1978). Indeed, even ordinary, inoffensive speech may be wholly unacceptable in some settings. See *Schenck v. United States*, 249 U.S. 47, 52, 39 S.Ct. 247, 249, 63 L.Ed. 470 (1919); *Pacifica, supra*, 438 U.S., at 744-745, 98 S.Ct., at 3038.

It seems fairly obvious that respondent's speech would be inappropriate in certain classroom and formal social settings. On the other hand, in a locker room or perhaps in a school corridor the metaphor in the speech might be regarded as rather routine comment. If this be true, and if respondent's audience consisted almost entirely of young people with whom he conversed on a daily basis, can we—at this distance—confidently assert that he must have known that the school administration would punish him for delivering it?

For three reasons, I think not. First, it seems highly unlikely that he would have decided to deliver the speech if he had known that it would result in his suspension and disqualification from delivering the school commencement address. Second, I believe a strong presumption in favor of free expression should apply whenever an issue of this kind is arguable. Third, because the Court has adopted the policy of applying contemporary community standards in evaluating expression with sexual connotations, this Court should defer to the views of the district and circuit judges who are in a much better position to evaluate this speech than we are.

I would affirm the judgment of the Court of Appeals.

JUSTICE BURGER'S OPINION NOTE

* Petitioners also challenge the ruling of the District Court that the removal of Fraser's name from the ballot for graduation speaker violated his due process rights because that sanction was not indicated as a potential punishment in the school's disciplinary rules. We agree with the Court of Appeals that this issue has become moot, since the graduation ceremony has long since passed and Fraser was permitted to speak in accordance with the District Court's injunction. No part of the damage award was based upon the removal of Fraser's name from the list, since damages were based upon the loss of two days schooling.

JUSTICE BRENNAN'S OPINION NOTES

1. In the course of its opinion, the Court makes certain remarks concerning the authority of school officials to regulate student language in public schools. For example, the Court notes that "[n]othing in the Constitution prohibits the states from insisting that certain modes of expression are inappropriate and subject to sanctions." *Ante,* at 3165. These statements obviously do not, and indeed given our prior precedents could not, refer to the government's authority generally to regulate the language used in public debate outside of the school environment.

2. The Court speculates that the speech was "insulting" to female students, and "seriously damaging" to 14-year-olds, so that school officials could legitimately suppress such expression in order to protect these groups. *Ante,* at 3165. There is no evidence in the record that any students, male or female, found the speech "insulting." And while it was not unreasonable for school officials to conclude that respondent's remarks were inappropriate for a school-sponsored assembly, the language respondent used does not even approach the sexually explicit speech regulated in *Ginsberg v. New York,* 390 U.S. 629, 88 S.Ct. 1274, 20 L.Ed.2d 195 (1968), or the indecent speech banned in *FCC v. Pacifica Foundation,* 438 U.S. 726, 98 S.Ct. 3026, 57 L.Ed.2d 1073 (1978). Indeed, to my mind, respondent's speech was no more "obscene," "lewd," or "sexually explicit" than the bulk of programs currently appearing on prime time television or in the local cinema. Thus, I disagree with the Court's suggestion that school officials could punish respondent's speech out of a need to protect younger students.

3. Respondent served two days' suspension and had his name removed from the list of candidates for graduation speaker at the school's commencement exercises, although he was eventually permitted to speak at the graduation. While I find this punishment somewhat severe in light of the nature of respondent's transgression, I cannot conclude that school officials exceeded the bounds of their disciplinary authority.

JUSTICE STEVENS' OPINION NOTES

1. "Because every university's resources are limited, an educational institution must routinely make decisions concerning the use of the time and space that is available for extracurricular activities. In my judgment, it is both necessary and appropriate for those decisions to evaluate the content of a proposed student activity. I should think it obvious, for example, that if two groups of 25 students requested the use of a room at a particular time—one to view Mickey Mouse cartoons and the other to rehearse an amateur performance of Hamlet—the First Amendment would not require that the room be reserved for the group that submitted its application first. Nor do I see why a university should have to establish a 'compelling state interest' to defend its decision to permit one group to use the facility and not the other. In my opinion, a university should be allowed to decide for itself whether a program that illuminates the genius of Walt Disney should be given precedence over one that may duplicate material adequately covered in the classroom. Judgments of this kind should be made by academicians, not by federal judges, and their standards for decision should not be encumbered with ambiguous phrases like 'compelling state interest.'" *Widmar v. Vincent,* 454 U.S. 263, 278-279, 102 S.Ct. 269, 279, 70 L.Ed.2d 440 (1981) (STEVENS, J., concurring in judgment) (footnotes omitted).

   "Any student of history who has been reprimanded for talking about the World Series during a class discussion of the First Amendment knows that it is incorrect to state that a 'time, place, or manner restriction may not be based upon either the content or subject matter of speech.'" *Consolidated Edison Co. v. Public Service Comm'n,* 447 U.S. 530, 544-545, 100 S.Ct. 2326, 2337, 65 L.Ed.2d 319 (1980) (STEVENS, J., concurring in judgment).

2. As the Court of Appeals noted, there "is no evidence in the record indicating that any students found the speech to be offensive." 755 F.2d 1356, 1361, n. 4 (CA9 1985).

   In its opinion today, the Court describes respondent as a "confused boy," *ante,* at 3165, and repeatedly characterizes his audience of high school students as "children," *ante,* at 3164, 3165. When a more orthodox message is being conveyed to a similar audience, four members of today's majority would treat high school students like college students rather than like children. See *Bender v. Williamsport Area School District,* 475 U.S.—, 106 S.Ct. 1326, 89 L.Ed.2d 501 (1986)(dissenting opinions).

3. See *Arnold v. Carpenter,* 459 F.2d 939, 944 (CA7 1972) (STEVENS, J., dissenting).

4. The Court's reliance on the school's authority to prohibit "unanticipated conduct disruptive of the educational process," *ante,* at 3166, is misplaced. The findings of the District Court, which were upheld by the Court of Appeals, established that the speech was not "disruptive." Departing from our normal practice concerning factual findings, the Court's decision rests on "utterly unproven, subjective impressions of some hypothetical students." *Bender v. Williamsport,* 475 U.S., at—, 106 S.Ct., at 1337 (BURGER, C.J., dissenting).

5. The school's disruptive conduct rule is entirely concerned with "the educational process." It does not expressly refer to extracurricular activities in general, or to student political campaigns or student debates. In contrast, "[i]n our Nation's legislative halls, where some of the most vigorous political debates in our society are carried on, there are rules prohibiting the use of expressions offensive to other participants in the debate." See *ante,* at 3164. If a written rule is needed to forewarn a United States Senator that the use of offensive speech may give rise to discipline, a high school student should be entitled to an equally unambiguous warning. Unlike the Manual of Parliamentary Practice drafted by Thomas Jefferson, this School District's rules of conduct contain no unequivocal prohibition against the use of "impertinent" speech or "indecent language."

Index